GLOBAL
EXPLORERS

The Next Generation of Leaders

J. Stewart Black, Ph.D.

Allen J. Morrison, Ph.D.

Hal B. Gregersen, Ph.D.

Foreword by Stephen R. Covey

ROUTLEDGE
New York and London

Published in 1999 by

Routledge
29 West 35th Street
New York, NY 10001

Published in Great Britain by

Routledge
11 New Fetter Lane
London EC4P 4EE

Copyright © 1999 by Routledge

Printed in the United States of America on acid-free paper.

Library of Congress Cataloging-in-Publication Data
Black, J. Stewart, 1959–
    Global explorers : the next generation of leaders / J. Stewart
Black, Allen J. Morrison, Hal B. Gregersen.
      p.   cm.
    Includes bibliographical references and index.
    ISBN 0–415–92148–1 (cloth)
    1. Leadership.   2. Executive ability.   3. International
business enterprises—Management.   I. Morrison, Allen J.
II. Gregersen, Hal B., 1958– .   III. Title.
HD57.7.B538   1999
658.4'092—DC21   98-49358
                              CIP

contents

foreword

In *Global Explorers: The Next Generation of Leaders,* my friends Stewart Black, Allen Morrison, and Hal Gregersen make a compelling case for the vital and growing need for global leaders who are equal to the challenges of today's global marketplace. With extensive research as a foundation, they do a masterful job of identifying the characteristics of a global leader. They lay out a practical, insightful path for leaders at every level of an organization to become global leaders, and provide living models of those who have successfully walked the path.

I personally believe that there are still relatively few who fully comprehend the significance of the global shift that has been set in motion and that continues to gather force and momentum in the world. One little personal anecdote comes to mind that illustrates how our everyday experiences can reinforce the need for this global awareness.

A few years ago, my mother attended one of my presentations. Arriving early, she sat near the front, and, like a mother, proudly awaited the introduction of her son. Right after I began, I caught a glimpse of her beaming face—nodding and encouraging at every phrase. You can just imagine it.

But all that changed. Before long, two people talking in the front row distracted her. It's not that they exchanged just a comment or two. They had the brazenness to carry on an extended conversation during *her* son's speech! With each minute that passed, she became more and more irritated. By the end she was absolutely fuming, tempted to give them a piece of her mind.

Instead, she went up to the person who had introduced me and said, "Could you believe how those two people in the front talked on and on through Stephen's whole presentation?" He replied, "Oh yes, that woman is from Korea and the person sitting next to her is an interpreter."

My mother's heart sank. Though ashamed at how severely she had judged them, she graciously approached the woman, greeted her, and wished her well. The new unexpected information my mother received created within her mind and heart what I call a paradigm shift—a new perspective, a new way of seeing things. And the new information transformed her whole experience. So instead of giving the Korean woman a piece of her mind, my mother constructed a new mind.

I am convinced that most significant paradigm shifts are preceded by the shock of new light, awareness, and understanding. And as *Global Explorers* points out, making major breakthroughs as a global leader is no different.

I love the statement made by business author Stan Davis: "When the infrastructure shifts, everything rumbles." Well, everything is rumbling because the old rules of traditional, hierarchical, high external control, top-down management in a local or national marketplace are being dismantled—they simply aren't working any longer. And why are they not working? It's because of the earthshaking force of global competition.

Global customers are demanding products and services of unprecedented quality, of high value and low cost, and that come with blinding speed to market. The problem is that the old forms of management produce organizational cultures mired in low trust, dependency, and inefficiency. They simply cannot perform to the level demanded. World-class quality, high trust, and innovation cannot be faked.

In my opinion, between the raised bar of global competition and the failure of most workers to stay at the cutting edge of their craft through training, broad reading, and continual development, at least twenty percent of the workforce in this country has become obsolete. In fact, I predict that if we stay on our current course, another twenty percent will be obsolete in another ten years. Such are the rumblings of the world we live in.

Although I don't necessarily agree with the East versus West thinking reflected in the following quote made years ago by Konosuke Matsushita, Executive Advisor to Matsushita Electric Industrial Co. of Japan, I do believe that most of the problems we face around the world are rooted in our paradigms. And I believe that the universality of the leadership principles that Mr. Matsushita champions have a deep resonance today:

> We are going to win and the industrial West is going to lose out. There's nothing much you can do about it, because the reasons for your failure are within yourselves. With your bosses doing the thinking while the workers wield the screwdrivers, you're convinced deep down that it is the right way to run a business—getting the ideas out of the heads of the bosses and into the hands of labor. For us, the core of management is the art of mobilizing and pulling together the intellectual resources of all employees in the service of the firm. . . . Only by drawing on the combined brainpower of all its employees can a firm face up to the turbulence and constraints of today's environment.

The good news is that the global marketplace that has emerged—especially over the last few years—has been the toughest best friend and teacher that we ever could have had. It has revealed the weaknesses that have always existed in our organizations and in our thinking—weaknesses that have been hidden by the luxury of having to compete only locally. It has awakened the giant that has grown sleepy, slow, fat, and content. The result is that we have a long way to go. Yet many organizations have made terrific strides in aligning themselves worldwide with the principles mentioned by Matsushita—as well as those found in *Global Explorers*. These principles produce trust, innovation, and empowerment in organizational cultures. They release the power and inherent gifts within people across the globe. And they ultimately create value for customers and shareholders.

As for the East winning and the West losing, most Asian countries, including Japan, are experiencing their own comeuppance—reinforcing the inescapable reality that no one is exempt from the consequences of the universal, timeless, self-evident principles that govern economic growth and prosperity. Yes, global competition has humbled the industrial West; it is also humbling the East. In the end, that's good for all of us.

Humility truly is the mother of all virtues. For when we are humble, teachable, and open—whether by our own wisdom or by the brutal force of circumstances—we can experience the paradigm shifts that open up the world to us. And when we are impacted by these illuminating moments and combine them with the courage and confidence born of hard-earned skill, experience, competence, and judgment, then we can become Global Explorers—bearing a mindset and skillset that match today's global reality. I wish you well on the sure path set out by the authors to become just that—leaders for the global frontier.

Stephen R. Covey
Vice-Chairman, Franklin Covey Co.
Author of *The 7 Habits of Highly Effective People*

preface

Today you can hardly pick up a newspaper or business magazine without reading about global leadership. However, when we conceived this project nearly five years ago, this was not the case. It is amazing how quickly things change. Consequently, while we devote some time and attention to the various driving forces of globalization, this book primarily focuses on the characteristics of effective global leaders and on how to develop these characteristics.

Developing a Global Leadership Model

Our basic premise is this: Corporations today need to look at the world on a global basis and develop products and strategies that work across borders, so today's corporate leaders need to develop business and leadership characteristics that are effective outside of their own national boundaries.

The Research

In examining global leadership we addressed two major questions: (1) What capabilities do leaders who are charged with directing operations that span an entire world of diverse cultures, capabilities, and customers need to acquire? (2) Given the growing need for global leaders, how can managers most effectively develop these characteristics?

We tackled these questions in a three-year research project. Our approach was simple. We interviewed over 130 senior-line and human-resource executives in 50 companies throughout Europe, North America, and Asia. We asked these individuals to describe the characteristics of effective global leaders and how those characteristics are best developed. We then asked these managers to identify "archetypal" global leaders, or executives in their companies who were recognized as global role models. We next interviewed the individuals identified, asking them the same pair of questions: "What are the characteristics of effective global leaders and what have been the most powerful experiences in your life in developing these attributes?" These interviews, along with the results of several different surveys that we have conducted over the same time, serve as the foundation for this book.

Relevance to You

Regardless of your current management position and responsibilities, if you want to lead organizations in the future, this book is required reading. Maybe you are a young manager and have little previous experience with international business issues. You might be on an international assignment right now. Perhaps you are serving on a task force or team grappling with an international challenge or opportunity for your firm. You might head a unit with global responsibility for products, services, or business functions. Whatever your current responsibilities are, and no matter how secure you feel today, you are not going to be able to avoid the effects of the growing tidal wave of globalization. Sooner or later *you* will need to master the key characteristics of global leadership.

Keep in mind, however, that we do not define leaders only as those in the upper echelons of corporations. Leadership is not a function of position as much as it is a function of action. Some of the most senior executives we have met were anything but real leaders. While they barked out orders and were greeted with compliance, they failed to inspire anyone. Leadership is about determining direction, and then inspiring and coordinating action.

Leadership is not just about coercion; it is about affecting people, what they do and what they believe. You do not need the vantage point of the pinnacle of the organization to see this. In our explorations, we have often found inspiring leaders deep within the lowest parts of organizations.

Structuring the Model

Our research objective was to identify a set of global leadership characteristics that was comprehensive and broad without being unwieldy. We were mindful that a number of companies have generated competency models that often provide little meaning for employees. Chase Manhattan Bank, for example, tracks almost 250 competencies, while IBM's executive leadership model contains 11. The complexity of these models has led to poor acceptance by some employees. Finding the right balance between identifying too many and too few competencies is always a challenge.

In our research, we found that overall global leadership success is a function of capabilities driven by both general global dynamics and business-specific dynamics. About two-thirds of the capabilities for success are driven by global dynamics, while the remaining one-third are driven by business-specific dynamics.

Global Characteristics. Our research and experience found that *every global leader must have a core set of global characteristics.* These attributes are essential for global leaders regardless of their countries of origin, the industries they work in, the companies they work for, or their functional orientations. In essence, these characteristics are driven by the global dynamics of business. Effective global leaders are different from average managers because they master these global aspects of leadership. Given our research and experience, we conclude that you cannot become an effective global leader without developing these core characteristics.

We found that global leaders are consistently competent in four important areas:

> *inquisitiveness*
> *perspective*
> *character*
> *savvy*

Inquisitiveness is both the glue that holds the other characteristics together and the source of energy that gives the model life. Effective global leaders are unceasingly inquisitive. Far from being overwhelmed by all the differences in language, culture, government regulations, and so on that exist from one country to another, they are invigorated by this diversity. They love to learn and are driven to understand and master the complexities of the global business environment.

Global leaders also have a unique perspective on the world around them. While most managers do all they can to avoid uncertainty and structure it out of existence, global leaders view uncertainty as an invigorating and natural aspect of international business. Likewise, while most managers hate competing pressures, global leaders relish the challenge of balancing the ever-present tensions between global integration and local adaptation.

Character is exhibited through the leader's ability to connect emotionally with people of different backgrounds and cultures and through the consistent demonstration of personal integrity in a world full of ethical conflicts. Both are essential for engendering goodwill and trust in a global workforce.

Savvy is demonstrated by the ability to recognize global business opportunities and then to mobilize organizational resources in order to capitalize on them. We found that global leaders are highly skilled at both identifying market opportunities and applying organizational resources to make the most of those opportunities.

Business-Specific Characteristics. While the focus of this book is on those characteristics of global leadership that are driven by global dynamics, there are charactersitics critical to overall success that are driven by other dynamics. Roughly one-third of what makes a global leader successful arises from these specific dynamics. These dynamics can be grouped into four major categories. The first important dynamic is *country affiliation*. Without doubt, certain leadership characteristics are vital in India, while others are essential in the United States, France, or Korea. The second dynamic is *industry*. Different industries have different product cycle times, roles for technology, and so on. Consequently, specific skills to deal with these dynamics vary from industry to industry. The third dynamic is *company affiliation*. Each company has a unique culture, set of values, and management philosophy. The skills and know-how associated with effective leadership at Toyota are in some ways unique and can be quite different from those required at Hitachi. The fourth dynamic is *functional responsibility*. Leading a team of software engineers requires different competencies than leading a team of auditors.

Each of these four dynamics plays an important, but supporting, role in determining the complete portfolio of competencies required for effective global leadership. We must be clear about this at the outset: *Every global leader requires a certain set of unique skills and abilities that arise from country affiliation, industry, company, and functional dynamics.* Every leader's personal situation differs and requires a number of unique skills that fit his or her specific context. Furthermore, whenever a manager changes contexts, an entirely new set of specific competencies may be required. However, while there are an almost limitless number of combinations of specific capabilities, these capabilities account for only one-third of what global leaders need to be successful. Therefore, though it is a natural temptation, it would be a mistake for any manager to myopically focus on the capabilities driven by specific dynamics versus the capabilities driven by global dynamics.

Becoming a Global Leader

After investigating the competencies needed for global leadership, we wanted to find out what it took to develop global leaders. We asked the question: "Are global leaders *born or made?*" The answer is that global leaders are born and then made. This means that your future as a global leader is a function of being *competent* at and being *interested* in global business. Exemplar global leaders are highly competent and interested. They are constantly pushing the frontiers of their own knowledge and understanding; they thrive in a chaotic, ambiguous environment; they love people; they have uncompromising ethical standards; they love global business; they are organizationally savvy. In reality, precious few fully competent global leaders exist. Many managers, however, have the potential to become global leaders.

This potential for leadership is innate: High-potential managers are born with a certain degree of inquisitiveness and ability much like the potential musician or athlete. You need some level of interest to even start off on the development journey. In addition, to be a good musician or athlete, you need some basic talent. Having met a certain threshold of raw talent, experience plays an essential role in "making" global leaders. Key experiences beget international curiosity and interest, which in turn foster the development of critical global competencies.

But which experiences are the most effective in accelerating your development as a global leader? In our research, we asked global leaders about their career and personal experiences. What experiences helped most in their development into capable global leaders?

The executives described four primary development options: Travel, Teams, Training, and Transfers (what we call the Four T's). While each kind of experience can provide valuable lessons, international transfers were judged to be by far the most powerful global leader development tool. Approximately 80 percent of participants in our research identified *living and working in a foreign country as the single most influential developmental experience in their lives.* However, taking advantage of all four types of experiences over the course of your career is the most effective way to acquire the complete set of global leadership competencies for your journey through the uncharted waters of today's business world: the New World of global commerce.

A Broader Approach to Global Leadership

This guidebook for your journey is organized into two main sections. Part One sets the stage. In Chapter 1, we briefly review the forces behind the globalization tsunami and the reason why there is such a shortage of quality global leaders. In Chapter 2, we describe the two fundamental global dynamics that drive the critical global leadership characteristics and we briefly introduce the overall global leadership model. Part Two includes detailed discussions of each of the global leadership characteristics. In Chapter 3, we describe the glue that holds it all together—unbridled inquisitiveness. In Chapter 4, we discuss the importance of proper perspective as a global leader. How will you manage the huge degree of uncertainty in the global business environment? How will you balance constant tensions between the demands for global integration and local responsiveness? In Chapter 5, we talk about the character and interpersonal abilities of global leaders by looking at the importance of connecting emotionally with people across the world. We also explore how you can tackle serious ethical conflicts and maintain your integrity. Chapter 6 shows you what you need to know in order to demonstrate global business and organizational savvy.

In Part Three, we show you how to become a better global leader. We discuss strategies you can pursue to master each global leadership competency. In Chapter 7, we show you how to use travel, teams, training, and transfers to develop greater global leader capabilities. In Chapter 8, we explain how you should vary the application of different development experiences, depending on your career stage. Finally, in Chapter 9, we discuss the conclusions we have arrived at and offer some final advice on how to reach your global leadership potential.

We have written this book for you—to inspire you and help you achieve your global leadership aspirations. As you set sail, keep in mind that all great explorers are driven by an innate sense of opportunity and yearning for challenge. They are not satisfied to stroll around in known and familiar territory. Instead, they push the envelop to discover new possibilities. Just like the Old World explorers, you must be excited by the opportunity and challenges of the uncharted global business frontier. We look forward to helping you build your ability to lead others on a thrilling and rewarding expedition. Bon Voyage!

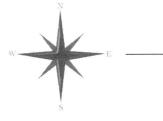

THE NEXT
GENERATION
OF LEADERS

one

EXPLORING THE GLOBAL FRONTIER

Over the past few years, globalization has moved from the periphery to center stage. Once the specialized responsibility of a few managers, it is now a core concern of nearly every senior executive. As international business consultants and professors, it used to be that we worked with a small and specialized group of managers within a company who had responsibility for international operations. Now prefixes such as Worldwide and Global are being added to standard titles such as Product Manager, Vice President of Marketing, Director of Quality, and so on. For many executives, it is not just the titles that are unfamiliar:

> I've got competitors now coming out of Peru, Hungry, and Taiwan that I didn't even know existed two years ago. They have cost structures that I have no idea how to compete against.

> I'm responsible for a worldwide product launch that requires me to bring people together who lie far outside my direct lines of authority. In some cases, I'm not even sure where the help I need is in the organization.

I've been given a mandate to lower our costs by 20 percent and to scour the earth for the highest quality, lowest cost components for our products. The world is a pretty big place when you've been using local suppliers for the last 25 years.

I'm in charge of a task force that has people on it from France, Germany, Italy, Canada, the United States, and Mexico. Even though we all speak English, it's clear to me that we do not speak the same language.

Sometimes I think I'm going nuts. How do you listen to "the voice of the customer" when they speak a hundred different languages and don't all want the same thing?

The company wants a worldwide standard of ethical conduct, but I'm losing business in some countries because it's against company policy to pay for things such as a golf game when we take out government officials.

It used to be that foreign exchange was something that the finance folks worried about. Thanks to the Asian debt crisis, now I have to worry about it. Should I keep our prices in Asia the same to protect our profit margins and risk our market share dropping like a rock, or should I lower our prices to maintain share and take a hit in profits?

Sometimes I feel almost overwhelmed. I've got seven major competitors from five different countries; 42 tier one suppliers representing 25 different currencies; governments ranging from dictatorships to open democracies; local customers in every major region of the world that want my services tailored to their needs; global customers that want my services standardized and delivered to all of their worldwide operations. I've never dealt with anything like this before and neither has anyone else in the company. No SOPs [Standard Operating Procedures] exist for the challenges we face today.

> I just returned from my first trip to China. It was a joint ven-
> ture negotiation. People have asked me, "Well how did it go?" I
> have to say I'm not sure. I couldn't get a direct answer or com-
> mitment from them. I sensed that something was going on in
> the background with their team but I have no idea what it was.

As these quotes demonstrate, many managers today have to navigate
with no mapped out answers. While the media make international business
seem glamorous, for managers who need new skills both to survive in their
current positions and to prepare for promotion opportunities, globalization feels more like a giant wave about to crash down on top of them. Consider the problems of a new factory in Vietnam that plays a significant role
in a major manufacturing firm's global strategy. The firm needs a low-cost
manufacturing base from which it can ship products throughout the Asian
region in order to compete with its major Japanese competitor which is
about to begin delivering product manufactured in its new factory in Indonesia. Since most of the Japanese competitor's raw materials are sourced
in Indonesia, the recent and dramatic depreciation of the Indonesian ru-
piah actually gives the Japanese an even greater cost advantage.

> We just opened up operations in Vietnam—a joint venture
> with the government. Guess what I found when I went to in-
> spect our new greenfield factory site: a green field all right—of
> rice, flooded with water. We have no usable road out there, no
> electricity, no sewer, no city water. I'm supposed to be turning
> out product six months from now. I'll be lucky if I can figure
> out how to get the field drained and construction started six
> months from now.

This manager is sailing in uncharted waters. For example, how does he
get a sewer line extended out to the factory site? Contact the local sewer department? There is no sewer department. Build a separate septic tank and
leachfield system for the factory? The problem here is that there are no specific regulations or specifications to comply with and no formal procedures
to follow for getting such a plan for a self-contained sewer system approved. And while the manager struggles for a solution, his company can-

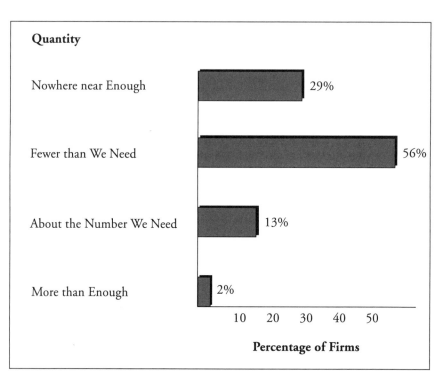

Figure 1.1 Quantity of Global Leaders

not afford to let its main global competitor gain a significant advantage in Asia—a major regional battleground.

Managers who are not trained to deal with international government relations, cultural issues, and global market uncertainty will not produce the results expected by the home office and will not achieve their own desired level of personal success.

In our consulting practice, we hear these frustrations often. This book is designed to give individuals the framework and the tools necessary to succeed in the new global business environment.

The Lack of Global Leaders

Globalization creates new opportunities that require new capabilities. However, these capabilities are not acquired overnight. Consequently, in nearly

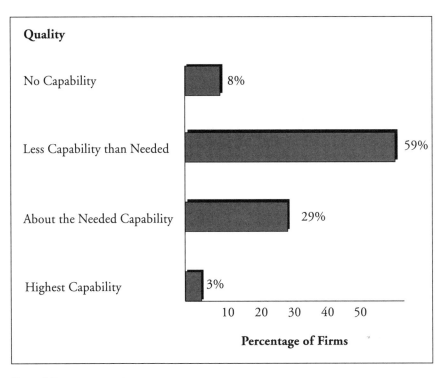

Figure 1.2 Quality of Global Leaders

every firm, the demand for global leaders far outstrips the supply. For example, in a survey of Fortune 500 firms that we completed in 1997, 85 percent of firms do not feel they have an adequate number of global leaders (see Figure 1.1).

Furthermore, as Figure 1.2 illustrates, these executives believe that even among those identified as global leaders the average skill level was not sufficient.

Surprised by these results, we conducted in-depth interviews in order to learn more about this leadership shortage and about the leadership competencies needed to manage successfully in the New World. Our research led us to two main conclusions:

1. The supply of global leaders is short because global leaders can't be developed overnight and because they haven't been developed in the past.

2. The demand for global leaders is high because of the pace and nature of globalization.

Let's first look briefly at the supply problem. As you progress through this book, you will see that the capabilities required to be a successful leader are not acquired overnight. No one can come along, sprinkle global leader dust over you and magically bestow these capabilities. Unfortunately, few corporations have sought to provide their employees with the experiences and training needed to develop global leadership capabilities. During the past 50 years, many firms have been able to focus on their domestic market and still grow and succeed. As a consequence, most managers developed into provincial rather than global leaders. For example, in the past Japanese managers dealt primarily with other Japanese managers. As a consequence, they developed provincial Japanese mental maps of leadership to help them captain their businesses. The same was true for U.S., French, German, Italian, British, and other managers.

While supply of global leaders is essentially flat, demand is growing almost exponentially. Many people say that the world is getting smaller. However, it is actually getting larger. For example, in how many countries did your firm operate twenty years ago? Ten years ago? Five years ago? How many countries does it operate in today? And five years from now? Clearly most firms are operating in more places today than ever before. For most executives the world they have to think about and understand is getting larger. Countries that didn't even show up on anyone's radar screen ten years ago present major market opportunities today. As a consequence, more global leaders are needed now and in the future because globalization means greater revenues, lower costs, and even corporate survival. Demand is also rising because there is no way to plot a reliable, lasting map of global business. The terrain is constantly changing. Consequently, it is not possible to simply develop a few global leaders and then have the masses follow the trails these leaders blaze.

Sailing in Uncharted Global Waters

Today you have the unprecedented opportunity and challenge of leading organizations into the new, unmapped frontiers of the global marketplace.

In that sense, global leadership has many parallels with global exploration of 500 years ago. In fact, one manager, working in China, said that he felt like Magellan sailing the uncharted Pacific Ocean.

As perspective, in the early sixteenth century, Ferdinand Magellan, a Portuguese sea captain, commanded the ship that was the first to sail around the world. His commission was to capture the spice trade for Spain. These excerpts from the ship's log convey the enormity of the challenge:

> The captain general Fernandez Magellan had resolved on un-dertaking a long voyage over the ocean, . . . a course as yet unex-plored by any navigator. . . . On Monday morning the 10th August 1519 foresail was set. . . . On Wednesday 28th November, we . . . entered the ocean to which we afterwards gave the de-nomination of Pacific and in which we sailed the space of three months and 20 days, without tasting any fresh provisions. The biscuit we were eating no longer deserved the name of bread; it was nothing but dust and worms, which had consumed the sub-stance. The water we were obliged to drink was equally putrid and offensive. . . . In the course of these three months and 20 days in the Ocean denominated by the Pacific . . . we saw no fish but sharks and if God had not granted us a fortunate voy-age, we should all have perished of hunger in so vast a sea. . . . We reckoned to have sailed upwards of 14,600 leagues, having circumnavigated the globe from east to west. I do not think that any one for the future will venture on a similar voyage. . . . On 8th September 1522, I presented to His Sacred Majesty Don Carlos neither gold nor silver . . . but a book written with my own hand, in which by day and day, I had set down every event on our voyage.
>
> *— Ship's log August 1519 to September 1522*
> *as kept by Antonio Pigafetta during Ferdinand Magellan's*
> *voyage around the world.*

Imagine what it must have been like for explorers such as Magellan as they scanned the horizon of the great Pacific Ocean for days on end—no reliable charts, the stars of an unfamiliar hemisphere often blocked from view by clouds, waves crashing over the ship's bow, wind howling threats of potential destruction, a crew losing confidence with each passing day of nothing but sea and sky, ravenous sharks ready to devour unfortunate seamates who slipped from the deck.

Now fast forward to the present. These descriptions may have a familiar ring. The global business opportunities today are vast, both for you personally and for your company. There are new markets to be developed, new territories to be explored. But just as the Pacific Ocean was for Magellan, our global marketplace is a shark-infested sea of danger. It is filled with brutal storms of competition, endless seas of change, confusing market channels, undiscovered frontiers of technology, and unseen threats. Like Magellan, the global manager of today must display unwavering leadership in the face of all these challenges.

While there are important similarities between then and now, there is one great difference—a difference that to you as a leader makes all the difference. In the Old World, once the seas and islands were accurately charted, once the rivers, valleys and mountains were properly mapped, the coordinates didn't change. The static nature of geographical landmarks allowed pioneers, and later settlers, to follow the maps of early explorers and move into the new territories. The first inquisitive footprints of the early explorers became well-beaten paths. Lands that were once hazardous and strange became safe and familiar.

Today's global business world is in a constant state of flux: markets, suppliers, competitors, technology, and customers constantly shift, which means that as quickly as the territory is mapped, it changes. As soon as the ink is dry, it's useless. The result? *The New World of global business requires that all leaders be explorers!*

The Tsunami of Globalization

Increasingly, you do not have to seek out global business opportunities—they are coming to you. In fact, whether we like it or not, the tsunami of globalization is inescapable. Tsunamis are fascinating phenomenon. These enormous waves are caused by volcanic eruptions or earthquakes far below the surface of the ocean. In deep waters of 20,000 feet or more, they appear at the surface merely as one- to two-foot swells, but they travel at over 600 miles per hour. They reveal their true force and size as they near shore and shallow water—sometimes towering 50 or 100 feet high. But even then, there is a "lull before the storm." An hour or so before the wave hits, the waters along the shore actually recede, usually to a point much lower than the lowest tide. Then just when the threat seems to have passed, the wave hits with mind-boggling force.

This proves to be a revealing analogy for businesses as they encounter the New World of global commerce. For example, consider the calm before the storm in the late 1980s for the private yacht building and refurbishing industry. Growth and profits for the industry were good, and competition was moderate and local. West Coast yacht builders and refurbishers rarely if ever competed with East Coast companies. In fact, in terms of refurbishing, companies in Washington and Oregon rarely even competed with companies in California.

This was the environment in which the manager of a small yacht company located in peaceful and sunny San Diego, California found himself. The company, with about 90 employees, made and repaired small- to medium-sized yachts. Life was great, and global business concerns were about as far away as icebergs from San Diego Bay. Then, the U.S. government put a 10 percent luxury tax on boats, even as the national economy took a nosedive. The company's workforce shrunk to about 30 employees. Suddenly they found that their customer base was turning to Korean, Indonesian, and Brazilian competitors that they never even knew existed. To survive these stormy seas, they reached out to customers in Japan and Saudi Arabia. They took advantage of the America's Cup race coming to San Diego to help boost their international contacts. When the U.S. economy rebounded, they were prepared to make the most of it. But the business was never the same. It was now a global business. Never again could the manager afford to take his eye off foreign competitors or ignore potential clients from throughout the world. The company he continues to manage, with its $15 million in annual revenue, may still be relatively small, but he now tracks the movement of foreign exchange rates on a daily basis.

Globalization is not a trend; it is not a fad; it is not an isolated phenomenon. It is an inescapable force. If anticipated and understood, it is a powerful opportunity. If not, it can swiftly destroy businesses and to drown careers.

Today's best global leaders, like Magellan, scan the horizon for subtle changes in the wind and waves. For example, by 2015 more business will be transacted between national borders than within them. Companies around the world are investing money in foreign countries at an unprecedented rate. In the last ten years, total foreign investment worldwide has skyrocketed from $60 billion to $350 billion annually. During the same period, the United States received a total of nearly $500 billion in investment from foreign countries (or $1,820 per person); the United Kingdom received approximately $200 billion (or $3,410 per person).[1] Savvy global leaders recognize that these statistics signal that everyone is playing in everyone else's backyard. We can no longer look just at our own domestic market, nor can we afford to ignore foreign competitors, and expect to survive.

Forces Driving Globalization

What do you do with these bits of information? Do you store them as discrete bytes or do you push yourself to speculate on their broad implications? Where do you look for the forces driving globalization? As with real tsunamis, we need to look far below the surface at the underlying tectonic plates of technology, costs, consumers, global customers, governments, and competitors in order to comprehend the powerful forces giving rise to the tsunami wave of globalization. Effective global leaders understand the power and dynamics of these tectonic plates of global business. Other recent books have been wholly devoted to explaining the drivers behind globalization; our purpose here is served with a brief review of them.

Technology

Technology is a wonderful and wicked thing. It is wonderful in terms of what it can do; it is wicked in what it can cost. For example, there is more computing power in one of today's leading edge personal computers than there was in the entire world in 1950! Today, 50 years later, a new fabrication plant that manufactures the computer's microprocessor costs over $2 billion dollars. "Fab plants" for the next two generations of microchips will cost $4 to $6 billion each. Consequently, chip makers, such as Intel, have no choice but to "go global." There is no single market large enough for them to recoup this level of investment. Consequently, their strategy is all about going after global sales.

The same is true for Boeing. Development costs for Boeing's new 777 were between $4 and $6 billion. This doesn't even take into account manufacturing costs. How will Boeing recover this investment? Even if every U.S. airline feel in love with the new 777 and ordered one for every possible route for which the 777 is appropriate, Boeing still could not recover its investment, let alone make enough money to fund the next generation of plane. Consequently, Boeing has no choice but to go after global sales.

The simple conclusion? As technology becomes an increasingly critical lever for competitive advantage and as development costs rise, the market required to recoup the investment must stretch beyond domestic shores and out into the world.

Costs

Costs are another tectonic plate driving the wave of globalization. Industrial customers as well as consumers increasingly have access to information that helps them compare product quality and price. To survive, companies must keep their costs competitive. To keep costs down, purchasing executives have no choice but to scour the earth in search of suppliers with the best products at the lowest possible prices. In Europe alone, GM saved over $1 billion through global sourcing. This savings is equivalent to GM buying a company with $15–$20 billion in annual revenues and good profit margins.

Consumers

Successful global leaders also understand the growing convergence of consumer preferences. Maybe everyone doesn't need a "2 in 1" shampoo that lets you shampoo and condition your hair at the same time, but the successful launch of Pert shampoo in 36 countries in 18 months suggests that at least some consumer preferences are converging.

Just look at the numbers and you can see the enormous potential for global success. In India alone, an estimated 100 million people make between U.S. $25,000 and $30,000 a year.[2] By 2005, there will be only one billion people in developed countries and five billion in developing countries.

McDonald's, for one, is very aware of these numbers. Of McDonald's first six restaurants in China, four set new opening-day records for sales. Or consider MTV, the Viacom division that now has more viewers in developing countries than in the United States.[3] From Beijing to London, from Montreal to Milan, Coca-Cola, Levi Strauss, Toyota, Kodak, Sony, and Swatch products are everywhere. While it would be a mistake to say that consumers have identical preferences around the world, global leaders recognize that those preferences are converging and consumers' capacity to buy products is rising.

Global Business Customers

As certain firms go global in response to technology, cost, and consumer drivers, they in turn pull many of their suppliers with them. Savvy suppliers recognize this as a tremendous opportunity to grow their businesses by following their leading customers overseas. For example, when GM committed billions to China, TRW recognized that expanding into China would enable them to continue to be a leading supplier to GM and would grow TRW's global business. In fact, not following key industrial customers may actually hurt the firm's domestic business with that customer. For example, as Toyota set up operations in the United States, it made it clear to its suppliers in Japan that if they did not follow suit, Toyota might look to "more committed" suppliers for some of its domestic (i.e., Japanese) purchases. Similarly, if you are a major supplier to Fiat or Daewoo or Shell, you may have no choice but to go global.

Governments

Global leaders also recognize the power of governments in today's global economy. Despite claims of "a borderless world," savvy global leaders recognize that national and local government officials the world over have no intention of meekly giving up their power to "transnational" companies or any other type of corporation. Governments can and do create both threats and opportunities. For example, pension fund managers at Fidelity can hardly contain their enthusiasm or fear as they eye the trillions of dollars in

Japanese pensions that will soon be open to foreign management. The government of Japan has created a huge opportunity for foreign firms, if these firms can figure out how to navigate the unmapped waters of this newly deregulated market. As this move toward deregulation is repeated in Korea, Indonesia, and Argentina, executives eye these developments both biting their nails and chomping at the bit.

Competitors

Today, competitors can come at you from virtually any country. Effective global leaders keep a vigilant watch on current and future competitors. The best global leaders recognize that they cannot afford to simply defend their home turf. For example, ten years ago, no one predicted that virtually every major U.S. TV manufacturer would be out of the business today. Would Zenith executives have predicted that they would have to sell 58 percent of the company to LG Group of Korea in order to survive? In turn, would LG executives have predicted that a few years later competition would have forced them to sell off major components of their conglomerate in order to survive?

The battle between Fuji and Kodak is another example. For years, Fuji has maintained a profit sanctuary in Japan that helps fund its war with Kodak in the United States and around the world. Recently, Kodak took its complaints about Fuji's unfair business practices in Japan and the United States to government authorities. Perhaps Kodak's complaints are legitimate. But the fact remains that because Kodak was a weak player in Japan, it allowed Fuji an important profit sanctuary, which Fuji has used to support campaigns against Kodak in the United States and elsewhere.

Globalization for U.S. Firms

Recently, we conducted a survey of over 100 medium and large U.S. companies in search of signs of globalization. We found that on average 38% of the survey firms' annual sales currently come from outside the United States. This is estimated to rise to nearly 50% over the next five years. Over the five years, the percentage of firms that get 75% or more of their sales

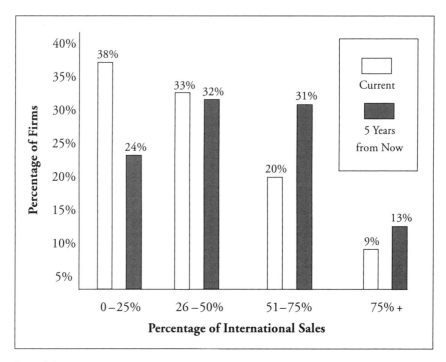

Figure 1.3 International Sales

from the U.S. domestic market is expected to drop from 38% to 24% (see Figure 1.3). The percentage of firms with one-half to three-quarters of their sales coming from overseas is expected to rise from 20% to 31%. These statistics clearly indicate that U.S. executives expect a international sales to account for an increasing portion of total sales.

We also asked these same firms about the relative strategic importance of their domestic versus international operations (see Figure 1.4). Among these firms, currently 46.6% have a strategic emphasis on domestic business; 12.6% have a balanced emphasis; and 40.8% have a strategic emphasis on international operations. Looking ahead five years, only 17.5% of these same firms estimated that they will emphasize domestic operations (a 62% decrease); 15.5% expected a balanced focus; and 67% stated that their firm would have a strategic focus on international operations (a 64% increase).

As a more direct assessment of global competition, we also asked these U.S.-based firms how many of their current top five competitors are foreign

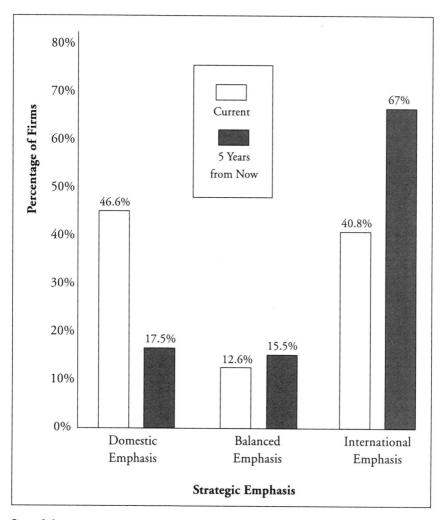

Figure 1.4 Strategic Emphasis

firms and how many they expected to be in the future. On average, 56% of their current top five competitors are foreign firms; they expect this to increase to 64% over the next five years. The percentage of firms with *all* of their top five competitors based in the United States is expected to drop significantly from 28% to 18%—a 36% decrease.

Effective global leaders realize that gone are the days when you could look across the street, or even within your own national borders, to find your competition and figure out what they were up to. Global leaders recognize that the tectonic plates of technology, costs, consumers, global customers, governments, and competitors have already collided. They are aware that the tsunami of globalization is surging forward at 600 miles an hour and that impact is unavoidable. They know that the provincial leadership models of the past will not work in a global future.

Globalization Demands a New Leadership Model

None of us can escape the tsunami of globalization. Consequently, if you have aspirations of leading any organization or significant business unit in the future, you must think as a global explorer; you must develop *global* leadership characteristics.

Provincial Leadership Models Worked in the Past

Leadership models that were once popular in the United States no longer work today. These old models were based on a strong belief in hierarchical command and control structures, and focused on the domestic environment. Executives who exemplified this model in turn hired and promoted others who shared this orientation. However, what worked in the past will not work in the future, and what worked in North America will not succeed in other parts of the world.

Recently, we met with a senior human resource manager at a primary division of Philip Morris. He had just returned from a tour of duty in Europe. From his comfortable New York office, he recalled the difficulty of trying to apply old models to the New World. "We wanted to get some consistency of direction in how we develop our people around the world," he explained. "So we developed a competency model for leadership. I think this was a good idea." But he went on to reveal that the company had made the error of assuming that the leadership model developed for North America could be reapplied everywhere else. "I was in Europe at the time as an HR director," he continued, "and thought this was just crazy. The words meant nothing to the Europeans." He was expected to measure his people in Europe against standards that had little meaning in their context. He shook his head, his voice still edged with frustration, "I could hear them say, 'Psst, it's American!' "

However, Americans are not the only ones guilt of taking a rather ethnocentric approach to leadership. Japanese, Korean, German, French, Swedish, British and other managers have the same tendency.

In one sense, this tendency is both natural and functional. It is natural because values across countries and even regions within countries do differ. The importance of relationships, short-term profits, hierarchies, ethics, and risk aversion and other factors varies from culture to culture.[4] For example, the Japanese adage "The nail that stands up gets hammered down" reflects a culture that places a priority on the group rather than on the individual. Consequently, consensus decision making rather than individual accountability prevails. Every country has a somewhat different leadership model, which in turn dictates different leadership practices. These models work fine as long as the leaders deal primarily with individuals from within the culture of the model. This has largely been true in the past. However, it will be increasingly less true in the future.

Global Leadership Models Work in the Future

Globalization is a major challenge to provincial leadership models. For a company to become more global, its leaders must look beyond familiar, provincial approaches. If becoming a global company means overcoming national differences, then becoming a global leader means the same thing.

Yet most of us are threatened by any change to the status quo. When facing new challenges, we tend to rely on what has worked well in the past. We work harder, put in longer hours, or try to think smarter; but, in the end, we usually come back to doing what we have always done—because what we've done is what we know. When faced with a new challenge, most of us try to meet that challenge by doing what we know a little bit better. Provincial leadership models of the past worked precisely because the past business environment was more provincial.

The wave of globalization requires something more than an American or European or Asian leadership model. It demands a global model that applies around the world, a model that transcends national perspectives and delivers a powerful tool for recruiting, developing, and retaining a company's future leaders. Jack Welch has preached to General Electric managers on many occasions that his example of leadership cannot last in a global company and that a new breed of leader is needed:

> The Jack Welch of the future cannot be like me. I spent my entire career in the United States. The next head of General Electric will be somebody who spent time in Bombay, in Hong Kong, in Buenos Aires. We have to send our best and brightest overseas and make sure they have the training that will allow them to be the global leaders who will make GE flourish in the future.

As this quote illustrates, both the characteristics and the development of future leaders needs to be different. Currently, companies all around the world face a serious global leadership gap (see Figure 1.5). Supply is low, and unless things change rather quickly and dramatically, supply will remain relatively flat. Demand, on the other hand, like a tsunami, is being driven by powerful tectonic plates at the very foundation of business.

For many corporations, this global leadership gap is a growing crisis. For you as an individual, it is an enormous opportunity. Global leaders are

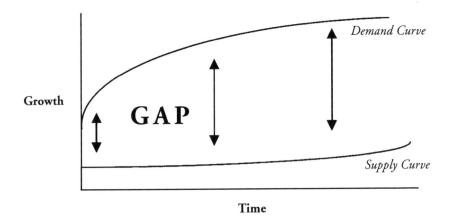

Figure 1.5 Global Leadership Gap

needed and are in short supply. If you have the interest and capabilities, you will be in great demand. It can also be a threat. If you have significant leadership aspirations but no interest in things global, you may face more career limitations in the future than at the present. For companies, this global leadership gap also presents both opportunity and danger. In an increasingly knowledge-based, global economy, having great global leaders today and a good bench strength for tomorrow is likely to provide significant competitive advantage. From our research, only 2 to 3 percent of firms have the quantity and quality of global leaders that they need. If ever statistics painted a picture of competitive white space, these do. Put another way, there are very few firms with first mover advantage in the area of global leadership. However, the current and future global leadership gap represents a significant threat to companies as well. It represents literally billions of dollars wasted in mistakes and bad decisions and even more in lost opportunities because of inadequate global leadership capabilities.

Having sketched the basic terrain of globalization, we now want to turn to a discussion of the key drivers behind what makes a successful global leader, and then turn to in-depth discussions of those capabilities and how you can develop them.

Notes

1. World Trade Organization (1996), "Trade and Foreign Investment: New Report by the WTO Secretariat." (Press Release) October 9.

2. For a more complete discussion on globalization pressures, see Morrison, A. (1990), *Strategies in Global Industries: How U.S. Businesses Compete.* Westport, CT: Quorum Books; Yip, G. (1992), *Total Global Strategy.* Englewood Cliffs, NJ: Prentice Hall.

3. Wysocki, B. (1997), "In the Emerging World, Many Youths Splurge, Mainly on U.S. Goods." *Wall Street Journal,* June 26, pp. A1, A12.

4. Kluckholn, F., and Strodtbeck, F. (1961), *Variations in Value Orientations.* Evanston, IL: Row, Peterson; Hofstede, G. (1980), *Culture's Consequences: International Differences in Work-Related Values.* Beverly Hills: Sage Publications; Boyacigiller, N. and Adler, N. (1991), "The Parochial Dinosaur: Organizational Science in a Global Context." *Academy of Management Review,* 16(2), pp. 262–90; Yeung, A. and Ready, D. (1995), "Developing Leadership Capabilities of Global Corporations: A Comparative Study in Eight Nations." *Human Resource Management,* Winter, vol. 34(4), pp. 529–47.

A FRAMEWORK FOR GLOBAL LEADERSHIP

In researching global leadership, we conducted interviews with over 130 senior executives in 50 firms based in Europe, North America, and Asia. We also interviewed managers who were identified in their firms as exemplars or role models of the future global leader. What we learned is that effective global leadership is composed of capabilities that are driven by fundamental dynamics. These dynamics can be segmented into those that are business-specific and those that are global.

Business-Specific Dynamics

This first set of dynamics results in a unique set of leadership capabilities that change depending upon the exact situation of the individual. We group these business-specific dynamics into four basic categories.

The first dynamic we have already touched on in Chapter 1—nationality. Even though we argue that the global future means that the provincial leadership models of the past are outdated, two facts remain true for the moment. First, even in companies with a high percentage of their sales out-

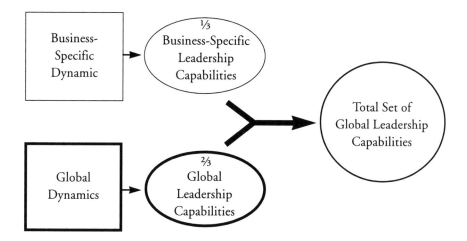

Figure 2.1 Business-Specific and Global Dynamics

side their domestic market, such as Nokia or Exxon, the executive ranks are still dominated by "home country nationals." Even though over 90 percent of Nokia's portable phone sales come from outside Finland, most of the senior managers are Finnish. Likewise, at Exxon 70 percent of revenues come from outside the United States, yet 70 percent of the company's senior managers are American. Consequently, not knowing how to deal effectively with American managers is a significant liability for an Exxon employee. The requirements for success in working with Americans are different than with Finns and vice versa. Clearly, some necessary leadership capabilities are unique to the culture of the home country of the individual's firm.

The second business-specific dynamic is that of industry. Clearly, business cycles, the role of technology, and other factors vary from industry to industry. As a consequence, so do a variety of leadership capabilities. For example, the decision-making skills that are particularly effective in the nuclear power plant construction business do not necessarily apply in the software development industry.

The third business-spcific dynamic is the company's culture. Even in the same country and within the same industry, success in a particular company may require unique leadership capabilities. For example, the factors that produce leadership success at Honda may differ in significant ways from those appropriate to Toyota.

The fourth business-specific dynamic is function. Even in the same country, industry, and company, some unique capabilities may be required depending on functional differences. For example, leading a group of engineers often requires capabilities different from those relied on when leading a group of marketers.

From our research, the unique leadership capabilities that arise as a function of these dynamics account for about one third of the complete set of capabilities required of successful global leaders. The remaining two thirds arise from global dynamics (see Figure 2.1). The important point here is that this second set of dynamics are essentially the same for every global leader and therefore give rise to a set of leadership characteristics that are relevant regardless of country, industry, company, or function. They are truly global.

Global Dynamics

Based on our interviews and experience, we have observed that two basic global dynamics drive the key required global leadership capabilities—the dynamics of dispersion and duality. These two dynamics are generated by the critical distinctions between domestic and global business.

The dynamics of dispersion revolve around the degree to which organizational resources, particularly people, are dispersed in a worldwide organization. These dynamics gain their power from the sheer scope of the global environment—no single domestic business environment even comes close. Though the Russian economy spans eleven different time zones, its diversity, however remarkable, does not begin to approach the enormity of the cultural, language, government, and market differences that exist across the globe.

In making this point, we do not want to create the impression that all domestic environments are somehow "simple" or even internally homogeneous. Clearly they are not. However, there is simply no comparison to the global environment. The consequences are plain. In the past, the scope of domestic initiatives undertaken by most managers was an appropriate fit with their command-and-control reach (see Figure 2.2).

Time and again, we have listened to executives with global responsibilities talk about the fact that the scope of global initiatives far exceeds the traditional reach of command-and-control (see Figure 2.3).

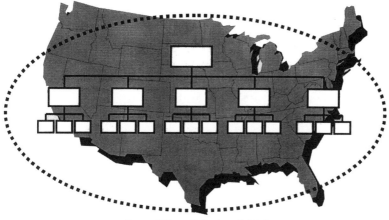

Scope of Domestic Business Initiative

Figure 2.2 Typical Match between Traditional Command and Control Reach and Scope of Domestic Business Initiative

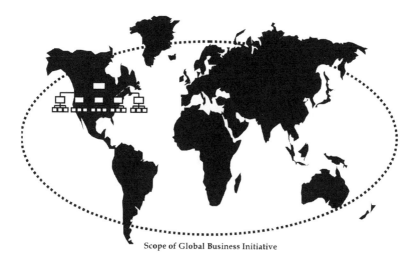

Scope of Global Business Initiative

Figure 2.3 Mismatch between Traditional Command and Control Reach and Scope of Global Business Initiative

Even the most senior executives—those who in theory have authority over virtually every employee in their companies—report that they need cooperation, goodwill, and trust in order to successfully implement global initiatives. The world is just too big—with too many time zones, languages, governments, traditions, customs, political systems, values, and miles—for executives to directly control it all.

For example, we listened to a senior executive at IBM lament his inability to get a specific global initiative effectively implemented. When we asked what the problem was, he responded, "People are just not going along with it." "But you have authority over 99.9 percent of the employees, how can that be?" we asked. "The world is a big place. I can't be everywhere at once. Someone in China, India, or Russia could sidestep me for months. By the time I found out about it and could force compliance, it would be too late," he responded. This was typical of many conversations on the topic.

The second global dynamic—dualism—revolves around the dual pressures for global integration and local adaptation. On the one hand, the push for global integration of activities is tremendous. In fact, most of the forces driving globalization that we discussed in the previous chapter create this pressure.

Yet despite the strength of these forces today and for the foreseable future, they are countered by forces for localization. For example, despite the growing convergence of consumer preferences, consumers around the world still do not universally aspire to the same exact things. Not everyone demands the level of precision engineering and safety found in a Mercedes, and of those who do not all are able to afford it. Likewise, despite the global trend towards deregulation over the last 50 years, governments still impose different standards, regulations, and statutes. The reality is that even while the forces for global integration have been steadily increasing, the forces for localization are not even close to dead (see Figure 2.4). While this dynamic of dualism has existed for some time and has been written about by other authors, it is especially relevant here because of its implications for effective global leadership.

A Model of Global Leadership

As mentioned previously, our model of global leadership is based on a rather extensive research study. The global leadership characteristics that

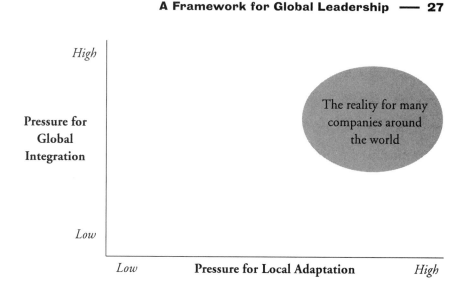

High

Pressure for Global Integration

Low

The reality for many companies around the world

Low   **Pressure for Local Adaptation**   *High*

Figure 2.4 Dynamics of Duality

emerged from our interviews were largely driven by the dynamics of dispersion and duality. However, not all the leadership characteristics were equally related to both dynamics. Consequently, as we introduce each characteristic, we will also briefly describe how it relates to the dynamics of dispersion and of duality. Figure 2.5 illustrates the characteristics of global leaders. Here we just want to briefly introduce each aspect; later in the book we devote full chapters to exploring each in greater depth.

Inquisitiveness is at the core of our global leadership model. Although inquisitiveness is a central characteristic of effective global leaders, it is more an attitude than a skill. Someone can be quite inquisitive without having well-honed skills or knowledge. For example, healthy babies are at the same time incredibly inquisitive and essentially devoid of skills. Inquisitiveness is a state of mind, and a vital characteristic of global leaders, providing the nourishment and sustenance required to keep the other three global leader characteristics at full strength. In many ways, leading a global organization is like leading a crew on a great voyage. And just as curiosity drove explorers to sail great distances through uncharted seas and trudge through dangerous, unmapped lands, inquisitiveness must drive your desire to understand

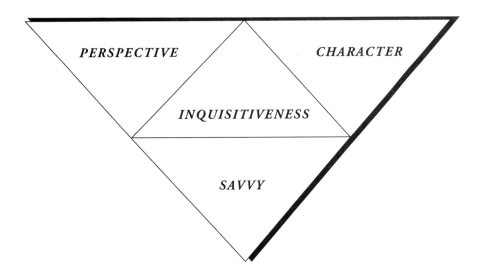

Figure 2.5   Effective Global Leader Characteristics

and explore new international markets. This is the core element of successful global leadership.

In our framework, inquisitiveness is the core; perspective, character, and savvy comprise a set of triangles around the core. This triangle represents the observable and measurable characteristics of successful global leaders. Each of the corners represents a different set of skills and knowledge, and each has two subsets.

Perspective is all about how leaders look at the world. It has two subcomponents: embracing uncertainty and balancing tensions. Later in the book we explore both of these dimensions in greater detail. Duality dynamics are the main driver behind the significance of perspective. The pressures for global integration and local adaptation each create tremendous uncertainties. While most managers shy away from these uncertainties, global leaders embrace them and are invigorated by them. In addition, the duality dynamics create tensions that have to be balanced. Successful global leaders do not have the luxury of simply ignoring one pressure in favor of another. They must often search for innovative ways to balance competing demands. Once again, while many managers are paralyzed by the clash of competing forces, global leaders view the same dynamic as an opportunity to find innovative solutions rather than to settle for mediocre compromises.

Character is the second corner of the model and has two subcomponents: emotional connection and unwavering integrity. Both are thoroughly explored in a separate chapter later in the book. This portion of the model is driven primarily by the dispersion dynamic. Successful global initiatives require the goodwill and trust of people outside your formal lines of authority—people who have different cultural paradigms from you and often from each other. Consequently, connecting with them emotionally and exhibiting unbending integrity are critical to engendering their goodwill and trust. These things cannot be commanded or controlled. They are freely given, not surrendered on demand.

Savvy represents the third corner of the model. Just as the great explorers displayed enormous skill in accessing money and provisions, as a global leader, you need to demonstrate both exceptional business savvy and organizational savvy. You must have a clear sense of what needs to be done and know how to access the resources to make it happen. Just as the great explorers enjoyed the confidence of their crews, you must also have the full support and commitment of your employees. This is crucial, because unlike yesterday's sailors who had little choice but to stay with their ship, employees today have many more options when it comes to abandoning the team or deserting their leader. The need for organizational savvy arises primarily from the dispersion dynamics. To successfully implement global initiatives, you need to know who to tap and what organizational resources are available in order to successfully reach beyond the limits of ordinary command and control. Business savvy, on the other hand, arises primarily in response to duality dynamics. You have to be able to figure out which activities need to be globally integrated and which need to be locally adapted, as well as how to simultaneously satisfy both demands, in order to maximize the moneymaking opportunities for your firm.

Figure 2.6 provides a graphic representation of how the global leadership characteristics relate to the two central global dynamics. As you can see, inquisitiveness is equally related to both dynamics. As we have already pointed out, inquisitiveness is not only the core of the leadership model but it is also the primary means by which global leaders transcend mere

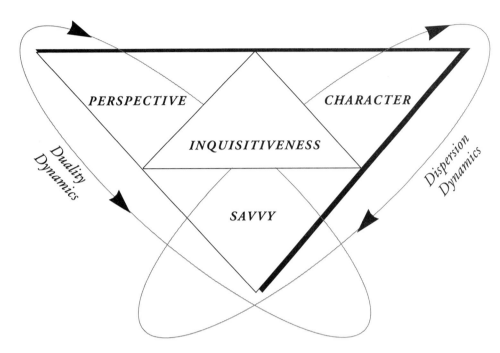

Figure 2.6 Alignment of Global Leadership Characteristics and Global Business Dynamics

coping strategies and actively engage with the dynamics of dispersion and duality. Perspective is critical in responding to duality dynamics, while character issues arise primarily because of dispersion dynamics. Savvy relates to both dynamics: organizational savvy to dispersion, and business savvy to duality.

Mapping Your Global Leadership Profile

Before the sixteenth and seventeenth centuries, mapmakers relied heavily on travelers' tales and explorers' rough sketches to construct their maps of the world. With the invention of more accurate measuring instruments and better mathematical techniques, mapmakers became increasingly precise. In fact, most sailing charts after the 1600s usually include an interesting series of connected triangles, which literally crisscross the entire map.

These patterns result from applying the cartographic principle of triangulation, which early explorers relied on to map their journeys. With some mathematical manipulation, they could figure out the exact dimensions of each side and angle in these triangles and then chart where they had been, where they were, and where they were going.

This whole process was facilitated by the use of control points. Control points are distant objects that allow cartographers to determine an exact position on the map. For example, by knowing the height of Mt. Everest beforehand, mapmakers can easily determine the exact height of adjacent peaks. When mapping your world of global leadership, you should create similar control points by comparing your leadership skills to others'. We would suggest that you start with the global leaders we describe throughout this book. They come from around the world and have been referred to as *exemplars* by their peers, subordinates, and bosses. These are men and women who can be your control points when constructing your global leadership triangle. They can be the peaks that guide you in your quest for global leadership success. Through these exemplars and others that you might know, you can more accurately determine how your global leadership triangle fits together.

Balance is Critical For Your Success

As you examine your global leadership characteristics, keep in mind that while some raw aptitude is necessary, exemplar global leaders must work hard to develop all four characteristics to ensure success. They know that success depends on a strong and balanced set of characteristics. In contrast, executives who are weak in one or two areas will find themselves significantly handicapped at some point in their careers. For example, managers who lack proper perspective and have difficulty embracing ambiguity and balancing tensions will not be effective global leaders. Without those skills, they can never achieve the proper medium between timidity and brazenness when acting in critical markets. They become paralyzed, incapable of making the types of decisions that set one apart as a global leader. Managers without character are similarly ineffective. They may be savvy and talented at spotting moneymaking opportunities, but without empathy and integrity, they become self-serving and lose the goodwill and trust of valuable employees. Managers who lack savvy are also ultimately of little use as leaders. While employees may perceive them as warm people, their lack of savvy makes them prone to costly business mistakes that eventually undercut their ability to lead.

Your Global Leadership Profile

Just as centuries ago each part of a triangle played an essential role for cartographers to chart unknown lands and waters, inquisitiveness, perspective, character, and savvy are *equally* important in effective global leadership. Building on the mapmakers' triangle, you can determine where you are and where you need to go as a global leader. Figures 2.7, 2.8, and 2.9 provide graphic examples of possible profiles. (See the Appendix for a set of questions and scoring procedures for mapping your profile.) Your profile may or may not be reflected in these examples, but they provide a general point of reference.

To begin to map your own profile, start with inquisitiveness. How curious are you about the world around you? Next, examine how you look at ambiguity and how well you balance tensions. Do they energize you or unnerve you? Similarly, take a look at how well you connect emotionally with people and how consistent you are in your ethical behavior. Do you inspire goodwill and trust in others? Finally, examine your organizational and business savvy. Do you know where critical resources are in your global organization and do you know how to tap them? Do you recognize business opportunities amidst the chaos of the global marketplace?

Assessing Your Global Leadership Characteristics

To help assess your global leader potential, consider your responses to the following questions:

Inquisitiveness
- Do you read everything you can get your hands on?
- Do you love to travel to new parts of the world?
- When in a foreign country, do you try to immerse yourself in the local culture?

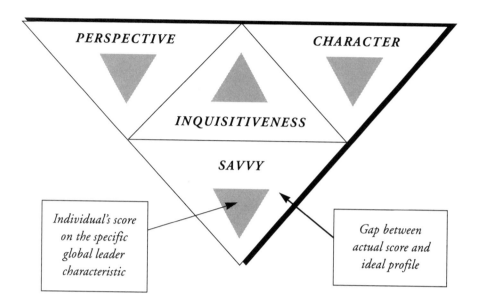

Figure 2.7 Balanced but Weak Profile

- No matter where you are in the world, do you really enjoy talking to customers or potential customers?
- Do you really enjoy learning and wish you had more time for it?

Perspective
- Are you comfortable with uncertainty?
- Do you enjoy not being told what to do?
- Are you good at differentiating between the policies and products that should be globally standardized and those that should be locally determined?
- Are you comfortable with applying company policies different ways in different circumstances?

Character
- Do you fully understand and embrace your company's ethical code of conduct?

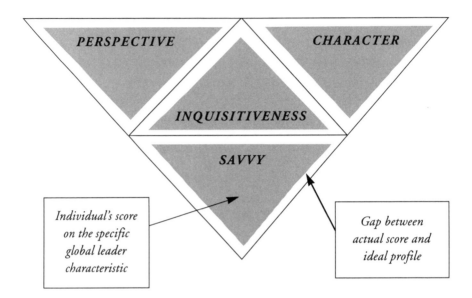

Figure 2.8 Balanced and Strong Profile

- Do the people you work with, both inside and outside the company, think you are an honest person?
- Do you genuinely like people—your employees, your customers, other people you work with?
- Do people find you easy to talk to?

Savvy
- Do you have a solid understanding of how money is made in your industry?
- Do you have a strong track record of making money for your company?
- Are you familiar with your company's strengths and weaknesses on a worldwide basis?
- Do you know who the key decision makers are throughout the company's worldwide operations?

Your responses to these questions can help you better understand your strengths and weaknesses, map your global leadership triangle, and guide

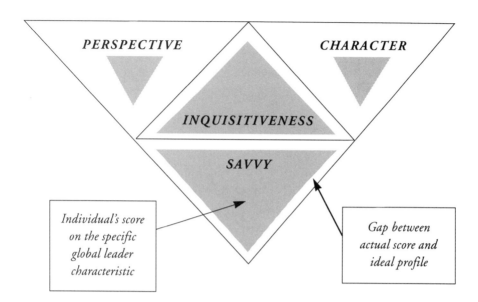

Figure 2.9 Unbalanced and Mixed Profile

your development as a global leader. Of course, these questions we provide here do not represent scientific measures of your potential as a global leader. Nor are they intended to assess how well you may or may not perform on an international assignment. They are, however, a valuable step toward a deeper understanding of your global leadership strengths and weaknesses. Much more comprehensive global leadership and international assignment assessment tools are available.

A few organizations have recently begun developing instruments to measure global leadership potential. Based on the research presented in this book, we have developed through the San Diego–based Global Leadership Institute a broad assessment tool (Global Explorer™) to help individuals and companies assess global leadership potential (a small sample of the instrument is presented in the Appendix). This instrument helps you get an idea of how balanced or unbalanced your characteristics are and what your personal strengths and weaknesses are relative to each of the four global leadership characteristics. For example, some individuals are strong in business and organizational savvy but weak on emotional connection. While this unbalanced profile may work for a time, at some point all the savvy in the world will not engender the goodwill and trust that comes with emotional connection. The feedback report not only gives individuals a profile of their global leadership characteristics but also what they can do to bolster weak areas and develop a more balanced profile.

Perhaps you are fortunate, and your global leadership triangle is not only well balanced, but quite large, suggesting significant strength in all areas of global leadership. More likely, though, your triangle is somewhat unbalanced, with a mix of strong and weak areas. In any case, each of us as global leaders still has room for improvement.

As we pointed out earlier, global leaders are in high demand, but in short supply. Consequently, competent global leaders are very valuable assets. While companies can find country experts, they find very few who are capable of effective leadership across multiple borders. One California-based senior executive explained that it was "easy to find country-competent people who can master a single market, but it is almost impossible to discover managers who are masters at multiple markets."

We saw this shortcoming again and again around the world. From Europe to North America to Asia, top managers had a difficult time identifying more than a few individuals in their own companies who could be counted on to effectively lead anywhere in the world. While European companies tend to have proportionately more leaders who are effective outside their home countries than firms in America and many Asian countries, many of these European leaders are focused on Europe and not the rest of the world. Their skills and knowledge base beyond Europe is not appreciably different from that of Americans outside the United States.

Because there is a severe global leader shortage and because the needed characteristics cannot be developed overnight, the sooner you launch full sail into the development of your global leadership characteristics, the sooner you will find yourself in a position to fill this leadership gap. Perhaps you lead a functional team like accounting, marketing, or purchasing; maybe you manage a business—small, medium, or large; perhaps you manage a particular geographic unit in your company or are in a corporate leadership position. No matter the position you hold, if you lead, the message is clear: *Your inquisitiveness, perspective, character, and savvy will have an enormous positive impact on the value you create for your company.* The stronger your competencies, the deeper and wider your impact will be on your firm's bottom line. And while the imperatives to develop these competencies are greater if you are a top manager, they will give you a personal competitive advantage no matter what your leadership position in your company.

THE ESSENCE

OF GLOBAL

LEADERSHIP

three

INQUISITIVENESS

In the Old World, inquisitiveness drove explorers beyond their limits to discover virgin territory and new trade routes. *In the New World marketplace, inquisitiveness is the essence of global leadership.* Inquisitiveness lies at the heart of exploration. Exemplar global leaders are constantly curious and eager for knowledge. They actively seek new information, investigate the world, and challenge what other people generally take for granted. As A. L. Flood, chairman and CEO of the Canadian Imperial Bank of Commerce, maintained, "Global leaders acquire new knowledge and skills precisely because it is something done *by* rather than *to* them."

Companies rich in international experience and those just beginning to internationalize seek out and develop executives with the skills to lead global operations, expand the corporation's global reach, and gain a competitive advantage for the company. Consider International Flowers and Fragrances (IFF), a company with over $1.5 billion in annual worldwide sales. It is the leading creator and manufacturer of flavors and fragrances for use as ingredients or elements in a wide variety of consumer products. Whether knowingly or not, we have all consumed and inhaled many an IFF product. The business originated in the 1800s as a joint venture between a Dutch company and a Dutch-American company, each contibuting extensive international operations. The company still reflects its international beginnings with a cadre of executives who come from around the globe.

From IFF's New York City headquarters, Eugene Grisanti, chairman and CEO, works closely with key worldwide product and functional executives, garnering over 70 percent of the company's business from outside the United States. Under the guidance of these executives, the fragrance division develops perfumes for global market appeal. In the flavors division, numerous overseas production facilities rely heavily on local country input to meet unique client demands by developing customized flavors for dozens of local markets (e.g., China, Indonesia, Thailand, Brazil, and France). Reflecting on IFF's competitive situation, Eric Campbell, corporate vice president of human resources, confided, "The best local and global leaders in our company are curious enough to pay attention to the extremely subtle nuances of any locale—whether in New York or Jakarta—as well as smart enough to notice consumer similarities around the world."

At IFF, as well as at any company with global aspirations, inquisitiveness is the essential leadership ingredient for seeing subtle local differences as well as noticing global similarities. Just as a specific fragrance becomes the essence of a perfume when mixed in a liquid base, inquisitiveness constitutes the essence of global leadership effectiveness when combined with the other key global leader characteristics. It is not only the essence, but *inquisitiveness is the fundamental driving force behind global leadership success.* Exemplar global leaders are incurably curious about every aspect of the world around them, much like kids in a candy shop. As Gilles Pellisson, CEO of Disneyland Paris, quipped, "they *always* have their antennas out" on the hunt for new knowledge, insight, and perspective. For global leaders, this hunt produces an almost inexhaustible fuel for keeping perspective, exhibiting character, and demonstrating savvy.

Inquisitiveness and Perspective

Inquisitive global leaders are curious in the face of uncertainty. Inquisitiveness not only helps global leaders seek out useful and timely data, it helps them sort through and make sense of that data. Global leaders know that inquisitiveness is the only prescription for uncertainty when facing a mountain of inconsistent information. This is precisely when global leaders manage their inquisitiveness most carefully. They know how to reign in curiosity and when to move forward. They choose to act in the face of uncertainty because they believe that their natural inquisitiveness will let them learn "on-the-fly" as a situation unfolds. They make constant, and more often than not, correct adjustments to prior decisions and actions. At Kraft Foods, they successfully made such adjustments in Beijing when the company decided to build a bicycle-based delivery system for ice cream products rather than try the typical distribution system prevalent in North America and Europe. For Corel software, adjustment meant creating unique graphics formats in its Word Perfect Presentations software program to make it attractive to Japanese end-users. And at the same time that McDonald's engages in endless wars with multinational competitors like Burger King in terms of pricing, production, and menu items, the company must develop different strategies for countries like the Philippines where local competitors dominate the fast food industry.

Without inquisitiveness, you cannot embrace the constant dualities that global leaders face when doing business internationally. The common trap is to do business the same way in all countries—the "cookie-cutter" management style carried over from the mass production era of the 1950s. Consider the difficulties that Steve Burke encountered when asked by Michael Eisner in 1993 to help turn around EuroDisney, a theme park then on its way to losing over U.S. $1 billion in a single year. The park was under fire from the local media and from shareholders understandably nervous about a possible park shutdown. Not only was Disney's reputation on the line, but so was Eisner's—it was *his* first theme park as a CEO.

In his new job as EuroDisney's vice president of operations and marketing, Steve balanced a myriad of tensions (such as pricing strategies, labor policies, and so forth) between corporate headquarters and the local operation. Understanding that no company can force its complete culture into new markets, he was challenged with either avoiding the problematic dualities, or soundly embracing them to help create a financially viable, competitive operation. For Steve, running away from these dualities could have been a way to avoid high levels of uncertainty and the difficulty of wrestling with and ultimately deciding between corporate traditions and local market pressures. At the time, the new park represented a significant financial stake for Disney and financial analysts were predicting a EuroDisney disaster, putting even more pressure on Steve. Instead of becoming a nervous wreck in this situation, unable to decide anything, Steve's high level of inquisitiveness pushed him to make tough choices that helped put the park back in the black financially.

Steve asked questions, listened carefuly, developed a strategy, and implemented a plan. He dug beyond the obvious in order to understand the assumptions and contexts for decision making and action, asking a slew of questions that focused on understanding customers' and key employees' values. He wanted to know what would bring more Disney magic into the park employees' work and at the same time, what would make a stay at EuroDisney more desirable to customers. For example, Steve wrestled with the issue of serving wine at EuroDisney. Back at company headquarters in Burbank, Steve probed senior executives with questions like, Does Europeans' desire to drink wine with lunch necessarily conflict with the need for a clean, safe, and fun atmosphere at the park? Over time, Steve came to see how headquarters executives had assumed that drinking wine would induce bad behavior, thus ruining other guests' experiences at the French theme park. In contrast, Steve's curiosity helped him understand that in France wine and beer were simply an essential part of meals and not drunk in isolation. Steve's inquisitiveness helped him work through the contradictory perspectives and find a way to serve wine with food while maintaining a clean, safe, and fun Disney park.

When managing the constant tensions that dominate international business environments, global leaders like Stephen Burke are unusually adept at learning everything possible about each side of the tension, each source of potential conflict, in order to balance those tensions and keep perspective. Only through the essence of global leadership—inquisitiveness—do global leaders comprehend the complex dynamics of a situation and accurately manage tensions, instead of working to destroy them.

Inquisitiveness and Character

Without inquisitiveness, you cannot maintain an emotional connection with people and consistently demonstrate the highest integrity. Neither the people you work with nor the ethical challenges you face stay constant. As one senior executive heading up new business development outside the United States maintained, "To connect with you when you are from a very different place than me, I must be curious or I am dead. If I don't pay attention to how you do things, why you do them, what the social and historical underpinnings are to your actions, what makes you tick, then forget it." Thus global leadership requires a huge, ongoing commitment to learn. For example, how can you connect with others on an emotional level if you don't seek an understanding of their world? If you are responsible for working with employees from 23 countries, how can you connect with them without knowing the subtle, but significant, nuances of each person?

Consider a mid-sized company that sent its marketing director to Asia. The marketing director did not want to go from the beginning and was essentially dragged overseas. As illustrated in the following situation, he was completely oblivious to any need for cultural sensitivity. During one visit to Korea he was socializing with a key client in front of a group of people. During the conversation, the client remarked, "No, this is the way it is." Immediately the marketing director shot back, "No, it is not!" Then, right in front of everyone, he took the Korean client to an exhibit area to prove (in public) that he was right and the client was wrong. The Korean client was thoroughly embarrassed in front of his peers. This marketing director's oblivious action devastated his company's relationship with the client's company for years. Afterwards, one senior executive inside the U.S. firm lamented, "There are people who are just oblivious and no matter what you do they are not going to pick up important cues during cross-cultural encounters." In this case, the result of not being inquisitive is self-evident; business with a key foreign client was lost for years.

Inquisitiveness is essential for global leaders to build the emotional connections required in high-performance, cross-cultural teams, as exemplified by one of our clients, a multinational petroleum exploration and production company. The company's major operations are in the rich offshore oil and gas fields of southeast Asia. Each of its offshore platforms has 100 employees working 12-hour shifts in 28-day cycles. The crews include Chinese, Malaysian, British, American, Indonesian, and Indian workers. Conditions on the rigs are crowded and noisy. Temperatures often hit 120° F, with high humidity. The situation is potentially explosive given the differences in language and culture. As this client knows, however, global leaders pick up subtle cues from employees and the company relies on very inquisitive team leaders who ask open-ended questions and use strong listening skills to learn about their crew members. These leaders engage employees in personal conversation: Where are you from? What is your family like? What kind of car do you want to buy? Simple but powerful questions, because through them people became more real to each another. Such banter between leader and crew gives everyone a much greater chance of working together as a cohesive team. Not a bad idea when offshore platforms cost well over $100,000 per day to operate. Whether in Asia or Africa, global leaders connect with others in every part of the world because they "always have their antennas out" for fresh information. As a senior executive at Merck suggested, "Wide eyes and closed mouth is probably one of the best prescriptions you could have going into a new culture."

How does inquisitiveness enhance your ability to demonstrate integrity? Curious global leaders carry a heightened awareness of potentially unethical contexts around them. They pay attention to the subtle cues that indicate that something is askew, something is out of place, something is *wrong*. In contrast, managers with limited inquisitiveness who work in multiple countries often act as if everything is just fine—and fail to notice when their own actions are unethical or illegal. For example, one manager at a European multinational wanted to see pictures of candidates for an engineering job in the United States and to know details about candidates' personal lives before hiring them for a U.S.-based research and development facility. This manager's actions were clearly against U.S. law, but he was oblivious to the fact. In this case, he found out about the law only after a lawsuit had been filed against his company for illegal hiring procedures.

Inquisitive global leaders ask difficult, proactive questions such as "How is it that one of your local managers lives such a lavish lifestyle on his base salary?" or "Is it normal for companies in this country to pay government officials for factory safety inspections?" Being an effective global leader requires asking these and many other questions, regularly. By developing a more inquisitive managerial approach, you gain the confidence of your employees and a more thorough understanding of the business context. Inquisitiveness becomes an insurance policy against accidentally crossing ethical boundaries—an act that almost always comes back to haunt both company and manager. In fact, it may prove helpful to assume that you *will* cross the boundary line of unethical behavior sooner or later, unless you exhibit constant vigilance through observation and inquiry.

Inquisitiveness and Savvy

Inquisitiveness helps global leaders see international and local business opportunities *and* take advantage of them through operations that span the world. For example, how can a worldwide president for a product line that is produced in 23 countries and distributed in 148 others learn all she needs to know without having a high level of inquisitiveness? How can someone in this situation keep from being overwhelmed without an inquisitive nature, a constant hunger for new information? They can't.

Global business and organizational savvy directly link to your methods for gathering knowledge of markets, competitors, best practices, internal organization, cultures, people, and technologies. Inquisitiveness helps you constantly retool in these areas. Technology, customer preferences, competitive products, and government regulations change constantly. Product and process innovations close in fast and furious. Volatile dynamics turn the global marketplace into a marathon in which the best global leaders know when to accelerate their pace as well as when to hold their position just long enough to see what the competition is going to do. Whether it is Gillette cutting production costs on the next generation of razors, Marriott International establishing new hotels around the world, or Sony introducing a stunning array of advanced digital sound devices, global leaders must constantly stay abreast of innovations and opportunities on a worldwide basis, or risk getting blindsided by more agile competitors. Levi Strauss faces this reality as the continued profitabilty of Dockers pants and 501 jeans is now threatened by dozens of upstart designer-brand and generic-brand denim pants producers in every part of the earth, all scratching away at Levi's global market share.

Without an insatiable desire to learn, you can easily miss key facts, important relationships, and critical connections that can help you improve your specific approach to a local market, or, conversely, systematize your overall business approach to obtain global market efficiencies. In either situation, the key to creating new sources of global competitive advantage comes from your constant inquisitiveness about unique market and organizational contexts. What you gain from these frequent learning adventures becomes the foundation for writing and rewriting the maps that guide your exploration into the ever-changing global marketplace.

Global Leaders Are Global Explorers

In our experience, companies hire, promote, and retain executives who demonstrate inquisitiveness, secure trust and goodwill in relationships with people dispersed around the world, and use their savvy to embrace duality and define new business opportunities. In short, these global leaders are global explorers. *They approach everyday business as an adventure and press beyond the horizon of everyone else's reality.* They ask penetrating (and sometimes irritating) questions. They marshal the courage to pursue those questions doggedly, sometimes at the risk of high personal costs. They are smart enough, when faced with tough questions themselves, to sort things through and come up with acceptable responses. They move forward boldly, yet pay careful attention to the terrain when traveling in unknown places. They map discoveries of new products, people, and processes, and share those maps with others, often challenging conventional wisdom about the marketplace.

Without exception, exemplar global leaders in each of our interviews excel at exploration; they work, live, play, and breath an inquisitive life that produces bottom-line business results. They are curious about almost every aspect of the world around them. As Pat Canavan at Motorola declared:

> They usually bring along something interesting to read when they travel, not to act smart at cocktail parties when they arrive, but because they want to be better able to perceive and understand the world around them wherever they are. If they are going to India for the first time and notice an Indian in the corporate cafeteria at headquarters, they sit down by them and ask questions. If they travel to Europe, they read the *International Herald Tribune* instead of *USA Today*. If they land in Hong Kong, they buy the *Hong Kong Standard*, not the *Asian Wall Street Journal*.

This kind of curiosity has made a big difference in Motorola's march around the world, producing better new market entries and more streamlined production processes.

Global leaders are the exact opposite of those whose lives revolve around how many points they collect in frequent flier and hotel programs and who will be out of work in the new millenium. Global explorers find rewards in the experience itself, where learning replaces consumption as the chosen mode of personal enrichment; and they view opportunities to learn as far more important than moving up the organizational chart.[1] They know through experience that inquisitiveness is necessary to give birth to any worthwhile adventure, and global leaders are adventurous. As one senior manager at GE Lighting remarked,

> One key to our global success has been developing leaders who see their work as a learning adventure both on and off the job. While they push hard to drive the bottom line of business—and ours is a cost-driven business—they are equally committed to sitting back, listening, learning, and understanding what's going on in the local environment. As a result, these global leaders thrive on the fundamental tension between a strong desire to make money today and an incredible interest in the immediate world around them.

Consider for a moment this endless spirit of inquiry that we cherish in a good friend and global leader, J. Bonner Ritchie. For decades, Bonner has engaged in extensive international consulting, ranging from organizational development issues at Exxon to Middle East peace negotiations. Several years ago, Bonner was driving with his wife and children on a German autobahn. As he sped down the road, he suddenly realized that he was headed away from his intended destination. After looking carefully both ways, he pulled over on the left shoulder near a median strip of grass separating the highways. With everything clear, he drove onto the grass to go over to the other side of the freeway. Suddenly, the Volvo he was driving rolled over, leaving Bonner and his family suspended upside down in a hidden gully.

As the family dangled by their seatbelts, Bonner's first question was not: "Is everyone OK?" or "Is anyone hurt?" Instead, the first words to his family were: "This is interesting. What can we learn from this?" Now most of us would have likely been more concerned about our safety than our education in this situation, but with Bonner the opposite has always been true: *He lives to learn.* His attitude of constant, almost boundless inquiry, mirrors what we see again and again in our work with exemplar global leaders around the world.

Global explorers make the wisdom of Henry David Thoreau a habit of their hearts. Thoreau said, "I wish to live deliberately. To learn what life has to teach me, and not, when I came to die, realize that I had not lived or learned." Instead of hunkering down in hotel rooms to watch cable movies after arriving in a new place, they immerse themselves in the local culture. On business trips, they avoid limousines like the plague. Instead, they walk the streets, venturing out into markets, stores, and museums. They read local papers and pose penetrating questions to people about their culture and history. Put simply, global leaders love to discover new things and their curiosity drives them to see and experience all that they possibly can.

Global leaders are content with nothing less than learning the feel of the very texture of any place they work in, any country they visit. They live the lifelong credo of Jacques Cousteau, the famous undersea explorer, whose ship *Calypso* carried the motto "Il faut aller voir" ("We must go and see for ourselves"). Global leaders never act like the tourists whom Carol Amore, a professional wildlife photographer and president of Management Leverage, encounters during her annual photo treks on the Serengeti plains of Africa: "A lot of people go to the wilds and are very protective, almost afraid of learning. They say, 'Oh, now I've seen a lion, now I've snapped a photo of a rhino. Let's go have lunch.'" Instead, be the global traveler whom Carol describes as "anyone going to Africa and seeing it as a tour of adventure. *You will get out of it just as much as you allow yourself to experience.* To capture these moments requires persevering, staying out, tracking, and having the staying power to follow the animals for hours." While Carol Amore's adventures have included polar bear attacks, facial visits by giant scorpions in the night, and huge rats chewing on her feet, she sees all these experiences as contributing to her intuitive "feel of the phenomenon," or what you will come to experience as the "texture of the place" in your work as a global leader.

Interestingly, a curious approach to new countries is no different from the way excellent global leaders operate within their home countries. Experiences in other areas of the world can create essential contrast points by which you can look at your part of the world in a different, and often illuminating light. Instead of being like a homesick tourist when meeting new people who come into your world, your inquisitiveness forces you to become a global traveler, at home and abroad. You remember that "an important difference between a tourist and traveler is that the former accepts his own civilization without question; not so the traveler, who compares it with the others, and rejects those elements he finds not to his liking."[2] Whether working at corporate headquarters or visiting far-flung subsidiary operations, seek out, compare, and contrast new data with the old information stored inside your head. By engaging in this process of constant compare-and-contrast, you gain the critical insights that global leaders need in order to transform the way global strategies are conceived and carried out. For example, a vice president of operations at Novell had never taken a business trip outside the United States and had difficulty understanding the value of conducting certain operations abroad at much cheaper manufacturing rates. As a result, Novell sent her on a series of one-month overseas stints over a three-year period. This extended foreign experience added up to a new perspective that resulted in the vice president deciding to place manufacturing operations in Ireland, Singapore, and Taiwan to achieve lower production costs.

Global Leaders Understand the Terrain

To know the terrain, or competitive context at home and abroad, inquisitiveness drives global leaders to challenge the outer edges of individual and organizational limits. Global leaders develop questions and look for opportunities to raise them in their business relationships. They ask tough questions, field tough questions, and doggedly pursue observations and inquiries—all in pursuit of the knowledge and experience that they can translate into seismic-level market impact.

Before joining EuroDisney in 1992, Steve Burke was responsible for growing part of Disney's consumer products business. He posed difficult questions to people throughout his unit and fielded a particularly challenging one from a Disney employee: "Why can't Disney have retail stores outside of theme parks, in regular places like shopping malls and airports?" Intrigued by the question, Steve pursued the issue for several years until the concept of a Disney store chain became reality. He began with a series of test stores in southern California and eventually expanded the concept at a swift pace around the world. Today the retail stores play a key role in the Disney portfolio, providing over $1 billion a year in annual revenue.

Global Leaders Crush Curiosity Killers

A famous Yiddish proverb suggests that a person should live if only to satisfy his curiosity, yet from our experience we observe the opposite in business: most managers live to kill the natural curiosity of people. Business managers are not alone. Studies show that children in the United States discover at a young age how not to learn in school. It becomes clear that giving the "right" answers—meaning the answers that the teacher wants to hear—is rewarded far more than asking the best questions. U.S. schools are more often than not "modeled after factories, putting children through a production line designed to turn out a uniform product, not original thinkers."[3] When these children reach adulthood and begin their careers, they face a hauntingly similar dilemma with managers who too frequently seek self-confirming information, acting like classic "confirmatory hypothesis testers."

Essentially, these managers want to confirm what they already believe and they ask questions that lead them directly to what they already know. They are anything but adventurers when trekking across the global marketplace. In the early 1980s, UPS slammed right into this dilemma when it entered the German market. With a senior management that was entirely made up of Americans with no international experience, UPS faced a real challenge getting beyond its highly domestic mindset. Because UPS was basically an unknown brand in Germany, local country managers painted a multicolored globe and flags on the brown delivery trucks to communicate the "global reach of UPS shipping." What seemed like a savvy local marketing tactic was quickly quashed by corporate headquarters and the trucks were dutifully repainted to conform to the worldwide standard, plain brown. The senior executives in the United States had no real curiosity about the local situation in Germany. As one German national executive who helped with the operation's start-up reflected, "How do you change mindsets when everyone at headquarters is American? How can a company really go global without changing worldviews?" It took years of below-par country performance before executives at "UPS headquarters ever took the time to really listen to what local managers were trying to tell them from Germany." Over time, these difficult experiences in Germany as well as in other countries have contributed to a major mind shift back at UPS headquarters. In fact, one senior executive confided that "the genie is out of the bottle and will never go back in"—that genie being a major strategic thrust to push decision-making authority down in the organization. This has resulted in much more local flexibility both abroad and in the United States.

Similar to the challenges UPS executives faced, we recently traveled to China to facilitate a global leadership program for a client. The company, a diversified U.S. multinational company, sent 20 senior executives on the excursion. The goal was to orient these senior managers with emerging markets. Many in the group had neither lived abroad nor done much international traveling. The most remarkable part of the entire experience for us was the different attitudes reflected by the people in our group.

To our chagrin, most of these executives had little international exposure and seemed quite uninterested in learning anything about China beyond the Great Wall and the Forbidden City. They were constantly on the phone to offices back in the United States. They spent evenings eating Western food in a Western hotel, and topped the day off with CNN International. These managers acted as if the China trip was simply an irritation; it interfered with what they believed were more important responsibilities. Even though they were in China physically, their minds were back home. They acted like tourists in search of what they already knew, matching quite well Mary Catherine Bateson's description of people who, given a choice, "choose not to learn and therefore not to change except in superficial ways."[4]

In stark contrast to the globally inexperienced, the more seasoned international executives created a much different experience for themselves in China. They actively sought out local street markets, as well as unique cultural sites off the tourist trail. They initiated, set up, and followed through on appointments with potential customers and suppliers. It seemed as though they had one primary goal on the trip: to stay as far away as possible from the hotel. For these highly inquisitive executives, the relatively brief time they had in which to experience China firsthand was of far more value than any task they might have left undone back home.

In contrast to sedate, routine-loving managers, inquisitive global leaders often ask questions about things that they don't know, believe, or understand, provoking interesting and enlightening responses. For example, David Ogilvy, co-founder of the global advertising agency Ogilvy and Mather, used to run several ad campaigns each year that his colleagues thought would be winners, though he was fundamentally convinced that they would be losers. He consciously chose to run a few of these campaigns to challenge, or disconfirm, his personal beliefs about what constituted a successful ad campaign. As one might expect, some failed, but just as many succeeded. David Ogilvy learned from those successes (that he thought would be failures) and built a better decision-making framework for developing successful advertising campaigns. He was inquisitive enough to challenge his own perspectives on how to do business.

Global Leaders Search for What They "Don't Know They Don't Know"

In any environment, global explorers possess sufficient self-awareness to be open to new experiences; experiences in which they often "don't know what they don't know." In any organization, there are managers "who assume that their prior experience is always 100 percent reality irrespective of the new environment or situation."[5] This sort is typified by one manager we met recently who was traveling throughout South America. At his first stop in São Paulo, he was introduced by his boss from corporate headquarters as "the man who thinks he knows everything." As one might expect, the moment was sobering, yet essential: he heard for the first time that his all-knowing style—as politely as he might be pulling it off—might not be the best approach. Compare this unfortunate experience with the counsel of a particularly insightful marketing executive at GE who advised: "You have to work to know that you don't know what you don't know. Whenever you enter any new environment, *you enter with a learning assumption that you always have something to learn*, rather than a knowing assumption." Global leaders overcome the arrogance of a knowing assumption through unbridled curiosity.

To illustrate the antithesis of an inquisitive nature, consider the plight of several senior marketing managers and engineers from a Fortune 50 firm. These men lived in upstate New York. They scheduled a three-day business trip to Montreal. Upon arriving at the airport, they were stunned to hear French, having simply assumed that all Canadians must speak English. After fumbling around, they hired an interpreter to help them conduct business in Montreal. Next stop—Toronto. Upon arrival at the at the Toronto airport, they met their potential clients by calling out a hearty "Bonjour!" To their embarrassment, they realized that people in Toronto generally do not speak French (and may not particularly care for those who do). The entire business trip was an expensive disaster. It had not occured to these executives that perhaps they didn't know some important things about Canadians before they ever began their journey to Montreal and Toronto. They came to a foreign country operating on automatic pilot, entered "thought-less," and paid the price.

Jon Huntsman, Jr., vice chairman of the Huntsman Corporation, presents the alternative, an ideal role model as you develop your leadership skills. Global leaders actively seek out those unfamiliar areas of knowledge and skill, an ignorance of which can lead to disaster, a lesson Jon Huntsman, Jr. has learned throughout his career:

> The most important, valuable asset that someone can derive from an overseas experience is learning what not to do. When you're doing international business, as important as knowing what you want to do is knowing what you shouldn't do. You can only learn that from experience. For example, we learned through experience in parts of South America, Mexico, and Russia that we simply could not maintain the high safety standards that are required in chemical production facilities. As a result, we decided to place fewer production facilities in those areas. After having been burned a few times here and there, the real value-add of overseas experiences is knowing how to react when inevitable surprises come along.

Global Leaders Know that the Best Answer is a Question

Inquisitive global leaders not only ask provocative questions, they also field them from people both inside and outside their organizations—even though such questions can often pose challenges to deeply held beliefs. Successful managers perceive others' tough questions as starting points for dialogue and understanding, rather than for argument and persuasion. They pay careful attention to probing questions from customers and employees at home and overseas. As Philip LaChapelle, recently corporate controller at Otis Elevator Company, observed:

> Global leaders know how to see, they make a conscious effort to learn. They invite me to talk and then they listen. When going overseas or when meeting someone new, I try really hard to

focus on asking questions and listening carefully. Ask questions, field questions—that is the key to discovering a part of their world that just might impact mine.

Global leaders create a culture around them that treasures inquisitiveness, that considers tough questions far more valuable than pat answers. At the very core, inquisitive global leaders work from an assumption that neither they nor their company has a corner on all the answers. As a result, they listen carefully to others' questions that may well challenge strongly held views on strategies, policies, or practices.

Global leaders not only ask and field tough questions, they also command the courage and the intellect to doggedly pursue those questions. They don't take "no" for an answer, at least not until they are convinced that "no" is the only answer that makes sense. Put simply, global leaders never give up in the face of extreme adversity. They are personally committed to gathering data—about markets, competitors, best practices, internal organization, cultures, people, and technologies—and to seeing how that data interconnects. They also engage others in this process and teach them the practical impact of inquisitiveness. Global leaders work hard to instill the value of learning deep into their organizations, often putting significant sums of money into building the intelligence-gathering and -dissemination capabilities of their people. The resulting information cache helps people throughout the organization see new market opportunities and marshal the resources to capitalize on them. Figure 3.1 provides a list of practical ways you can change your own level of inquisitiveness.

Global Leaders Master the Terrain

Exemplar global leaders not only gather facts and gain experience, but they master the application of facts and experience in the global marketplace. They consciously seek out a sophisticated understanding of how complex data fit together, an understanding that has to be lived, not taught. Norm Merritt, an executive at Warner Brothers Studio, articulated this opportunity and challenge quite well:

> Out there you have to be smart, you must have the gray matter
> to manage the complexity and ambiguity. The last six months

Action Steps for Understanding the Terrain

1. Seek out the unexpected, unknown, or novel. Surround yourself with people, books, ideas, and movies with perspectives different from your own. Maximize the number of experiences at work and home that create contrast in your head. When confronted by disconfirming information, don't discount it—savor it.
2. Actively challenge your own perspectives. Engage in regular self-debate—use a mirror if you need to. Seek opinions inside *and* outside both your company *and* your industry—especially on key decisions.
3. Make the time to learn—don't leave it up to chance. Provide a resource margin for making little mistakes today to avoid making big ones tomorrow. Celebrate failure in your world as much as success.
4. Regularly check whether you are approaching life with a learning assumption ("I need to learn") or a knowing assumption ("I don't need to tell").
5. Construct head-jerking questions—ones that challenge core assumptions of yourself or others: individuals, groups, or organizations.
6. Model question-asking, then foster question-asking in those around you.
7. Respect and value others' questions as much as your own.
8. Never accept "I don't know" as an answer. Seek a deeper understanding of the situation individually or collectively.
9. Maximize your question-answer ratio. In other words, contribute more questions than answers to each hallway conversation, conference call, memo, or team meeting you engage in.

Figure 3.1

have been an incredible learning experience figuring out how international activities fit together, how wholesale relates to domestic markets, and how that relates directly to the consumer. Underneath it all, there seems to be a complex algorithm of how all these things fit together in a very sophisticated pattern, and you must have a strategic mind to recognize what really matters.

To capture these complexities, global leaders observe, deliberate, and ponder. They know that reflection, or meditative thinking, "does not just happen by itself. It demands of us not to cling one-sidedly to a single idea, nor to run down a one-track course of ideas. Meditative thinking requires that we engage ourselves with what at first sight does not go together at all. . . . It is one thing to have heard and read something, that is, to merely take notice; *it is another thing to understand what we have heard and read, that is, to ponder.*"[6] Such reflection requires significant effort and demands the subordination of one's belief systems, assumptions, and customary mental maps in order to consider other versions of reality. When mastering complex interrelationships, global leaders know how to bide their time, letting ideas ferment. They know when to stop seeking out more experiences and start making sense of what they've encountered, instead of continuing on with sense-less experiences like those destined to be global failures.

On the positive side, one global leader we interviewed who just itched to get from one place to the next on his business trips also built in self-financed side trips to places like Vietnam and Turkey—countries where his company had no formal business activities. These excursions gave him the chance to step back and contemplate the places he had just visited and what he had learned there. When describing these reflective moments, this executive reiterated a favorite quotation from Albert Einstein: "No problem can be solved by the same consciousness that created it." We could tell that he lived by those words.

Often global leaders are at a loss when asked to describe the rich, complex knowledge that results from reflective learning, or explain precisely how they developed it through experience, because "the greater the master (of any skill or art), the more completely his person vanishes behind the work."[7] For example, when Tony Wang brought Kentucky Fried Chicken (KFC) to China for the first time, he had no accurate market entry data and felt that collecting it through traditional marketing tools would prove unproductive. As a Taiwanese native who had traveled extensively in China, Tony turned to his own experience and pulled together various tidbits of information to predict how the Chinese would likely respond to KFC products. He had watched their buying habits in small shops, observed their use of spices in food, and noticed their liking for chicken in general. By combining these data points with his extensive fast-food industry experience, Tony could confidently forecast how KFC would fare in China. When we asked Tony to articulate why he was convinced that KFC would prosper, all he could say was, "I just knew the Chinese would like it. I can't exactly say how I knew this, but I could *feel* the Chinese would love us." In fact, his years of fast food industry experience combined with astute observation and probing of local customer preferences and habits gave Tony Wang an instinctive mastery of the competitive business terrain that concluded with a lucrative business result for KFC.

Having this kind of "feel" for markets and employees is key for global leadership. There are times when one simply knows what to do. While it takes a lot of work to acquire the necessary depth of knowledge, it is not impossible. It reflects years, and at times, decades of business experience— combined with an inquisitive nature that refuses to let prior experience sediment over present reality. This is where inquisitiveness plays a remarkably powerful role: helping global leaders build on past experience to make better sense of the present. The result is by far the most significant type of knowledge required for global leadership— worth more than its weight in gold. It can not be easily copied or downloaded like a computer file, and it will prove to be an invaluable source of competitive advantage for you, as a global leader. Companies cannot buy this kind of knowledge as if it was a commodity; it does not come off the shelf packaged in a new and shiny box. Instead, companies build it in their people over long periods of time, or seek out those few who have worked through the years to acquire it themselves.

Learning to know *and* feel these complex interrelationships may be no easy task at first for young global leaders, especially as they crisscross a growing number of international borders. Yet the exemplar global leaders we interviewed move with ease from one paradigm to another, while global failures find it impossible to actually learn and act beyond their own small, provincial worlds. These folks are essentially nonexplorers, people who "rather naively assume that once they have a clear sharp picture in mind of where they are going, they can trust that picture through to the end."[8] In contrast, the best global leaders often resemble chameleons as they move from culture to culture, paradigm to paradigm. At times, they show surprisingly little loyalty to *any* single perspective. They are "zigzag people" who switch the angle of their point-of-view from one cycle to the next, like a sailboat tacking into the wind. Their ability to change, adapt, and truly embrace what works helps them piece together the complexity and master the chaos.

Developing this kind of mastery is a real challenge. As one senior executive in our study warned:

> You can find cross-cultural people a dime a dozen, but they're single market managers. If you wanted me to, I could easily grab fifteen people from our company who could work extremely well between the U.S. and Japan. But don't send those same people to Korea, and never send them to Europe. It is far more challenging to ferret out people who can move through multiple markets and master a much trickier and far more valuable world.

Precisely because these skills are relatively rare, global leaders not only actively seek out learning experiences for themselves, they also create opportunities for subordinates to learn through exposure to a broad range of cultures and markets. At a major consumer goods firm one senior executive whom we interviewed practices this principle regularly for himself and his team, as exhibited in the following example:

> I just itch to get to the next new place and learn what it is like. In fact, my work is like living in a big theme park and the theme park is the world. For example, I have taken a personal side trip to Vietnam after a business trip to Japan—just because I was dying to learn more about Vietnam. I did not have anyone meet me at the airport. I simply did it on my own. On another trip, I went to Turkey because it was a convenient place to visit for two days before going home. Most of my team doesn't take diversions, but if I'm along, they have to. Recently we had some business meetings in Munich, Germany. I knew that it was not that far to visit Salzburg, so we finished our three o'clock meeting, rented a car, and I said, "I am going and if anyone else wants to come along, that's great." We made the trip and created an important learning experience.

Action Steps for Mastering the Terrain

1. Identify and gain the knowledge base required for mastering your territory— functional, organizational, industry, and geographical. Carve out the time to master each knowledge base. Do this by relying on "to learn" lists more than on "to do" lists.
2. Find a regular time and place for reflection. Construct your own version of a Japanese rock garden where you can sit, ponder, and make sense of things without interruption.
3. Seek out opportunities to test your mastery of the terrain by applying your knowledge in real-time profit-and-loss settings.

Figure 3.2

Global leaders not only embrace experience, they make sense of it. They know the difference between and the relative impact of watching someone else exercise and exercising oneself. They create experiences for themselves and others in order to magnify their understanding and ultimately master the local or global competitive business terrain. Figure 3.2 provides some concrete steps you can take to master the territory.

Inquisitiveness Nurtures Our Capacity to See and Make Sense of New Terrain

Inquisitiveness allows one to view a paradigm like the pattern in a kaleidoscope. Experience, like turning a kaleidoscope, alters paradigms and expands our knowledge—if we are inquisitive. So as global leaders encounter new paradigms, like the changing images in a kaleidoscope, they view these paradigms as if they were actual maps, conveying entire histories of cultural bias and acquisition. Recently, one of us worked through this process while teaching an executive program in Scandinavia. Like many consultants, Hal used the classic perceptual deception image of an old and young woman in the same picture:

Thinking he knew exactly what there was to see in the image, he asked the participants, "What is in that picture?" followed quickly by, "Do you see an old woman or a young woman?" Immediately a man in the back of the room raised his hand and said, "I don't get it, Gregersen. There is not an old woman in the picture. I don't see one. There is not a young woman either." Then the man stated matter-of-factly, "All I see is a bear eating a woman's head." Hal's first thought was, "How ludicrous, a bear eating a woman's head!" Then the participant outlined the bear's head on the screen, and sure enough, it was eating the woman's head.

What did Hal learn from this relatively simple experience? First, he confronted his own arrogance and unwillingness to see the personal layers of cultural acquisition that had kept him from seeing anything else than what he was used to seeing. Second, he gained an insight into the cultural heritage of the person who did see the bear eating the woman's head. It was no wonder that this man, having grown up in Finland, where the bear has great symbolic power, saw a bear virtually leap from the screen upon first viewing the classic optical illusion.

Cultural Baggage Destroys Our Capacity to See and Make Sense of New Terrain

To illustrate the challenges associated with learning and unlearning the layers of core assumptions, or worldviews, that we all carry around in our heads, consider this historical example. For centuries, Europeans were entranced by legends of far-distant islands endowed with unimaginable wealth and resources. In 1541, Hernán Cortés and a group of adventurers set sail from Spain to discover such an island. Cortés —at least as interested in his own glory as he was in that of Spain—sailed across the Atlantic, portaged through Mexico, and then set sail again up the Strait of California. Eventually, his provisions low, his crew close to mutiny, he was forced to an unhapppy decision: to turn back, having apparently failed in his goal. For Cortés, failure was unacceptable, and so with a little wishful thinking, he created a success. To the east and west, land was in view; to the north and south, water. Cortés reached a conclusion that seemed perfectly logical: he was in search of an island, and an island he found—La Isla de California. Cortés returned to Spain and reported to the king and queen exactly what they wanted to hear (and what he wanted to believe): *California is an island* (see Figure 3.3).

Figure 3.3 Map of the Island of California (circa 1656)

Shortly after Cortés's discovery, another expedition was sent to confirm the find. This one traveled far up along the Pacific coast, past present-day San Francisco. This over-ambitious expedition also ran low on supplies, and by the time they reached the mouth of the Mendocino River on the coast of northern California, the crew was stricken with scurvy. With no inclination to dispute Cortés and no absolute proof that he was wrong, they concluded that the river was really a strait that separated the northern part of the island of California from the rest of the continent. This cartographic myth persisted throughout Europe for over two centuries—in spite of overwhelming evidence to the contrary collected by numerous other explorers—until a royal proclamation from Spain finally declared that California was not an island.

For the monarchies and mapmakers alike, paradigms took a great amount of time and a great many challenges to change. The experiences of those who held such worldviews so deeply only served to confirm them, since for these true believers, "contrary evidence was simply invisible."[9] In fact, they lived the reality of Machiavelli's oft-quoted observation:

> There is nothing more difficult to carry out or more doubtful of success than to initiate a new order of things. For the reformer has enemies in all those who profit by the old order, and only lukewarm defenders by all those who can profit by the new order. This lukewarmness arises from the incredulity of mankind who do not truly believe in anything new until they have had experience with it.

Once the belief that California was an island became established, reports from later explorers were filtered to fit the reigning paradigm; anything contradictory was labeled as false or impossible. Arrogance ruled: "I'm the king, please bow." Pure self-interest governed: "As king, I must possess this island for its great bounty." Poor communication continued: "Don't tell me things that I don't want to believe or that are refuted anyway by our exquisite maps." All these things conspired to keep the myth of California as an island quite alive within European courts for over two hundred years; those who profited from the order of which this myth was a part could not believe in anything new until they had experienced it.

Just as resistance to learning has shaped much of history—and resulted in thousands of inaccurate maps of the Old World—it can also undermine the effectiveness of global leaders in our New World. For example, IKEA, a global powerhouse in retail furniture, expanded in the 1980s from its Scandinavian roots to continental Europe, and then moved across the Atlantic to North America. A key component of IKEA's competitive strategy is sourcing extremely large volumes of moderate quality goods at an incredibly low cost. As a result, it can sell its items to customers for prices lower than its rivals'—a perfect competitive position. This strategy works well around the world for most of the products that IKEA offers, such as curtains or dinnerware, but it failed miserably in the United States for some items, like beds and sheets.

When IKEA began its operations on this continent, it shipped low-priced, moderate-quality, *metric*-sized beds and bedding to all of its North American stores. As one might expect, these items were not exactly hot sellers in the United States. In fact, they quickly became category failures, filling up entire warehouses. Local store and regional managers tried to communicate to corporate headquarters in Sweden that metric-sized beds and bedding were not selling in the United States—in spite of the fact that they were priced lower than the king, queen, full, and twin-size bedding found in competitors' furniture stores. How did IKEA's senior managers, who were seven time zones away at corporate headquarters, respond to this local dilemma? "Be more creative. *Pull* the customers into your store. Any good retailer *can* sell metric sized bedding; that's the solution to your inventory problems." Despite local and regional U.S. managers' constant attempts to convince headquarters otherwise, their bosses in Sweden held to this position for more than two years. Finally, the bursting warehouses won, and metric-sized bedding was reluctantly discontinued in the U.S. market.

Any global leader or leading global company can easily make the same kind of mistake IKEA made by getting sucked into the comfort zone of their own unexamined cultural heritage. For example, executives at Kmart were slow to challenge its decades-old assumption that big retail stores belong only in big cities, leaving many vital markets in smaller cities untapped for years. Top managers at Apple Computer still find it incredibly difficult to realize that proprietary operating systems are not the future of the global personal computer market. For executives in these and many other companies, strategic choices, policies, and practices based in the past can create significant roadblocks to efforts at moving constructively toward the future. Too frequently, such executives fail to reexamine their *feel for the business*, until that feel is completely out of touch with market reality.

Instead, they must learn to heed the counsel of T. S. Eliot: "We shall not cease from exploration, and the end of all our exploring, will be to arrive where we started, and *know the place for the first time.*" Global leaders take Eliot's message to heart as they move from market to market, shift from worldview to worldview, see and question their assumptions, and in the end see places and things as they really are. They not only explore around them, but they also search inside themselves and their organizations to observe their own cultural inheritance in stark clarity not only the "first time," but time and time again, knowing that *any* worldview offers both insight and ignorance.

Inquisitiveness Impacts Performance

In brief, persistent inquisitiveness guides global leaders to new insights which they can then translate into seismic-level market impacts. One good example of a company that prizes inquisitiveness is Japan-based NEC, whose global leaders have a model track record for the use of alliances as hothouses of innovation. Inquisitive NEC executives view external alliances as a means to an end, that end being knowledge acquisition by NEC. Whether they are aware of it or not, NEC's partners provide opportunities for the company's very curious managers and engineers to discover new product technology, new process technology, and advantageous internal policies and systems.

If you only look carefully, wellsprings of innovation and impact exist right inside your own company. As Larry Kahaner, author of *Competitive Intelligence*, states, "90% of what you need to know to improve sales performance is within your own company. The other 10% comes from public information."[10] Consider the open-minded marketing executives at Cincinnati-based Proctor & Gamble who discovered that the company's Taiwan subsidiary was unsurpassed in running international media campaigns, or the inquisitive U.S. managers at Scott Paper who learned about jumbo toilet paper rolls from the company's Italian subsidiary. Consider Unilever, whose German subsidiary created Kuschelweich brand fabric softener (in English, Cuddles). Persistent local managers helped receptive executives at Unilever's headquarters discover the brand, with its teddy bear logo, and transfer it around the world. In the United States alone, Snuggle brand fabric softener has tripled Unilever's market share for that segment.

Inquisitiveness Keeps Global Leaders above Water

Inquisitiveness provides a clear benefit for global leaders: it is the life-preserver that keeps them afloat. Without a constant, childlike fascination for people, cultures, and ideas, global leaders can become overwhelmed by the daily rigors of conducting international business. Incessant travel, time zone changes, complicated multilingual discussions, strange foods, and often difficult living conditions wear down managers, both physically and mentally.

In these challenging circumstances, the fuel for managers is inquisitiveness, a constant fascination with the world and their jobs. We saw a great example of this during one of our recent trips to Asia. While in Shanghai, we interviewed the Dutch president of a European-Canadian joint venture. His factory employed 450 people, all Chinese except for himself and two other expatriates. His office was sparsely furnished and looked like it had last been redecorated in the 1950s. On the summer day we met, his air conditioning wasn't working properly. The elevator was broken. The linoleum tiles on the floor were gritty with dirt and dust. We were inclined to wonder, "Who in their right mind would want to be here when they could stay in a plush high-rise office tower in Toronto or Frankfurt?" We asked the Dutchman what kept him going in the face of adversity. His comments are revealing:

> Working in China can be tough. A contract here is like the minutes of the last meeting. It is viewed by the Chinese as the start, not the end of negotiations. Also, in China, so long as your customer acknowledges that he owes you money, you can't take him to court. I have seen disagreements drag on for years. It can be frustrating and exhausting. I see a lot of people give up. You have to want to be here. In the mid-1980s, we made a decision to become a major TV manufacturer in China. The government encouraged us and before long, there were 113 assembly lines for TVs owned by 88 manufacturers in China. The government knew that the market needed consolidation but didn't have the courage to do it themselves. So they decided to simply open the doors to imports and essentially, we went out of business overnight. We ended up with nothing for our investment, but I didn't leave. The thought of going back to a job at headquarters in Europe was depressing. China is a real adventure. The wild

west. So, I found another Western partner. The parent's owner-
ship dropped to less than 40 percent, so I don't really work for
them anymore. We changed our strategy and began focusing on
making semiconductors for export. We are now making money
while the rest all left and went back home. The country is
changing so fast that my job is always new. There is something
new to learn everyday. I must be crazy, but I love the job.

A genuine interest in everything the world has to offer rewards global
leaders with the gift of personal renewal. Global leaders are driven not so
much by wealth or power, rather they share a burning desire to explore new
frontiers. Their strength and their rewards come from the same powerful
energy source: an insatiable love of learning. As Pat Canavan at Motorola
pointed out:

> To be fascinated with the world around you is central to psy-
> chological patience, stamina, acuity, and attention. I think the
> fascination of traveling the world, doing business, making
> deals results in renewal. It is not only more complex work, it is
> an opportunity to learn and enlighten. When you hear a lot of
> whining and moaning like, "Isn't it awful?" "I expected an air-
> port!" or "You just can't trust these people," you know that the
> renewal process has stopped and the fascination is gone. As a
> result, people get worse and worse at what they do. They gnaw
> at themselves, feeling like they have to do what they have to do.
> This results in either a terrible product or no product at all. In
> contrast, renewal through constant learning snaps this down-
> ward cycle and keeps your personal edge in the global market-
> place.

What is the bottom line for inquisitiveness? Global leaders don't go a
day without learning. They are much more likely to pay attention to "to
learn" lists rather than "to do" lists. Everyone can benefit from a role model
like psychologist Leo Buscaglia's father, a parent who wouldn't let his child
go to sleep at night until he answered a simple question, "What did you
learn today?" Buscaglia's father asked him this question every day. It got to
the point that he and his siblings would often run to the encyclopedia just

before dad came home to find some trivial fact to share. Only in adulthood did Buscaglia discover that *what was most important in his childhood was not what he learned, but the fact that he learned, and learned, and learned.*[11] Indeed, exemplar global leaders are no different in their daily quest for understanding and insight.

Exemplar Global Leader:
Mikell Rigg McGuire

In one of the fastest growing divisions of Franklin Covey, Mikell Rigg McGuire plays a key role as vice president of international. From her perspective, inquisitiveness is tightly linked to the mental flexibility global leaders require. She feels that:

> If you do international business without preconceived notions, having an open mind, looking, and learning, you communicate well, ask questions, and listen. You are flexible enough to say, "Your comment is not in my comfort zone. I may not like what I am hearing, but the reality of the situation is that that is the reality. Your perception is my reality for the moment."

To Mikell, differences in perception demand flexibility, which encompasses more than a management style. It includes "flexibility in systems and thinking processes."

Meeting with her CFO, Mikell discussed how to finalize a policy manual to standardize a number of practices throughout the company. She appreciates the fact that he understands standardization and localization, having come from a career at General Electric, and more recently, having been CFO of Rubbermaid. When they talk about global standards, according to Mikell, they both agree that:

> You don't cookie-cutter stamp what the U.S. wants around the world and make it fit your mold. Standardization is creating a guideline, taking it overseas, and asking, "How do we adapt this to your market?" Flexibility shows not only in your style, but in systems, structures, policies, and your questions. Inquisitiveness

and flexibility combine to help global companies wrestle with these constant standardization and localization issues.

On her international team, Mikell expects inquisitiveness and openness in her people. For example, her finance manager recently spent five years as treasurer of a European company with annual revenues equivalent to $6 billion. Europe provided valuable experience, but "when he goes to the Asia Pacific region, he must learn to go in blind. He can't go over with his U.S. *or* European notions. To be truly international, he must *understand the perspective of every single country he walks into. He must learn to tune into their reality.*"

Inquisitiveness Starts at Home

Mikell acquired habits of inquiry quite young in her life. She didn't grow up in a family that traveled the world. In Mikell's words:

> I was always curious and exploratory. My sisters were not big risk-takers, but I was. My mother was a stay-at-home mom and would take us to the library, science center, and art gallery. Learning was certainly a part of our home, but in comparison to my sisters, I would ask more questions on these excursions. I would explore the experience. They would see the same thing that I did and not have much interest in it. Perhaps part of curiosity is simply who you are.

Canadian-born, Mikell believes that "when you are forced as a Canadian to be in bed with an elephant—the U.S., a massive, all-encompassing, and all-consuming place—you have to search out and discover your own identity."

Mikell's journey of discovery eventually brought her to university where she obtained a joint degree in finance and sociology. Reflecting back on her schooling, she feels that:

> Taking a sociology degree was certainly open-minded and ex-ploratory. It was theoretical and philosophical and forced me to open my mind. Before entering the university, I was taught

facts, practical things in great quantity, volumes of stuff just pushed through my head. My university experience was a totally different thing. They taught theory. They taught me to think with an open mind, to explore, to act creatively.

Mikell's pursuit of her joint degree also demonstrates her understanding of the importance of combining business skills with cultural awareness. Today she continues to value this approach as she observes certain employees: some who may know the language and even the culture of a foreign country, but lack the technical or business savvy required to create and sustain viable organizations in distant corners of the world; and others who exhibit strong technical skills in marketing, operations, or finance, but don't have the necessary degree of social competence or understanding of the local language. From Mikell's perspective, linguistic capability cannot overcome the lack of business competence and vice versa. Instead, global leaders must be "multidexterous given the demands for different behaviors depending upon the country they are operating in." Inquisitiveness keeps people like Mikell from resting on their laurels, and drives them to understand their weaknesses and figure out how to turn them into strengths. Only inquisitiveness can produce a truly well-rounded global leader.

Making Inquisitiveness Work at Work

When Mikell graduated from the University of Western Ontario, her entrepreneurial side kicked in. She built and ultimately sold a business, Carefree Cottaging, in Canada. After the sale, she joined Franklin Quest Canada, the national branch of a leading worldwide firm that delivers seminars and planners to improve time management skills. Mikell was responsible for selling Franklin materials to the entire Canadian student market. This position was a natural step for her since she had been actively involved in student government during her college years and understood the student's world. Her approach was successful, but at the time, Franklin Quest's Canadian unit as a whole was approaching the point of bankruptcy. Mikell was asked to take over as country manager and she immediately began restructuring. Today the unit is one of the strongest in the company. From her country manager position in

Canada, Mikell was transferred to corporate headquarters in Utah to head up the international division.

In her new job, the first thing Mikell did was call her uncle, the CFO of Dr. Pepper, who had been responsible for opening up the Asia Pacific region for the soft drink manufacturer. Mikell recalls saying to him, "I am a Canadian and I am not global. I am not an American, which makes me partially suspect at corporate headquarters in the U.S. How should we go into Asia? How can I know what to do when I go to Japan?" She asked a lot of questions and her uncle gave her some particularly helpful assistance: he connected her with one of his Japanese colleagues and suggested a certain book to read on her plane flight over. Her curiosity led her to read about and reflect on the unfamiliar world she was entering. Upon arriving in Japan, she could see that she was "walking into a totally different country where they not only lived, but also thought differently."

Today Mikell follows this same ritual of preparation before entering any new environment, a result of the same natural curiosity that led her to contact her internationally savvy uncle. Before heading overseas, Mikell diligently prepares by watching international news networks and reading international magazines, finding books and articles, collecting information. She talks to friends who may know people in the country where she is going, calling them up and making the open-ended request: "Help me understand a little bit about what I am walking into." A friend might send her a book on art, "which reflects what is important to them about the country." Mikell starts to learn before she even begins her journey and continues to learn as she pursues her travels in order to *"get that feel for the place."*

Transition Zones Are Essential for Mikell's Inquisitiveness

Two weeks after Mikell formed her international team at corporate headquarters, they hit the road to familiarize themselves with the company's overseas operations. They didn't really have time to learn and were plunged straight into dealing with whatever fires they encountered at operations in each country. As a matter of fact, her team would often hit the ground running and work from seven o'clock in the morning until midnight, fall into bed and get up first thing the next morning. As a result, Mikell told us that, "they were not learning *as a team* on that first trip. In fact, the team would joke and say, 'What's New Zealand like?' and the response would be, 'a plane change' or 'a hotel.' " As the trip continued, team members started to notice Mikell's approach to international business. They would observe her behavior in a given country and ask her, "How did you know that about England?" She would respond, "Because I read this book. Do you want to read a bit of it?" If one or more team members took her up on the offer, she would later start a discussion on the material they'd read. By the end of their first year traveling together as extensively as they were, all of the team members had become more inquisitive. They were all conscious of the learning process and had discussed its importance. As a result, learning had become a regular ritual not only for Mikell, but for her entire team as well.

When Mikell and her team go to a new country today, they read a book on different cultural and business issues in that country. She described the general process: "We get in the mind-set that anything we learned in the country we just left, we must now forget. We are going to this new place and reading things as we go. We say to each other, 'Wow! I didn't know that.' We can't pretend to walk into their world with a preconceived notion. When we're on their ground, we're in their land." Mikell and her team have found that bringing something to read, something to learn as they travel from place to place helps them make the transition. Her team is constantly flying on planes, spending a week here, two days there. With that kind of schedule, she knows that "the plane ride *is* our transition point. It is really a time to say, 'The curtain is shutting on this country, and a new curtain is opening on that country.' "

Mikell finds opportunitites for *inquisitive transition zones*—time set aside and devoted to mind shifts—not only during airplane flights. On a recent trip, her team committed to spend at least one evening out on each leg of the trip to explore the culture of whatever country they happened to be in. For example, in Sydney, they might go to the opera house. Basically, they try to "take in a piece or flavor of that country to experience it." At times they stay in traditional local hotels, instead of generic American ones. While this works well at an old bed-and-breakfast place in London, it has created problems in places like Taiwan. For example, the first time Mikell's team flew to Taipei, the local managers put them up at a traditional Taiwanese hotel. The team members couldn't breath or sleep because of the dust. After a miserable night, the entire team woke up the next morning with big, puffy eyes. From this experience, they learned to focus their inquisitiveness, understanding that while local hotels can be a great source of learning, they are not necessarily the most productive ones in every country.

Mikell Builds Inquisitiveness into the Organization

Mikell's approach to building inquisitiveness into Franklin Covey rests on her assumption that:

> It is pretty tough to create open-mindedness. It is almost starts from infancy and increases from all of your experiences. Instead, I prefer building a team around individuals who show a nugget of inquisitiveness and open-mindedness. Then, you mentor them from top management down. It is an ongoing process to build these capabilities, not something that happens overnight.

Mikell believes that such inquisitiveness is fostered by experience. She told us that the most powerful experience for her is "living in another culture, immersing in it for an extended time. At Franklin we say that it takes at least 21 days to change a behavior. After a training course, you can easily fall back in old habits. But immerse someone in a society for a period of time and they might become more open-minded, more curious." Mikell knows that not all people *do* become that way through experience and she prefers to send people abroad who are like a manager she recently assigned from Canada to Southeast Asia. He has traveled all his life and loves what he calls "extreme culture," avoiding expatriate enclaves overseas "because they're full of people who have been there for three years, don't speak the language, and never really experience anything outside their mini-America village. They're people with little spark for exploration. In fact, they work at avoiding discovery." In contrast, this manager

> wanted to live in the trenches, because he was open-minded before he ever got there. Now when I send a person overseas, I make sure that person does not slip into their comfort zone and

hide away in an expat village. If they really want to be a leader, especially in a remote country, they must be inquisitive and open-minded to create new ways of doing things.

While actually living in a new country is an invaluable way to learn, Mikell also fosters inquisitiveness in her team through other kinds of travel experience. For her, it is most important to get her team members right into new countries, even if only for a few days. As she explained, "Toss them in and let them learn a new way of life, bit by bit." Not too long ago a manager at Franklin was having difficulty understanding production problems in a foreign country. Instead of just talking about it, Mikell went with the manager to the country and learned first hand how distribution worked and why inventory was arriving three weeks late because it came by boat. To Mikell, "The only way to learn some things is to experience them." Mikell's inquisitiveness not only pushes her to learn about other countries, but also about other business practices outside Franklin Covey. For example, she constantly benchmarks other firms to understand state-of-the-art practices and recently took her customer service manager on a site visit to L. L. Bean's facilities in order to discover innovative approaches to customer service.

At the home office, Mikell works with her team to bring in other people with international backgrounds who see the world from different perspectives. She invites international managers to visit headquarters, meet with other people, and "make the global part of Franklin Covey more visible." Currently, Mikell and her team are putting together a slide and video show illustrating operations and markets around the world. As her team travels, they take pictures of landmarks, places, and people. They videotape overseas offices and do narratives on local employees and vendors. They also collect information to complement the media show. Then they use these materials in U.S.-based meetings and conferences to help make international operations more real to people focusing on the domestic side. Mikell wants people at headquarters to see that international clients and employees really exist, that they are more than mere rumors. Through these various activities, Mikell hopes to fan the sparks of inquisitiveness into flames for domestically oriented executives, helping illuminate a new, international world for them.

For Mikell Rigg McGuire, an inquisitiveness that started at a young age continues to grow. With the world as her playground, she never gets bored.

Inquisitiveness fuels her passion for her job and her vision for her company. Mikell knows that "to truly become a global company, every single person must think globally." One essential key to making this happen at Franklin Covey is Mikell's consistent approach to life, an inquisitive approach representing the essence of global leadership—Mikell's and yours.

Conclusions

Inquisitiveness helps global leaders maintain their edge in a world that moves faster and grows *larger*, not *smaller*, a world constantly shifting, changing both at home and abroad. They know that doing business in today's global markets requires personal mapmaking skills, and they know not to rely on anyone else's chart to guide them across terrain that is always altering, always transforming. Inquisitiveness is the foundation from which you, as a global leader, can maintain a sharp personal edge and develop an enduring reservoir of knowledge and skills. It is a reservoir that is filled by your capacity to see things that others miss, to sense patterns where others find only confusion. It is a reservoir that gives you the desire and strength you need to handle an overwhelming amount of work and information. Although making time to learn presents a real challenge for any global leader, your commitment to learning constitutes the solid core, the essence of your ability to build business savvy, exhibit character, keep perspective, and create value in a hypercompetitive marketplace.

Notes

1. M. C. Bateson, *Peripheral Visions: Learning Along the Way*. 1994. New York: Harper Collins, p. 74.

2. P. Bowles, *The Sheltering Sky*. 1949. New York: Vintage International, p. 6.

3. M. C. Bateson, *Peripheral Visions: Learning Along the Way*. 1994. New York: Harper Collins, p. 166.

4. M. C. Bateson, *Peripheral Visions: Learning Along the Way*. 1994. New York: Harper Collins, p. 68.

5. Interview with Ray Arlinghaus, Proctor and Gamble.

6. M. Heidegger, *Discourse on Thinking*. 1966. New York: Harper Torchbooks, p. 45. Emphasis added.

7. Ibid.

8. P. Vaill, *Learning as a Way of Being*. 1996. San Francisco: Jossey-Bass, p. 207.

9. M. C. Bateson, *Peripheral Visions: Learning Along the Way*. 1994. New York: Harper Collins, p. 187.

10. L. Kahaner, *Competitive Intelligence: How to Gather, Analyse, and Use Information to Move Your Business to the Top*. 1998. New York: Touchstone Books, p. xx.

11. L. Buscaglia, *Papa, My Father*. 1989. New York: Fawcett Columbine.

PERSPECTIVE

Remember the last time you flew overseas, crossing borders into new territories? Did you observe how the business practices, social norms, values, regulations, marketing channels, languages, and opportunities all changed? Global leaders can't help but notice these shifts as they move from place to place. They know that their work is done in a world full of borders, even though communications and travel technology have created a "borderless world."[1] When crossing national, cultural, and language boundaries, they confront a fundamental challenge, as pointed out by a Wal-Mart executive: "One of the biggest obstacles we face when traversing country markets is learning to get the right mix at the right time, learning and relearning what each area really wants." Global leaders at Wal-Mart, like those in all globally competitive firms, learn to thrive on duality instead of working to destroy it. This perspective lets them master a myriad of border crossings instead of being overwhelmed by them. This perspective balances global with local and action with patience.

Global leaders take advantage of perspective through two critical skills that help them confront and overcome two key conflicts in the global marketplace. The first is the capacity to manage uncertainty—global leaders know when to gather more information and when to act. The second is the ability to balance tensions—global leaders understand what needs to change and what needs to stay the same from country to country, region to region. The ability to constantly balance tensions rests at the core of a perspective that embraces duality. The notion of duality suggests the simultaneous existence of two contradictory conditions, for example, sweet *and* sour. The essence of duality exists when two opposing conditions coexist and their continued coexistence is seen as being *good*. For example, if Asian cuisine allowed for sauce that was *only* sweet or *only* sour, the unique savor of sweet *and* sour could not be experienced. Such dualities can prove beneficial in the business world as well, but only when we gain the perspective that allows for the simultaneous occurence of opposites and that relishes their coexistence.

In a global marketplace, leaders face two sets of opposing demands: seeking information or acting on it and localizing products/processes or globalizing them. When global leaders learn to balance these constant tensions and ultimately embrace duality, they act far more effectively in the international business world. Global leaders do not just tolerate duality; nor do they try to avoid it; instead, they develop a perspective that embraces duality with a passion. They thrive in a world full of contradictions, a world laden with global *and* local demands. In fact, duality is an inescapable aspect of doing international business. As a leader, you face diverse demands from employees, customers, suppliers, and situations in which you need to gain as many perspectives as you can in order to solve the puzzle. Finding the puzzle pieces and fitting them together, however, becomes incredibly difficult when crossing multiple international borders. In fact, this process is so challenging that in our recently completed survey of over 100 U.S. multinational firms, we found that most executives and managers are consistently *weakest* in their ability to embrace duality as they do business around the world.

Some managers respond to the myriad of country and market differences with an almost instinctive drive to standardize products, policies, and practices. For example, a team of executives at the headquarters of a major U.S. software firm recently insisted that a holiday closure be held the same week in every part of the world. However, one company executive with significant international experience recognized that the week designated as a worldwide "holiday" had absolutely no meaning to Asian employees in

Asian countries. So he proposed an alternative: Let Asian countries take a week off during one of their local holidays, such as the Chinese New Year. Unfortunately, the executives at headquarters insisted that the holiday be held on the same week worldwide to "ensure consistency throughout the company." Standardization works fine if a product, service, or policy is brilliant enough that the entire world wants to buy in. However, in most instances it is unlikely that a company's standardized offering will be accepted as inherently valuable in each and every country simply because it comes from corporate headquarters! In fact, the reverse bias may be more common (and more accurate).

At a fundamental level, the present-day dynamics of globalization reflect a powerful convergence of companies and markets. Yet global leaders still determine on a day-to-day and quarter-to-quarter basis what to standardize globally and what to customize locally. They know that global *and* local must coexist within many areas of their companies. They embrace this duality by suspending prior beliefs about the present situation, creating fresh, new perspectives on the issue at hand, and—most important—acting on their insights. Put simply, they embrace the duality of a situation in order to formulate better definitions of problems and opportunities; to make better sense of an international marketplace laden with complex, and often conflicting, data; and to act on those insights in spite of significant uncertainties. A human resources executive from Colgate-Palmolive captures these dynamics quite well:

> We must populate our company with strong people who are not going to burn out, but rather *flourish* in a job where strong functional, strong P&L divisional, strong regional, strong category, and strong corporate managers are all pulling their strings. *Global leaders need the ability to operate in a world with shades of ambiguity, filled with creative tension, constantly balancing the priorities of a business.* This creative tension tends to shake out the best people. Some people can do it and some people can't.

Historically, strong country managers running largely independent operations have fueled Colgate-Palmolive's global growth. Recently, shifting customer demands, rapidly emerging markets, and increasing competitive cost pressures have combined to create an ultimatum for greater global brand consistency at Colgate-Palmolive. Today the company constantly balances the expertise and knowledge of local managers with ever stronger brand managers attempting to extract lower costs and more consistency. To compete in the tumultuous waters of the global marketplace, global leaders at companies like Colgate-Palmolive have learned how to perform superbly in a sea of ambiguity while facing the constantly crashing waves of competing tensions.

Embracing Uncertainty

At the heart of running your global organization, uncertainty reigns supreme. Every day, you face a dearth of quality data and a staggering number of questions that arise when your company crosses national, cultural, social, economic, or language borders: Who are your competitors? Where are your competitors located in the world? What are their competitive advantages? What is the real market potential of a particular country? Is this country a good platform for global operations? How easily can you train local workers? How secure is the government? How stable is the local currency?

While executives operating in only one country certainly confront some of these questions, the degree of uncertainty you face as a global leader increases exponentially. In fact, managers with responsibilities spanning dozens of countries face remarkable levels of uncertainty, as well as an incredible volume of data, both good and bad. JoAnn Cordary, international director of revenue management at Marriott Lodging International lives this uncertain, complex reality everyday. She is charged with finding and sorting through endless reams of information for dozens of countries and deciding on an appropriate hotel rate structure that combines some level of global rate consistency with local rate competitiveness. One of the biggest challenges she faces is deciding what data matters most, finding it, making sense of it, and then acting on it—in spite of the fact that she never has perfect information on competitive conditions at every Marriott hotel and resort location around the world.

To help sort through and then decide what matters most in this mass of information, JoAnn uses three fundamental criteria. First, she understands the current and future strategic direction of the firm and seeks out information for a pricing structure that makes strategic sense. Second, she understands the globalization trends in the hospitality industry. This knowledge helps her focus on competitors' key moves around the globe, not just in North America. Third, she works to see information that is contrary to Marriott's strategy or industry trends, particularly information that surfaces at a local level. In other words, she keeps her eyes focused on the strategic company goals and industry trends and she uses her peripheral vision to gather information around the margins of her reality.

Global Leaders Master Environmental Complexity

In an increasingly complex international business environment, global leaders demonstrate a very high capacity for managing uncertainty. Consider the complexity that Claire Bilby confronts daily as director of international marketing at Disney Attractions. Claire's former colleague, Norm Merritt, shared what it takes for her to manage the messy ambiguity of international business:

> What makes Claire so effective is her ability to keep a lot of balls in the air at the same time . . . and still get things done! She has an incredible memory that's not just recalling a myriad of facts and figures. She also draws on an intricate recall of spaghetti-like relationships spanning the globe. She plays in a global marketplace that is extremely complicated. It's hard to remember how things fit together, because they fit together quite differently in every market. Yet Claire is absolutely superb at moving in and out of a market and remembering, "Oh yeah, the marketing channels are very different here."
>
> For example, a tour operator in the U.K. is very different from a tour operator in Japan. It's different in terms of structure. It's different in terms of margin. It's different in terms of approach. It's different in terms of how they access the market. Everything's different, and in particular, relationships are different. Memory is key when sorting through endless reams of information and then making multicountry decisions. Claire has total recall of key components in complex situations. It's like she's

playing fifteen complex jigsaw puzzles simultaneously with each puzzle presenting a different picture and never knowing exactly what each picture looks like before you start. Claire thrives in that kind of world. She knows the subtleties of sorting through messy data and ultimately patching together a collage of colors that represent each puzzle's unique logic.

Like an expert game player putting together multiple jigsaw puzzles or playing several chess games simultaneously, global leaders—like Claire Bilby—have the capacity to cut through uncertainty and comprehend key activities. They make the appropriate moves and move forward boldly. They enter a new country and ask themselves, "What are the contexts? What are the relationships? What do I need to remember? Who are the real players?" To master this global game, they ask insightful questions, master the connections, make the relationships, and then do it all over again as soon as they arrive in another country. In sum, the global leaders we interviewed know how to identify, remember, and act on what is most important when facing a mass of confusing, complex information.

Many global leaders confront high levels of uncertainty that are actually built into their multinational organization's structure. Kraft Foods International, for example, has fewer than 100 people at corporate headquarters. Headquarters houses specialists in strategy, legal affairs, human resources, manufacturing, and so forth. While these managers report directly to the president, most decisions are made in the field. In Europe, the company has a regional headquarters with regional vice presidents in charge of production and R&D. Yet country presidents make key brand decisions. Within Europe, power is fluid. Individual leaders determine how to make things work. According to Simon Nash, a British national and director of management development at Kraft General Foods International, "The structure here will always be ambiguous, and our best leaders flourish in unstructured environments."

Relatively few executives are adept at moving forward in the face of incredible uncertainty. Yet global leaders are particularly agile at developing new market opportunities, as well as cutting to the heart of key issues in mature international operations. Global leaders not only feel comfortable, they actually thrive when dropping down like a paratrooper into virtually any city in the world. They say to themselves, "Yes, *I can navigate*; I know how to get to a hotel; I know how to start this operation; I know how to sniff out new market opportunities"—even though they may land in a city or country where they have never been before. They understand that prior experience may have nothing to do with the present. They confront ambiguity, attack uncertainty, and enter the market. Put simply, global leaders just do it, even when their information and preparation may be less than perfect. This attitude and approach is reflected in the following observation made by a senior executive in Asia working for a Fortune 500 firm: "Innovation is highly valued, recognized, and rewarded in our company. We haven't become a global leader in our industry by waiting to be 100 percent sure all of the time. Indeed, a significant level of risk taking is inherent in any leadership role."

Global Leaders Follow the "80/20" Rule

Many—if not most—managers who are far more comfortable directing their little dinghies in domestic waters are tempted to do endless research when facing the high uncertainty of international seas. They do this to avoid the risk of making a poor decision. Furthermore, corporate headquarters often demand research that is frequently purposeless, as confessed to us by the subsidiary president of a large transportation equipment company in Thailand:

> My head office keeps asking for reports that I have no ability to generate. The data they want do not exist here nor do my people have the skills to generate what they want. We might spend a month preparing a report that gets done in three days in the States. Headquarters thinks it is just a matter of hiring more people with better skills. But after being here a while, I realized headquarters has got it mostly wrong. While we can always use more good people, the American way of running the business just doesn't work here. *The reports are not only a waste of time, they actually lead us in the wrong direction.*

In today's hypercompetitive business environment, engaging in too much research and waiting for complete clarity is an invitation to trouble. The competition simply does not stand still waiting for executives to figure out what to do. IBM provides a classic case in point.

Before Lou Gerstner arrived at IBM, managers there had a history of avoiding uncertainty. While the company produced some of the best technology in the industry, IBM's corporate culture in the early 1990s emphasized getting the product "right" before going to market. Every line of code was checked and rechecked, every piece of hardware had to perform *perfectly*. This policy minimized risk for employees and conformed with IBM's "product out" strategy. As technological change accelerated and customer choices increased, however, IBM's risk-averse approach did not work very well.

Delayed by the need to "get things right," IBM's newest products often arrived on the market months late and over budget. When the products finally arrived, many customers had already moved past what IBM was trying to offer as cutting-edge technolgy. According to Tom Bouchard, senior vice president for Human Resources at IBM, "We no longer had the luxury of getting everything 'just right.' Once we embraced a 'customer in' strategy, the qualities for effective leadership changed." Beginning in 1995, executives at IBM actively promoted a new 80/20 rule. They would go to market with the product 80 percent "right" and 20 percent still unproven. The features they focused on getting right were those the customers cared most about. The result? Sales increased, enormous amounts of money were saved, and most important, customers were happier. Global leaders at IBM learned to quickly separate "the figure from the background." Today, Lou Gerstner and other executives do not wait for the entire picture to come into focus before moving ahead. They know that speed to market is key to competitive success. Some at IBM have even considered switching the 80/20 rule to a 20/80 rule for even greater speed in the rapidly changing global markets. Under such a rule, managers must identify the critical 20 percent of all customer needs which, if addressed well, will satisfy 80 percent of the customers. By quickly identifying this critical 20 percent, they can make a quantum leap in overall speed to market.

Global Leaders Do Their Homework

We find it amazing that many executives approach business uncertainty by copying others, like teenagers following fashion fads. If they don't know what to do, they impulsively watch what others do. They follow the leader. Yet benchmarking or following without thinking can be incredibly dangerous in the global marketplace. It's not much different than dancing blindfolded near the edge of a cliff. Consider for a moment the generally disastrous attempts by many U.S. and some foreign airlines to mimic Herb Kelleher's highly competitive operations strategy at Southwest Airlines. Southwest started with and still focuses on short-haul flight routes, relying on standardized aircraft and rapid turnaround at airport gates. This results in rates of operating efficiency and aircraft utilization for Southwest that are much higher than those of other airlines in this capital intensive industry. Executives at Southwest's competitors have learned that it is one thing to notice what others do well and quite a different matter to imitate their actions.

In overseas markets, multinational firms blunder around in the dark when they fail to acquire the contacts, relationships, and connections—the essential conduits of information—that are held by local companies. When this happens, executives tend to do what they have always done, or they simply start imitating what others do. Inevitably, problems result. For example, when UPS first entered the European market and established operations in Germany, it tried to attract quality drivers with the same pay and policies that had worked in the United States. However, the wages offered were too low to attract experienced drivers in Germany, and the traditional brown UPS uniforms put many potential employees off. The uniforms were too similar in color to those worn by the Nazi youth groups during World War II. By focusing on what made a job attractive to an experienced German truck driver, UPS finally came to understand that it had to offer higher wages and clarify in its recruiting advertisements that brown uniforms were required UPS dress in all parts of the world. In sum, doing effective homework helps global leaders understand their target constituency, be they customers or potential employees.

Global Leaders Are Open to Uncertainty

In the global marketplace, creative leadership in the midst of uncertainty is not an option. It is a mandate. For example, corporate executives at one major consumer products firm were set on selling bubble bath in Hong Kong. The only trouble was that people don't have bathtubs in Hong

Kong. For this consumer products company, it had no choice but to do things differently. Realizing their mistake, senior executives learned the right lesson and paid closer attention to local input. This resulted in a number of innovative ideas, and the company ultimately relaunched the bubble bath as body soap packaged with a washcloth—with highly successful market results. To offset local surprises when entering new markets, global leaders exploit local understanding and global capabilities to achieve lower costs and superior product and service offerings.

Global leaders can rarely predict where new product development and process improvements will come from. As Kazutami Komada, general manager of the Visual and Audio Products Division of the Toshiba Corporation recognized:

> In our industry, product differences remain significant between Europe and North America. We do the basic design work for consumer electronics in Japan, but the models change in each region. In fact, we encourage local and in some cases regional production and want our local managers to take initiative. As an example, in the late 1980s our U.K. subsidiary developed closed caption television and stereo broadcasting. We have learned that we simply can't do everything in Tokyo.

Managing uncertainty effectively means feeling comfortable with the unknown. Remember the global leader we mentioned in Chapter 1 who was recently responsible for setting up a production operation in Vietnam for one of the largest multinational firms in the world? As we said earlier, after taking the assignment and arriving in Vietnam, he discovered that the land on which the firm intended to build the production facility was a fully flooded rice paddy. He had never encountered this kind of challenge back at corporate headquarters and had limited staff to turn to for solutions. His mind raced with questions, like: Whom do I contact to get the water off the land? What government officials might have to approve the land use change? Can we predict how long it will take to drain the water and stay on production and costs schedules? This executive learned firsthand the truth of what Sven Grasshoff, vice president international corporate human resources, Citibank, expressed: "Global leaders in developing countries *are* the infrastructure." This Vietnam-based manager built a government strategy to accomplish the business strategy. In collaboration with a few, key local employees, he learned how to effectively petition the proper government officials and negotiate for assistance in clearing the land. Furthermore, he had also built up substantial influence and contacts within the company that enabled him to mobilize its resources in response to the emergency. Working with his local team, the local government, and his company's regional headquarters, he discovered a way to clear the land, put the factory in place, and stay basically on schedule. Effective global leaders do not shy away from these types of situations. Instead, they seek out opportunities where uncertainty rules. They ask smart questions in these complex situations, they sift through a myriad of unknowns, and ultimately, they act.

Doing International Business Resembles White-Water Rafting

While plans can be critical to international success, global leaders appreciate that doing international business in a world teeming with unknowns resembles white-water rafting, requiring both preparation and improvisation. Experienced white-water rafters first scout the river from the shoreline. They study maps, survey routes, and plan the attack. Yet no matter how valuable this preparation is, white-water rafters understand that once on the water, they must often make decisions in a split-second. Even though they may be following a particular, planned route, rafters must make constant adjustments in real time, on-line. In this fluid decision-making context, studying every detail of a river beforehand provides little direction in the swirling moments of decision that are forced by a river's unpredictable currents. Even more importantly, rafters know that if they approach large rapids timidly or with the slightest degree of hesitation, the water's powerful force will easily flip and sink their boat.

The skills required to succeed as a white-water rafter are quite similar to those needed for success in the global marketplace. Even with the best market intelligence and the most up-to-date, comprehensive databases, global leaders can never know all the answers beforehand because they simply can not anticipate every question and because the scenery changes so rapidly. There are always new and unexpected elements to be reckoned with. Remember that just ten years ago, there was no such thing as a corporate website. Today, most companies tout their presence on the Internet in every

form of advertising. Not even Bill Gates, CEO at Microsoft, fully anticipated the tidal wave of change that launched the rapid growth of the Internet with its compressed web-years of 90—not 365—days. In the global
marketplace, change is constant and global leaders know that they must
make effective adjustments in real time. One European global marketing
executive disclosed: "Global leaders exhibit the ability to accept whatever
comes at them in their jobs. They do away with whatever they thought was
fixed to traverse the unpredictable terrain of international business."

Conoco's CEO Archie Dunham is the kind of leader who understands
the truth of this statement. As CEO of a large U.S. oil and gas company,
Dunham was asked by the chief of the Nenets, a reindeer-herding people
in Russia, to meet face-to-face on the Arctic tundra to finalize negotiations
on an oil and gas lease. After taking a routine flight to Russia and a heli-
copter lift to the village, Dunham began an encounter atypical in every way
of the normal life of an American CEO. He started by sitting cross-legged
in a tent pitched on the snow. Then he offered a number of gifts to the
Nenet chief. These were not letter openers or paperweights, but hatchets,
matches, and ropes. In return, the chief of the Nenets respectfully rose,
chopped a piece of reindeer meat from a carcass hanging in the tent,
dipped the meat in a bowl of fresh reindeer blood, and held it out for Mr.
Dunham to eat. What to do? Test the meat for food poisoning? Visit a library about the health benefits of eating fresh reindeer blood? Call a culture consultant to consider the possible responses when offered such a gift
by the chief of the Nenets? Dunham chose none of these options. Instead,
he took the meat graciously and swallowed it whole.[2]

As companies cross borders, uncertainty increases exponentially. Figuring out how every piece of the puzzle fits together before acting is not only
impossible, but in the international business domain is plain foolish. Gary
Griffiths of Marriott International learned this lesson well, as evident in his
experiences opening up the first Marriott hotel in Poland.

Exemplar Global Leader
Gary Griffiths

After working as a controller at Marriott hotels in the United States, Gary
Griffiths was asked to become director of finance for the company's first
hotel in Poland, the Warsaw Marriott—then still some months from open-

ing. While Gary's previous experience in the United States was invaluable, it did little to prepare him for the extreme uncertainty he was to encounter in Poland. Several months before this assignment came, Gary had requested an international posting; expecting a position in one of Marriott's Mexico resorts, he had instead got the call to Warsaw. He was chosen largely because of his sound financial skills, honed while working for years in a U.S. public accounting firm before joining Marriott. Most hotel controllers have purely operational roles and do not have full charge of the balance sheet, but corporate executives knew that the director of finance for the Warsaw Marriott would need a broader mandate. He or she would work on a management team facing incredible levels of uncertainty, without the typical safety net of standard operating procedures. Gary was their choice.

The Warsaw Marriott was still under construction as the opening team of 23 employees and their families flew in. One of the first challenges Gary faced was finding a telephone for his family's home in Warsaw. His wife and five children had never been to Eastern Europe, didn't speak Polish, and were worried about being able to contact Gary at work in case of an emergency. To get a phone line, Gary had to find the right contact people in the local telephone company, pull some "pretty impressive strings," and then pay $600 (an enormous sum of money at that time in Poland) out of his own pocket for the telephone company to extend a main trunk line into his subdivision. After six months, the Griffiths family got the phone. (Ironically, during the first week of the hotel's grand opening, over 200 telephone sets were stolen by guests. Fortunately, Gary and his team were well prepared and had already purchased extra phones.) The refrigerator that Gary's wife ordered for their house was delivered at eleven o'clock at night in an unmarked truck and had to be paid for in cash with American dollars. While Gary and his family struggled (and laughed a lot) through the difficulties and surprises they encountered at home, he also faced an endless stream of significant unknowns on an everyday basis at work.

For several months before and after the hotel opened, uncertainty was the order of the day for Gary. First, he needed to set up a bank account in the country. Gary telephoned the local bank that planned to open a branch in the hotel complex and invited the bank's vice president over to his office to discuss the hotel's banking requirements. At the end of the conversation, the vice president declared, "Great! It's now April. We're opening our branch in your building in October and we'll open your accounts then."

Gary, thinking they had "lost something in the translation," tried once again to explain the current and future banking requirements of the Warsaw Marriott. This time the bank vice president responded, "I understand what you need, but we do not have room in our system for your accounts until we open our new branch. I'm sorry, but we can't help you." Gary had never heard of a bank that didn't want money, yet this one seemed to have a "No Vacancy" sign hanging on the door. At this point, Gary was exasperated and ready to walk out of the meeting. The bank vice president stood up and suggested: "You know, I can't open a business account for your company, but let me open a personal account so you can at least take care of yourself."

To open a "personal account" to run the entire Warsaw Marriott, Gary called the treasurer of the Marriott Corporation in the United States. Gary said that he was ready for the first transfer of cash to the hotel, $200,000. The treasurer answered, "Terrific! I am glad you finally got that one figured out. Give me the bank routing address." When Gary told it to him, the treasurer asked, "Give me the name on the account." Gary hesitantly responded, "Gary Griffiths." There was a long, strained pause. The funds were ultimately transferred to Gary's *personal* account, but they were declared "missing" in the bank's system for 56 days. As a result, the Warsaw Marriott still had no operating cash. The only option Gary could think of to get the necessary cash for operating the hotel was to drive to the Marriott hotel in Vienna, Austria, pick up $25,000 in cash, and bring it back to Poland. Reentering Poland alone with the money, Gary was fairly scared. He had to declare to a machine-gun toting border guard that he was carrying $25,000. The cash in Gary's car was the equivalent of more than 50 years of wages for the border guard. Fortunately, Gary made it safely through the crossing, returned to the hotel, and deposited the money—in his personal account.

The management team in Warsaw faced other surprises during the startup in Poland. With no beef suppliers available to age their beef, they decided to build a meat locker room in the basement of the hotel. They then ordered fresh beef carcasses to put in the locker—something that had never been done before at any Marriott hotel. They also imported celery seed and gave it to farmers so that the Marriott restaurants could be supplied with celery. On the day the restaurants in the hotel complex opened their doors, they served 2,200 meals. Everything in the country worked on a cash basis at that time, and given the exchange rate in zlotys for a $10 meal, Gary had an unexpected problem the next morning. His night clerk, finishing up the shift, called Gary to ask, "How should we get the cash to the bank?" Gary responded with the standard operating procedure: "You get the cash, put it in a deposit bag, and take it to the bank." The clerk told Gary he probably ought to come down to the general cashier's office. Frustrated, Gary went to the room and was stunned at what he encountered. The room was literally full of zloty bills, lining the walls from floor to ceiling. The clerk asked, "How am I going to get *this* to the bank?" Gary gave some thought to the problem and decided to have the engineering department build a cash trunk, complete with two large padlocks, to replace the standard issue cash bag. Day after day, week after week, Gary sent the clerk with four very large men to deliver the trunk full of cash to the bank.

After living through all the uncertainty in Warsaw, Gary Griffiths concluded,

> Things are not the same when you get out there in the world. You have to be willing to understand new environments and figure out how to deal with them. You have to learn to improvise. You must be ready to change your fundamental paradigms of how you do business. These frames of reference are educated into us at school and work as standard business practices, but when you go overseas, those same frames often become massive blinders. My experience in Warsaw drove home the point that you simply have to find new ways of doing things, you have to get around typical business practices when bumping up against the constant unknowns of running an operation in a developing economy.

For Gary Griffiths at Marriott, for Claire Bilby at Disney, or for you, encountering extreme uncertainty and acting comfortably in the face of it constitutes one essential foundation of your perspective as a global leader. Another important component is your ability to balance tensions in the global marketplace.

Balancing Tensions

Global leaders demonstrate the ability to constantly balance tensions and by so doing, act far more effectively in the global marketplace. Comments by a senior finance executive at Proctor & Gamble reinforce this point: "The secret is the balance. Global leaders know how to keep one eye on bottom-line business results and the other eye open to the local customer. To the degree to which global leaders do that well, I believe that a firm will succeed globally." Pat Canavan, a director and corporate vice president for leadership development at Motorola, extends this idea:

> Global leaders who make the largest difference at any level of our corporation are able to think and act on a scale which is different from acting only at a country or regional level. They have a way of thinking about the planet that they are on, a way of understanding where customers are coming from. It's built into their understanding of any situation.

At Proctor & Gamble or Motorola—as well as at other corporations around the world—global leaders can move in and out of various worlds, balancing the inherent tensions experienced during those transitions and understanding the underlying global and local pressures that create constant tensions.

Pressures for Global Integration Impact Global Leaders

As you face competing pressures of global integration and local responsiveness, enormous conflicts often arise. Consider the experience of Colgate-Palmolive as described by Brian Smith, former director of global HR Strategy:

> The country manager used to be king of the hill in our company. They would come up with a nifty project and get approval to launch it. You'd get a German brand and a French brand and maybe it would translate across borders. It would take a great deal of time and create enormous redundancy. That approach is now over. Today, we have global bundles. While the big red, standard anticavity Colgate used to look 60 different ways around the world, now you can walk into any store in any market in any part of the world and Colgate is Colgate. It's a truly global brand.

How did Colgate-Palmolive move to this global brand position? Through the constant resolution of conflicts that occurred between country and global brand managers about packaging, pricing, and production sites. To negotiate these conflicts successfully, managers did several things. First, country managers were willing to bend on strongly held views that product packaging must always contain their personal, local touch. Second, global brand managers were willing to change their perspective, valuing local country input as they implemented global packaging, pricing, and production procedures. Third, all parties worked for creative solutions to the conflicts rather than seeking the lowest common denominator compromise. These actions resulted in decisions on product packaging and other matters that now work very well throughout the world.

Like Nestlé, Unilever, and Sony, Colgate has customers whose fundamental needs are the same across the globe. For example, a Sony Walkman cassette or CD player meets a customer need that is fairly universal: a small, portable machine with which to play music. Similarly, Gillette can sell the same razors worldwide because customers have a fairly universal need to remove hair.

Just as universal customer needs create pressures for global integration, global competitors can also force companies to more closely integrate their worldwide operations. In the photographic film market, U.S.-based Kodak faces competitors like Fuji from Japan. Fuji's continued attempts to increase U.S. market share forces Kodak executives not only to compete against Fuji in the United States, but has also to enter and stay in the Japanese market—even though Kodak loses money there. If Kodak failed to compete in this global fashion, Fuji could easily leverage increased profits from Japan, increasing its profit sanctuary to fund market battles in the United States.

In the development and production of innovative products, major capital and technological investments can also push firms to look beyond the borders of their home country. Recently, executives at Phillips in the Netherlands chose to spend millions of dollars in developing a leading-edge home entertainment system to compete against Sega and Nintendo. The high development costs for this product forced executives at Phillips to integrate global operations even further and attempt to market the product worldwide.

Pressures for Local Responsiveness Impact Global Leaders

In stark contrast to these global integration pressures, global leaders also encounter significant pressures for local responsiveness. The expansion of Domino's Pizza into Japan provided a fun example of localization pressures. To meet the unique taste preferences of Japanese customers, Domino's added chicken teriyaki, corn, squid, tuna, and sautéed burdock root as pizza toppings. While you might think that pizzas are a globally standardized product, what goes on top of the pizza is definitely not the same in Tokyo and Chicago.

Not only can tastes differ, but so can even more significant customer needs. Wal-Mart learned this lesson the hard way when it entered several countries in Asia and stocked its stores with thick flannel shirts. These shirts sold well in Wisconsin, but they were useless in hot, humid Asian climates.

Differences in laws and regulations can also create significant localization demands. In Europe, computer monitor emission restrictions are far more stringent than those found in the United States. As a result, NEC of Japan had to customize monitors to meet local regulatory demands and compete with European manufacturers like Nokia.

Pressures for speedy delivery often require a local presence to deliver products and services as quickly as local competitors. Effective global leaders, understanding this dynamic, strategically locate operations close to the customer to enhance delivery speed as well as increase the ultimate value perception of each country's customer set. For example, as Japanese auto manufacturers set up operations in the United States and Europe, parts suppliers follow close behind with production operations located next to the auto factories to ensure speedy and reliable delivery.

Global Leaders Balance Tensions

To balance tensions in the global marketplace, global leaders accept and ultimately exploit competing ways of doing things. Customer demands, employee practices, government policies, production technologies, and competitor responses often differ greatly between countries. As a result, the policies your company establishes in one country may need significant revisions for other countries. Furthermore, the ways in which global leaders respond to these tensions differs between companies as well. Consider the differences between executives at Frito Lay and Wal-Mart as they attempt to balance the inherent tensions in international business. Frito Lay has almost 50,000 route sales representatives around the world. They must develop close personal relationships with everyone on their routes. For Frito Lay, this system is very expensive, but effective. In contrast, Wal-Mart has invested lavishly on Electronic Data Interchange technology and downplayed the role of personal relationships in the sales process. Wal-Mart's EDI system is also very expensive, but it better facilitates the company's globalization efforts. To prioritize what might seem like hopelessly conflicting demands in situations like these, effective global leaders rely on several criteria to guide their choices. First, they pay particular attention to countries that are competitively consequential to their industry. For example, personal computer makers cannot afford to ignore the U.S. consumer market. Second, they track key competitors around the world and regularly reverse-engineer their successes. In the automotive industry, for instance, every manufacturer knows every part of its competitors' vehicles. Finally, they know their own companies' competitive advantages and leverage them to create value for the customer.

Beyond the tensions that result from global-local differences, traditions established in one part of your company are often inappropriate for other parts of the organization. As the company expands overseas, global leaders regularly sort out which traditions will work and which ones won't. Understanding what, when, and how to change your company's strategies, processes, practices, and policies is at the heart of a global leader's capacity to balance tensions and embrace duality. Paul Cook, a vice president for international HR at Novell, captures this inherent tension:

> Our biggest challenge is, how do we motivate our people worldwide, in so many countries, and still create some level of acceptable consistency to balance it out? It's a complete balancing act that never ends.

Several years ago one of the largest banks in the United States attempted to motivate its employees worldwide by handing out a small number of company stock certificates to each employee. While this incentive worked well for financially savvy employees, employees in many countries, perceiving the stock certificates as relatively worthless, simply gave them to other employees in the bank who saw their worth. The savvy employees actually accumulated more significant financial gains from the gifts of fellow employees' stock than from the increase in market value of their own stock.

Executives adopt polices to provide organizational discipline, reduce repetition in decision making, minimize risk, and maximize efficiency. Once established, though, standardized policies can easily shut down the critical judgment aspects of decision-making processes. Unfortunately, managers who don't like balancing tensions typically cling rigidly to company policies. They want the security blanket of being told clearly what to do and how to do it, no matter the circumstances. Global leaders, on the other hand, understand that the system of company policies should be considered something like a great bridge—stable enough to cross, but flexible enough to sway. As any engineer will tell you, environmental conditions (temperature, wind, humidity, and so on) change constantly and a long bridge, such as the Golden Gate in San Francisco or the Rainbow in Yokohama, must not be constructed too rigidly. In fact, a bridge built too unyielding will quickly collapse under stress.

In a global context, relatively few policies can be implemented uniformly throughout the world. As Figure 4.1 shows, certain core elements, such as superior customer service, should be globally standardized. Other elements, such as leadership style, may vary from region to region. Finally, some elements, such as specific recruiting tactics, may vary widely from local operation to local operation.

Global leaders know when to follow the rules, when to bend them, and when to break them at each level of their organization. Steve Holliday, managing director of British-Borneo Oil & Gas, describes these dynamics well:

> We always have a concern that our people will "go local." When this happens, our team risks making decisions based on personal relations to the exclusion of the interests of the business. Going local has its limits. When necessary, the relationship has to be subordinated to the business. If your team has gone local, they almost always support excuses from the local partner when things don't happen. In reality, global business represents a com-

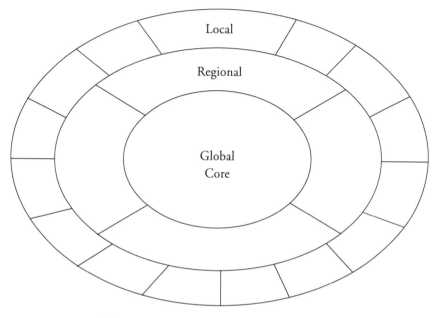

Global Core: Examples may include customer service
Regional: Examples may include management style
Local: Examples may include recruiting tactics

Figure 4.1 Managing Globalization-Localization Tensions

promise. If you are doing business in China, you can't do it 100 percent the Chinese way. They need to live with our way and we need to live with their way. Global leaders must decide how, when, and what to compromise.

Clearly, one of the keys to balancing tensions is recognizing that not everything needs to be either universal or unique and local. In deciding when a policy should be universal and when it should be flexible, begin by examining the global integration and local responsiveness pressures in your particular industry.

As Figure 4.2 shows, global leaders in each industry face a unique set of pressures for global integration and local responsiveness. At the industry level, funeral homes are a great example of an industry that faces pressures primarily of local responsiveness. The watch industry, in contrast, has been

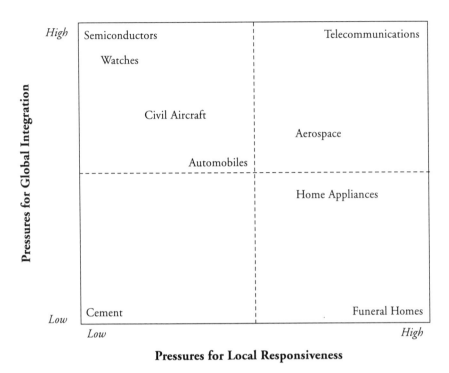

Figure 4.2 Locating Industries on a Globalization-Localization Matrix

dominated by global integration pressures for over 100 years. Some industries, such as telecommunications, face strong pressures for both global integration and local responsiveness. The need for worldwide routing of voice and data transmission creates strong global integration pressures, yet different government regulations exert tremendous localization pressures.

Consider how David Janke, vice president for international at Evans & Sutherland, daily encounters competing pressures in the United States:

> One of our main products, an F-16 fighter jet simulator, has some parts that stay the same wherever we sell it in the world and other parts that need major modification. In my experience, every sale is unique and usually customized. For instance, if I sell a visual system to a flight simulator in Korea, I sell the hardware—the computers that draw the pictures—but the software that goes on there—the database—models some specific area of

the world. The Koreans want to train over Korea. Forget those Nevada deserts; they want to train over Korea. So, we have to model that area of the world for their pilots. Furthermore, Korean F-16s need certain specific markings. Pilots fly and land them in certain ways, and their airfields look different. So, we have to model and customize the software to the Koreans. In our business, any day of the week I have customers from some part of the world here meeting with my team to customize their simulator database.

When faced with dual pressures at an industry level, companies sometimes choose to reduce the tension by focusing on one set of pressures over the other. For example, at Lego Toy Company in Denmark, senior executives have decided to focus on global integration pressures, since they believe that many of children's play needs are essentially the same around the world. Lego produces hundreds of different toy kits. Prototypes are designed in Denmark on the basis of global market research. Although Lego has multiple manufacturing sites, each kit is designed to meet worldwide market demands and is sold on a global basis. Lego boxes have no writing, instructions are pictorial, and play figures are devoid of racial features.

In direct contrast to Lego, executives at Nestlé take a much different approach to competing pressures. The Swiss-based company has a history of building and supporting powerful country organizations, focusing on each nation's different food-taste preferences. Country managers supervise research and development. They decide which products to sell, at what prices, and through which channels. Power in the organization has resided, at least historically, directly in the hands of country managers. Executives and managers at Nestlé's head office have traditionally played a facilitative, fairly hands-off role. Leaders have been chosen primarily on their ability to work successfully in their home country.

In reality, very few companies that face globalization-localization pressures organize as strongly in one direction or the other as executives at Nestlé and Lego have historically done. In fact, it is rare for senior executives to globalize *all* activities in their companies; similarly, it is rare for them to turn complete strategy-formulation authority over to country presidents. Thus the vast majority of executives today live a real-life balancing act of globalizing and localizing activities. Global leaders become walking paradoxes as they engage in a mixture of activities that result in complex—and in many ways incomprehensible—structures and systems. In these companies, R&D may be global for some products, but regional for others; product policies might be global and advertising programs local; manufacturing might be local, regional, or global.

We found a case of these complex dynamics at play at Pfizer in Europe, where the discovery, development, and registration of products are all globally managed. Pricing and work with physicians are the responsibility of local subsidiaries. Subsidiary leaders are not allowed to take initiatives toward the discovery of new products because regulations are so different in each country throughout the world. For example, the U.S. Food and Drug Administration does not accept clinical tests from Japan, and Japan does not accept clinical tests from the United States. In contrast, Malaysia and the Philippines accept both U.S. and European testing. Frank Hickson, senior vice president for pharmaceutical marketing and development at Pfizer Pharmaceuticals Japan, explains his response to these challenges: "We can and do take initiatives here in Japan in areas of distribution and marketing. We can also decide how aggressively we will push clinical trials. What we really control in Japan is the speed and competence of bringing products through clinical trials and marketing."

The following chart helps us visualize how one firm decides where to locate activities in terms of globalization and localization. Figure 4.3 demonstrates how global leaders need to look below the industry level to see how globalization-localization pressures impact activities in their own organizations. As you look at how executives at the Coca-Cola Company generally approach the location of their company's different value chain activities, as shown in Figure 4.3, you might consider where your company's key activities should be conducted.

When you focus on competitiveness at the activity level, you can develop far greater precision in determining the optimal level of globalization for your company. Clearly, globalization does not produce scale or scope advantages for all activities. In the final analysis, you may optimize some activities at the global level—with resulting global scale and scope advantages—and optimize others at the local level.

As a global leader, you are responsible for determining what should be globally integrated and what should be locally adapted in your company. When you optimize activities—whether at the local, regional, or global

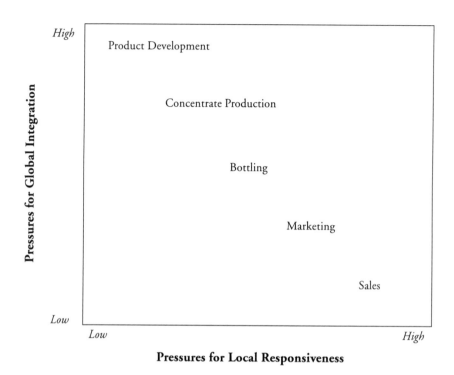

Figure 4.3 Globalization and Localization Pressures at Coca-Cola, by Activity

level—you maximize efficiencies and serve customers best. Keep in mind that you can make mistakes in either direction. You may try to globalize activities that should be localized, and you may mistakenly try to localize things that should be globalized. As one senior finance executive from a major consumer products firm reasoned,

> Global leaders must have the capability to see an idea, a process, a technology, an approach to business, and be willing to not only reapply it, but to modify it to the degree and only to the degree that it is *absolutely* necessary for its success.

Indeed, F. Scott Fitzgerald observed that "the test of a first rate intelligence is the ability to hold two simultaneous ideas in mind and still keep the ability to function." Global leaders do just that, while global followers either freeze up in these decision situations, or simply give in to one set of pressures while ignoring others.

Global Leaders Face Tensions in New Markets

Perhaps at no time is the conflict between global and local more apparent than when your company moves into new markets. Here, opportunities for effective global leadership are at their greatest. For example, the Big Three U.S. auto makers face vast, untapped opportunities in Asia Pacific markets. After essentially ignoring the region for decades, managers must now make momentous decisions about everything their companies do and how they do it. As an example, CEOs at GM and Ford have pushed "global cars" as a tactic for cutting costs and speeding market entry. Now executives face many perplexing questions: Will global cars work in China, the Philippines, and Thailand? Should corporate policies for gifts and gratuities be applied to new operations in Asia Pacific and Africa? Should exclusive distributors be used, or should the automakers invest heavily in establishing networks of independent dealers, much as they do in the United States and Europe? Your ability to embrace duality will be tested by questions just like these.

The degree to which you are able to embrace duality is closely related to your capacity to manage headquarters versus field relationships. As a senior HR executive at Pepsi counseled,

> This skill turned out to be incredibly important for our global leaders and if you think about it, it makes a lot of sense. If I'm in China, I've got to establish my business and know how things work in China—the political system, the values, the culture. At the same time, I've got my boss saying, "I want something implemented this year." Then I've got to find a way to do it within the kinds of ways that are acceptable in China and at the same time not have the people back home think I'm not getting their job done. It's a very delicate balance you have to strike and it's a key competency in our company.

Maintaining this balance is key as Pepsi continues to fight the cola war in countries around the world. For instance, its key competitor, Coca-Cola, has recently reentered India after a sixteen-year absence from the country. In 1993, Coca-Cola bought a local bottler of Thums Up, a popular Indian drink that tastes almost exactly like Coca-Cola and commands a significant market share. Unfortunately for Pepsi, corporate executives at Coca-Cola have finally warmed up to the idea of pushing two cola drinks in India to try and take away sales from Pepsi. Pepsi continues to hold on to a strong market share, but the Indian cola market is now hotly contested.

This powerful dynamic between global and local demands is not unique to the soft drink industry, as was borne out by one of our interviews with a senior executive at Merck:

> When you are sent from head office to another country, there is often a tension between your responsibility to be a loyal corporate representative and the need to be very responsive to and learn from the local environment. In many cases you are sent to an overseas subsidiary to do something. You still have a tie back to head office and you have a three- or four-year deadline to get some major things accomplished. Yet, what happens when you learn that the original objectives and plan you had going in to the new country is clearly not the appropriate plan after you arrive in the country? This produces real tension, tension as powerful as that found on a high-voltage power line. This tension is even more acute if you are brought in as a hit man from head office. When you are in the subsidiary, though, I think that you must work for the subsidiary and work to make that subsidiary succeed. Trying to split those loyalties is very difficult, and at times almost impossible.

In reality, global leaders know that hard and fast corporate goals and policies must be supported *and* circumvented—at the same time. Many managers are driven crazy by the personal risk and uncertainty associated with dynamic situations; they feel as if they're bumping their heads against the wall everyday, all day long. Global leaders, on the other hand, emulate tightrope walkers, who maintain their balance by constantly adjusting the angle of their poles. Freeze the angle of the pole by grasping for certainty in uncertain situations—and you fall. Those who do not understand this, who are unwilling or unable to balance the necessary tensions of international business—they fail.

In contrast, managers who succeed keep their perspective and thrill at traversing this tightrope of tensions. Managing the tensions requires what a senior executive at Disney referred to as

> global leaders' ability to accept whatever comes at them, whenever it comes, and wherever it comes from. They have to do away with whatever they thought was fixed and become extremely flexible.

This point became reality for Steve Burke, our exemplar for balancing tensions, when he was asked by Michael Eisner, CEO of Disney, to help turn around the Eurodisney theme park in 1992.

Exemplar Global Leader
Stephen B. Burke

Steve Burke was asked personally by Michael Eisner, CEO of the Walt Disney Company, to take the position of vice president in charge of operations and marketing at the EuroDisney theme park on virtually a moment's notice. The official announcement was made on a Monday morning in October, 1992, and Steve was on a plane for Paris that very afternoon.

Before Steve joined the Walt Disney Company in 1986 at the age of thirty, he had already received his MBA from Harvard and worked for two years at General Foods. As a brand manager for Post Raisin Bran cereal, Steve began early in his career to learn the meaning of a "balancing act," since he had to manage the tension between localized pricing and promotion strategies, and regional or national demands for consistency in the breakfast food market. These lessons were helpful when he joined Disney as the director of business development at the consumer products division.

Paying careful attention to employees' input, Steve launched the idea for a Disney retail store, and then grew it into a nearly half-billion-dollar business, paying close attention to consistency in operations at each store—visiting them whenever possible. These visits set off what came to be known as the "Burke alert"—a store that had just been visited would call other stores in the region to warn them. Steve was understanding, however, recognizing the local challenges confronted by each store and working with them to improve their unique situations. In 1990, Steve became executive vice president of consumer products with the Disney Stores, which were averaging $600-800 in sales per square foot, more than twice the U.S. national average for specialty retail.

Building on his success at Disney Stores, Steve was asked to help turn around Disney's biggest financial disaster—EuroDisney, a (quasi) joint venture between Disney and the French government that had opened in April 1992 amid a storm of bad publicity. From the beginning, the project was beset with problems:

- Attendance was off 10 percent from projections.
- Per person spending in the park was less than half that at Disney's theme park in Japan.
- Hotel occupancy rates were 37 percent versus 92 percent at Disney's U.S. properties.
- Labor costs were significantly higher than in the United States because of labor contracts that made it impossible to dramatically increase and decrease staff during peak and off seasons.
- Negative publicity abounded, with newspaper headlines like "Disney is Cultural Chernobyl."
- The French government's appropriation of farm land for the theme park had led to continuing protests from French farmers.
- Workers resisted the Disney management style and dress code.
- Construction cost overruns were nearly $2 billion.

It was expected that the park would post upwards of $300 million in net losses for the first year of operations, even with total attendance at ten million guests. Many executives within Disney were beginning to feel that it would be years before the park became profitable.

Despite this bleak picture, CEO Michael Eisner remained optimistic about the venture: "Instant hits are things that go away quickly, and things that grow slowly and are part of the culture are what we look for. What we created in France is the biggest private investment in a foreign country by an American company ever. And it's gonna pay off."[3] Steve's job was to work closely with Philippe Bourguignon, EuroDisney's president and a French national, to make sure Eisner would be proven right. Things were a bit chaotic at first. Steve didn't speak any French and he had never met Phillipe Bourguignon, who was soon to become CEO and chairman of the board of the European theme park. Steve wasn't at all sure how he and Phillipe would get along. Furthermore, his predecessor had left France to return to the United States three days after Steve arrived, providing no transition period. All this meant that Steve had to jump directly into a very uncertain situation.

Some days it was difficult for Steve to keep track of everything he was doing; many Disney expatriates were preparing to go back to the States, leaving the office in a constant state of change and turmoil. As more expatriates left, Steve took on additional responsibilities, including human resources and support, hotels, and day-to-day park activities. Although Steve might have liked more time to adjust to the new office environment, the fact remained that he was sent to EuroDisney to maintain the Disney way in Paris *and* bring about changes to the troubled park. Steve quickly realized that this was not going to be an easy task.

Touring the park on his first day, he thought to himself, "This is just *not* how Disney does it!" While the rides and cartoon characters were in place, dirty dishes and trays abounded on tables in the restaurants, and garbage bins were overflowing in the restrooms and walkways. Even areas that he had just seen the maintenance crew sweep up still had pieces of litter strewn about.

After reviewing some of the reports he had requested, Steve was particularly concerned about park guest attendance figures, especially among the French. Hotel occupancy rates were alarmingly low, and guests were not spending much money in the restaurants or souvenir shops. With revenues much lower than projected, Steve recognized that labor costs were a serious concern. This problem was augmented by the French government's resistance to allowing Disney to use part-time or seasonal workers as the company was accustomed to doing in its U.S. and Japanese theme parks. In addition to establishing a culture and attitude in the park more faithful to Disney traditions, Steve needed to find ways to attract more French visitors and persuade the government to allow seasonal employment.

Steve also faced the task of devising and implementing strategic changes that would ensure that the park could grow and stay healthy. The first significant change was renaming the park. Without a name change, Steve felt that nobody would really give the park a "fresh start." The very name "EuroDisney" had become identified with the prevailing view of the theme park as an invasive force whose only mission was to make a lot of money for the Walt Disney Company. Further, "Euro" sounded more like a chemical prefix than an attractive tourist destination. The name Disneyland, in contrast, implied someplace magical. In addition, Steve felt that while many Europeans outside of France might harbor a dislike of the country and its people, everyone loved Paris. "With Disneyland you get a magical place; with Paris you say where it is, and everybody loves Paris. And by including 'Paris' in the name, the French will be more receptive to the park. Also, by definition, we can tie the park to the city in our marketing and advertising campaigns. We don't have to have a big press release. We'll just change the name, make our logo bigger and bolder, use different colors. We'll change the merchandise over slowly; this doesn't all have to be overnight. But I think the end results will be very positive for us." And with that, the name was localized to Disneyland Paris.

After changing the park's name, Steve continued to struggle with a central challenge: How to put the park in the black financially, while at the same time maintaining what needed to be universally the same at all Disney parks and adapting those noncore elements that needed to be localized. In the end, Steve made a number of key changes, some that reinforced the traditional Disney image and approach, others that changed things many back at headquarters thought were too sacred even to touch:

Keeping Disney Disney
- Improved hiring to focus on outgoing, friendly Disney cast members.
- Increased training to emphasize and teach friendly service and Disney-level cleanliness.
- Introduced seasonal pricing for entry to the park.
- Used traditional Disney characters throughout the park.

Adapting Disney to France
- Removed traditional ban on alcohol in the theme parks.
- Lowered customary Disney premium prices by 20–30 percent on admission, merchandise, and food.
- Relaxed Disney's normal hierarchical managerial style and encouraged more individual initiative.
- Cut managerial staff by almost 1000.
- Changed the name to Disneyland Paris.

These and other changes helped make a positive impact on the park's financial results. Attendance figures rose approximately 17 percent in one year. Hotel occupancy rates went up. Visitors were spending more in the park. For the third quarter of the 1995 fiscal year, the park posted its first profits ever. Space Mountain was introduced as the park's fortieth attraction; billed as the fastest thrill ride in any Disney theme park anywhere in the world, it was a big hit. By 1997, the press were saying mostly positive things about the park, quite a shift from when the park first opened.

Throughout the entire experience at EuroDisney, Steve kept perspective—not only managing well in the face of great uncertainty, but balancing constant tensions between headquarters in Burbank and executives in Paris. Steve balanced tensions between Disney management and local employees. He balanced financial tensions between banks, creditors, the parent company, and EuroDisney's own interests. He balanced tensions between employee practices that had been standard worldwide and those that were most appropriate for continental Europe. He balanced tensions between Disney's traditional idea of clean, safe fun in theme parks without alcoholic beverages against the French need for a theme park that could serve wine and still provide the renowned Disney environment. He balanced the tensions between Disney's typical global approach to its brand name as a premium price product with the need to reduce prices to attract local customers. He balanced the park's precarious cash position with the need to build more rides—such as Space Mountain, which cost $120 million—to continue attracting visitors.

Steve grappled with these tensions (as well as numerous others we haven't mentioned) for several years, always maintaining the required perspective to manage them well. Eventually he returned to a new position in the United States. With Disney's acquisition of ABC/Capital Cities, a whole new world opened up in the company, and Steve became president of broadcasting at ABC, ready to face yet another turnaround situation.

Conclusions

Whether they are aware of it or not, superb global leaders like Steve Burke have the perspective and experience to see what the designers of the F-16 fighter plane knew years ago: *high performance requires the creation and support of dynamic tension, not its elimination.* While the F-16 is one of the world's most agile fighter jets, it is an inherently unstable plane. To maximize maneuverability in sharp turns, the plane is designed to create opposing yaw and pitch forces. Without proper management of these aerodynamic forces, the plane would crash and burn. To handle the incredibly complex set of tensions, an onboard computer makes nearly a hundred complex calculations and adjustments per second. It is the continued existence of these contradictory forces *and* their effective management that contributes directly to the F-16 fighter jet's stellar maneuvering capabilities. Attempting to eliminate tensions would destroy exactly what makes the F-16 so effecive.

Like those who design and fly the world's most sophisticated fighter planes, effective global leaders know that the dynamic tensions they encounter in international markets must be carefully managed. They live the advice of fighter pilot Chuck Yeager: "If you want to grow old as a pilot, you've got to know when to push and when to back off." Global leaders know when to push and when to back off. They recognize that tensions are absolutely necessary for high performance and that their focus on constant management and real-time adjustment are the keys to outmaneuvering the competition in global market dogfights. They embrace dualities by looking at a situation, suspending prior beliefs about it, creating a fresh perspective on the issue at hand, and—most important—acting on their insights. They embrace the duality of situations to arive at better definitions of problems *and* opportunities; then they make choices based on these insights and act in spite of significant uncertainties. Gaining the perspective to master dualities is fundamental to *your* development as a global leader.

Notes

1. K. Omae, *The Borderless World.* 1990. New York: HarperBusiness.
2. *Wall Street Journal,* June 3, 1997, p. B4. "Conoco's Dunham Makes Bold Moves to Hit Goal."
3. D. Jefferson, "American Quits Chairman Post at Euro Disney." *Wall Street Journal,* January 18, 1993, p. B1.

five

CHARACTER

A leader's personal character forges a critical dimension of global leadership. As an effective global leader, you must get close to people and gain their trust and goodwill. By doing so, you gain critical insights into your company, competitors, and customers. Your strong personal character sets an example within the company and creates a working environment that supports your implementation plans.

Driven primarily by the dispersion dynamic, character is critically important in engendering the goodwill and trust of people. Such credit can only exist when it is given freely; it cannot be exacted from employees by their superiors. The daunting challenge for global leaders is to earn the goodwill and trust of employees whose values and expectations can vary widely. Personal character is essential in carrying this out.

From our research, we found that global explorers demonstrate personal character in two ways. The first is the ability to connect emotionally with people from various backgrounds. Emotional connection is essentially a two-way process, involving you as a leader and others—from subordinates, to peers, to business partners, and everyone in between. The second component of personal character is integrity. Integrity means holding firm to high ethical standards and consistently supporting your company's interests.

Emotional Connection

A global leader must connect emotionally with people inside the company as well as in the broader community. Connecting emotionally means establishing personal, empathetic relationships. These relationships are essential for you to learn about markets and customers, understand local conditions within the company, and mentor future leaders. Emotional connections constitute a critical lubricant in the often unwieldy decision-making process of global organizations. Because globalization is built on the principle of integration, a leader who connects with people is particularly valuable. The greater the need to integrate people and activities around the world, the more important it is for global leaders to connect emotionally with people.

You need three distinct abilities in order to connect emotionally with people: (1) sincere interest in and concern for others; (2) a heightened ability to listen to people; and (3) a strong capacity to clearly understand different viewpoints. Global leaders possess all three abilities and can use them effectively across cultures.

Showing Sincere Interest

If you are not genuinely interested in personal relationships, you simply will not be able to do business in many countries. In our research and work around the world, we found that trusting relationships are the foundation of business in many countries. Showing a sincere interest in people is the first step in building these relationships.

As we spoke with Ravi Agarwal, general manager of the Components Group at Intel Japan, he explained the real challenge for Intel in Japan: "We need very close relationships with our customers here in Japan. It needs to be almost like a family." It is not enough for suppliers to be merely reliable; they must look after their customers' interests. "They need to feel that their problem is your problem," Agarwal continued. "How does an

American company supply global Japanese consumer electronics and computer companies?" he asked. "It all comes down to relationships."

Many others shared the same view, including David Janke, vice president of business development at Evans & Sutherland: "International customers are not buying equipment, they are buying a relationship with the company they're going to have to trust." According to Janke, the product often takes a back seat to the relationship with the company's people. In Janke's words,

> We're not selling equipment: we're selling somebody's career because she's got her neck on the line, buying something, making a large investment. If it doesn't work, everybody points the finger at her, so she wants to deal with a company and people—and a company *is* people—to do the work that she trusts. As a result, we spend a lot of time just cultivating those relationships.

Obstacles to Overcome. Despite the importance of relationships, U.S. managers in particular have a difficult time appreciating them. Because relationships take time and provide benefits that are difficult to quantify, managers who are fixated on short-term results see little value in establishing lasting relationships. "As Americans we are not very good at relationships," chided Richard Bahner, a seasoned international human resource management executive. "In the U.S., it's basically 'Let's do business and then we'll develop the relationship.' The rest of the world is juxtaposed to that." Bahner complained that too many Americans place little value on developing a relationship "with the faith that business will come."

Our research found that effective global leaders actually like people. They successfully form business relationships because they enjoy talking with people and spending time with them. They seek out rich personal relationships. They care about people and want in some way to make their lives better. Their interest is sincere; it is not an act, and it goes much deeper than Rolodex management.

Some have argued against expatriate managers establishing close relationships with local people, out of a belief that relationships actually hinder a global leader's ability to exert control and a fear that the manager will "go native." In many companies, a gulf—a sort of "us" versus "them" dichotomy—separates head office expatriate managers from overseas employees. Rather than close the gulf, some head office managers seek to exploit the gap as a legitimate barrier separating the corporate "aristocracy" from the "masses." According to this line of reasoning, developing relationships with locals breaks the command and control system through which power is maintained. The conclusion of this logic: emotional connections diminish the leader's power and should be avoided.

Such a narrow-minded perspective, although not uncommon, can be disastrous. A Japanese deputy general manager of a multinational U.S. chemical company we interviewed was dealing with this very problem. The subsidiary's general manager was an American from the international division. The deputy general manager was frustrated because his superior seemed interested only in maintaining the corporate perspective and discouraged any subsidiary initiatives. "There seems to be little room to maneuver because of the American general manager," he lamented. "He speaks little Japanese and puts out very little effort to learn. He just seems eager to finish his assignment as soon as possible and go home." The Japanese manager had been with the company for twenty years and had witnessed this pattern of remoteness in every general manager he had worked under. "They don't understand us," he said with a shake of his head. "They act like they don't want to be here."

This difficulty in communication and lack of mutual respect is not an uncommon problem for expatriate head office managers and it can be tremendously destructive. Without close personal relationships with expatriate managers, good local people lose commitment or leave the organization entirely. Even with the best products, global companies cannot succeed overseas without strong local support. Establishing sincere relationships is essential in developing local leaders and in getting the most out of the global organization. To the degree that local leaders can empathize with global leaders as people, they are more likely to want and be able to emulate global leader behaviors. Black & Decker's Robyn Mingle reported that her company's leaders are expected to develop the people they work with and "make them as passionate about our business as we are." Further, the ability to connect empathetically with people is an important factor for senior advancement:

> At senior management levels including country managers and presidents, empathy is a major indicator of success. Leaving

"dead bodies behind," or not showing regard to the human aspect of doing business, can be devastating for a business on both a short- and long-term basis. Empathy is one of those things we seek to develop in our leaders.

Demonstrating an Interest. Demonstrating a sincere interest takes effort. It requires that you spend quality time with people and have frequent interactions. Many of your interactions must have high social and low business content. George Cohen, president of McDonald's Canada, estimated that he made over 100 trips to Russia before opening McDonald's first fast-food restaurant in Moscow in 1990. Although a great deal of business was done, particularly during latter trips, time after time he returned to Russia solely to build relationships. His commitment to establishing sincere relationships was at the core of the venture's success.

In many cases, locals *want* business deals to take time. They want the time to build the relationship and may even be somewhat cynical of foreigners' efforts to play the relationship game. A Saudi Arabia–based country manager for a Canadian health care company explained that as he tried to develop a relationship with a senior government decision maker, he suspected that the official "thought I was just going through the motions and the relationship didn't really mean anything to me." The Canadian manager brought gifts for the official's children, called on him regularly, took him out to dinner, and returned every few months to follow up, but "it still took years until he trusted me."

When a leader sets out to establish emotional connections, pride and position must typically be subordinated. Some executives are simply too proud to go through the relationship-building process, particularly when it comes to interactions with low-ranking employees in the company. Not Sony's president, Nobuyuki Idei. He is known in the company as "salary-man shacho," or the president who has risen from the bottom. Idei maintains close ties to rank-and-file employees in part by inviting groups to his home for late-night feasting. Idei's approach is unusual for a global chieftain, many of whom are known for their aloofness.[1]

Others demonstrate an interest simply by treating people with respect. Successful global leaders think of things like flying the flag of a foreign customer's home country during a business trip or arranging for special meals or site visits. Simple things like avoiding the use of jargon and speaking slowly also show respect. One of the American companies we worked with was hosting a delegation from an Israeli client. Even though all of the visitors spoke good English, the company's director of business development arranged for presentations to be done in Hebrew. The visitors were impressed that so much effort was made to make them feel at ease. It was a simple gesture that generated valuable goodwill.

Learning, or attempting to learn, a foreign language is a highly effective way to demonstrate interest in other people. People appreciate the gesture because they know that learning a foreign language is difficult and represents the leader's personal commitment to the country and customer. One senior international human resource executive at Merck believed that language was the *most* critical determinant of demonstrating a sincere interest:

> At some point you have to have some visible signs that you respect the people, the culture, the history, that you are going into. And it could be anything from sincere, honest, ongoing efforts to learn and speak their language, to understanding their cultures, their customers, and their foods. What I've found is even if you stumble through the language, the fact that you're making some real, honest, sincere efforts, that in and of itself really broke down some barriers. Initially, you may be met with a lot of laughter, but taking the time to learn the language is important to connecting with the people.

Genuinely Listening to People

Being interested in people is not the same as genuinely listening to people. For others to feel understood, you must not only have a genuine interest but also excel at picking up verbal and nonverbal communication. It is an active rather than passive process.

In an international setting especially, it can be exceedingly difficult to listen effectively. We found several barriers to effective listening: (1) managers falsely assume that everyone already thinks the way they do; (2) managers mistakenly believe that everyone *should* think the way they do; and (3) managers let language and cultural differences impede communication.

The "Everyone Thinks the Same" Assumption. Naive international managers often make the mistake of believing that everyone within the company thinks the same. In most cases, this could not be further from the truth. Cultural differences, background, position in the hierarchy, training, proximity to the market and perceived self-interest are all reasons why people view things differently. Unfortunately, many managers leave their common sense at home when they travel overseas. When we asked a British executive of a U.S. multinational about her perception of executives from headquarters, she related the following:

> I too often watch our senior managers come to England from the head office in the U.S. They make a big speech to a group in London and assume the audience has the same background, beliefs, and sense of humor as he or she does. They try to ingratiate themselves, and yet they end up alienating themselves even further.

Believing that people think the same way around the world is a problem rooted in low inquisitiveness and is a key barrier to emotionally connecting with people. It suggests a superficial understanding of the aspirations, interests, and feelings of people. It is a problem not limited to American managers. One noteworthy example occurred when Stephen Covey's book *Seven Habits of Highly Effective People* was first published in Japan. It sold less than 5,000 copies. Given that it was a number-one best seller in the United States, many observers were surprised. In their analysis of the problem, Covey's associates focused on the Japanese translation of the book. A virtually direct translation of the book into Japanese had been made, out of the belief that what worked in the United States would work just as well in Japan. A new, more culturally aware translation was then commissioned. Instead of a literal translation from English, the book was reworked to convey meaning in a style that fit Japanese ways of thinking. This new version sold over 500,000 copies and, for a period of time, was the number-one best-selling book in Japan.

The "Everyone *Should* Think the Same Way" Mistake. An even more difficult problem arises when managers believe that everyone—both inside and outside the company—*should* think the same way. Americans in particular have been accused of this sort of cultural arrogance in international business. Around the world, many believe that Americans think they have all the answers and know how to solve every problem. They are offended when Americans try to impose their management systems and values on others. This view was expressed by a vice president at Cargill, one of the largest private companies in the world. This vice president commented on what he had observed in the course of making a number of trips to Brazil to negotiate two separate joint ventures:

> The Brazilians are generally a very friendly people. They ask how my children are doing. They want to see pictures. They want you to meet their families. If you don't genuinely like these people, it will come through. Sometimes they feel that Americans believe that the U.S. is the only place where things are done right. Many think we are culturally arrogant. Too many Americans come to Brazil hoping to change the way Brazilians do business. If we want to be successful in Brazil, I've learned we need to do business the way the Brazilians do business.

While this example involves American ethnocentrism, we heard many similar examples involving managers from other countries. In one increasingly costly example, Sitix, a silicon wafer–manufacturing division of Japanese-based Sumitomo, constructed a $400 million plant in north Phoenix, Arizona. The plant, which came on line in mid-1997, was built only three quarters of a mile from an upscale residential neighborhood. In Japan, Sitix has plants that are located across the street from residential housing. Japanese managers felt that because locals in Japan never complained about the plants there, Americans *shouldn't* either. To their shock, lawsuits and regular picketing by local residents disrupted the Phoenix plant's construction. What the Japanese has failed to understand was the degree to which local residents valued the pristine, high-desert environment of north Phoenix. Local residents moved to the area *to get away* from the pollution and factories that Sitix represented. The inability of the Japanese to understand deep-seated local concerns has led to accusations of cultural and corporate arrogance. Not only did the conflict disrupt the plant's start-up schedule, it also resulted in an embarrassing loss of face for the company and its Japanese managers.

Within companies, another type of arrogance is often observed: the assumption that the head office knows best and need never change its beliefs. A senior human resource executive at a large U.S. consumer products company shared with us an incident that occurred at a meeting in Amsterdam involving managers from the company's Northern European offices and American headquarters. A manager from the company's Amsterdam office asked the American vice president of human resources some tough, critical questions during a presentation. In the Netherlands, managers are expected to be "very forceful in making objections and so forth," he explained. "And this guy from Amsterdam took a very much 'in your face' type of approach. But it was done with respect." While the man from Amsterdam was asserting himself, an American sitting next to the executive we interviewed leaned over and whispered, "I hope that guy has a big bank account." The message was clear to the executive we interviewed: "The guy from Amsterdam was not doing it the American way, which is to bow humbly and say, 'He's our leader so I won't ask these types of questions in a public forum—probably not even in a private forum.'" In this example, the American did not think overseas managers should have a significant role in decision making. Given this, there was no point in listening to what they had to say. In fact, global leaders know that it is the very rare idea or product that is perfect enough to sweep the world without undergoing some adaptation for foreign markets. Global leaders understand that good ideas can come from every corner of the world.

Genuine Cultural Barriers. Despite the best intentions, cultural and language barriers can severely restrict your ability to listen effectively. It takes great effort and patience to understand the heart and soul of people. Working out the cultural nuances of communication can be a painstaking process. In Japan, for example, the word *kekko* can mean both "yes" and "no." Determining when "yes" means "yes" and "no" means "no" requires a deep understanding of context and nonverbal communication. Lack of this understanding can be a huge problem in such activities as negotiating contracts, working with government regulators, and establishing employee work expectations.

Overcoming genuine cultural barriers is a real issue for anyone working in a foreign environment. We found an interesting example of cultural miscommunication in a recent newspaper article entitled "Most Misunderstood Passenger":

As the plane left the runway, the German tourist bolted from his seat, shoving aside a flight attendant who tried to stop him. He had to go to the bathroom, he later told a judge.

But on that January flight from Fort Lauderdale to Hanover, Germany, something got lost in the translation.

"The roof is going to go!" was what the flight attendant said she heard him say, as he made a sweeping gesture with his arms as if to indicate a gigantic explosion.

The plane was brought back to Fort Lauderdale, and the passenger was arrested on federal charges of interfering with a flight crew and making a bomb threat.

The tourist spent nine months in jail, until a German-speaking judge released him. Apparently, the German expression "then the roof flies" is slang for having to use the bathroom.[2]

Similar cases of cultural misunderstanding can have a severe adverse effect on your company's business interests. So great are the consequences of cultural miscommunication that an increasing number of companies are specifying official company languages. Nestlé, Nokia, and ABB, for example, all use English as their official language. Managers in these companies, whether English is their first, second, or third language, must all communicate in the same language with each other when they cross borders. While this obligation imposes a heavy burden on some, the standardization of business language is increasingly seen as essential in many global organizations.

In the absence of cultural sensitivity, mistakes frequently occur. One example arose in our interviews with a seasoned American manager based in Singapore. This manager, who had over ten years experience in Asia, described an insensitive American superior, who was placed in charge of the entire Asian region, as "an American cowboy, acting just like a bull in a china shop when he'd go into a meeting with Asians." Because he had never lived in Asia, the American superior had no understanding of the subtle cultural nuances that exist there. "He was just kind of a Wild West American, six-gun on the side, and away he went. He offended quite a few, and in the end he was terminated."

Understanding Different Viewpoints

Emotionally connecting with people requires more than sincere interest and skillful listening. It requires that you be able to understand many different sorts of people. To understand people, you need to be familiar with local conditions. Local conditions establish the context from which people develop and express their viewpoints. To understand different viewpoints, global leaders must relate personally to the lives of employees, customers, and others who are relevant to the business. Robert Bennett, U.S. Senator from Utah and former president of California-based Microsonics, explains the benefits of understanding different viewpoints:

> Global leaders need lots of empathy. They need to love the people they work with. Without empathy, they lose loyalty. And without loyalty, they lose the ability to work together. If you cannot empathize with people, you become like the manager who is good with a hammer who sees every problem as a nail. Empathy enables managers to see problems differently and, together with others, determine appropriate solutions.

You must understand context to determine how to interact with people in general and, more specifically, how to provide appropriate leadership. For example, how a 40-year-old American expatriate manager delegates to a 35-year-old Japanese subordinate with a U.S. MBA needs to differ significantly from the way in which she delegates to a 55-year-old Japanese subordinate with no U.S. experience. To delegate successfully, the American manager should pay much greater deference to the 55-year-old Japanese subordinate. Global leadership requires the uncommon ability to understand the myriad of subtle, cultural nuances that govern a wide range of beliefs and behaviors within each country's context.

We worked closely with a U.S.-based petroleum exploration company that had set up offices in southern China. To entice American managers to leave their comfortable homes in the U.S., the company moved its expatriates into a gated housing compound not far from its Chinese headquarters. Expatriates were given subsidized housing comparable to U.S. standards—3,000 to 4,000 square feet in size, Western-style washing machines, dishwashers, etc.—plus a car and driver. Many expatriates expected these "perks" to soften the challenges of what they perceived as a hardship posting. Many local Chinese had a much different response. They had a clear view of the American compound from the top floors of the subsidiary's offices. The Chinese lived in much smaller and far less appealing apartments. As was the norm for China, the U.S. company did not provide the Chinese with washing machines, dishwashers, or cars and drivers. Even though the Americans listened to the concerns of the Chinese managers, they could not fully relate to their local counterparts' experience. In an attempt to improve relations, American managers sometimes invited the Chinese to their homes for social functions. Embarrassed by their poor living conditions, the Chinese felt they could not reciprocate, leaving them in an awkward position and even more aware of the inequities that existed. This situation provides a classic example of listening without really understanding.

Not surprisingly, neither side fully understood the other. Many of the Chinese employees felt that although the Americans lived in China, their hearts were still back home in the United States. In contrast, many expatriate Americans blamed the Chinese for being lazy, unappreciative, and difficult to train. What the Americans failed to appreciate was the concern of the Chinese employees that no matter how well they performed, they could never receive the benefits Americans had come to expect. They simply lacked a comparable incentive for self-improvement. The Americans listened, but were too absorbed in their own difficulties to fully understand; similarly, the Chinese listened but also failed to fully understand the business performance stresses the Americans were under. The result was friction in the relationship that compromised the ability of the Americans to lead as effectively as they wanted in the Chinese venture.

Understanding differing viewpoints is a proactive process. Global leaders go out of their way to connect with individuals in far-flung locations. They shake hands, eat with employees, and pay attention with all of their senses. They visit customers in their offices and homes. The don't try to "get through" to people, but rather work hard at "being with" people—all kinds of people.

How far should you go in working to understand different viewpoints? Is it possible to go so far that you lose your own distinctiveness? Steve Holliday at British-Borneo offers some interesting insights into how global leaders approach very real cultural gaps:

Over the years, I have worked with some great global leaders. What I see in these leaders is the ability to become like the people they are with. Teenagers are good at this. They can pick out the subtleties of fitting in. They can move from group to group and know what shoes to wear, what brand of jeans to wear, and so on. In some ways global leaders have the same basic skills that teenagers display. Instead of clothes, they seem to be very good at picking out a couple of key things that let them fit in. Global leaders are experts at figuring out the few things they need to say or do that will enable them to communicate effectively with people from different cultures. These tricks help them establish close personal relationships with people.

Emotional Connections Improve Decision Making

By emotionally connecting with people, you can significantly improve the quality of your decision making. Global leaders, except in very limited cases, cannot in isolation fully understand current and evolving customer needs, competitors, and local conditions. You must have at your disposal the eyes, ears, and goodwill of your corporation. Connecting with people—both inside the company and out—provides quality data that can differentiate your company in the global marketplace.

This point was underscored by an international marketing executive in a Fortune 500 company. "I just love being around people and talking to people," he began. He told us that he typically spends about 80 percent of his time out in the field with the sales force versus 20 percent of his time with the departments in his home country. He continued:

> This approach gives me a clearer understanding of the sales force's needs. Then when I spend that 20 percent of my time with staff, I can actually talk to them based on a real understanding of the field, rather than trying to learn details through e-mails across the water. Global leaders must know the people who make their business work. They are more important to you than anything else, because if you don't connect with them, you should just write off the deal.

Emotionally connecting with people improves the quality of your decisions in two ways. First, when you have close relationships with people in the field, you are far more likely to be fully accepted by them when you are overseas. Employees and customers open up more readily when they feel at ease with a visiting executive. They are much more prone to make honest and forthright comments when they feel understood by an outsider. Second, when you have close relationships with people in the field, you will receive more unsolicited intelligence data from them. Subordinates open up when they feel they are being listened to and understood, when they know that what they say matters. Intelligence from the field is frequently more useful than financial performance in measuring your unit's success and in directing future changes. Greg Geiger, director of finance for international automotive operations at Ford, shares this view:

> Financial tools are useful only at diagnosing things. They are not helpful at all in solving things because things are solved with people. People, in order to be effective, . . . have to understand what needs to be accomplished, and finance can be a part of that in terms of planning goals, but it cannot be the only thing.

Connecting with People Promotes Trust and Goodwill

Trust is a critical issue in global organizations. To work effectively in a global context, you must develop and be able to rely on relationships of trust. In today's complex and far-reaching organizations, solutions to problems and customers' needs come more from cooperation than from command-and-control processes. Effective global leaders need webs of influence rather than "solid line" authority and reporting relationships. To be successful, you need to establish mutual trust with a host of other people. Double-checking, monitoring, and spending hours persuading others is costly in both time and money. And spending too much time or money can be the difference between winning and losing in the global market place. For all its "soft" connotations, trust leads to very real, powerful, and hard economic payoffs. Emotionally connecting with people through sincere interest, listening, and understanding is key to establishing trust and capturing economic benefits.

Emotionally connecting with people also promotes goodwill. Goodwill goes a long way in facilitating strategy implementation. It encourages your employees to give you the benefit of the doubt on difficult matters. It also helps secure your employees' best efforts. In many cases employees will make huge sacrifices to help you out when goodwill is present. We saw examples of this throughout the world.

While in Japan, we were told an interesting story that illustrates the benefits of emotional connections. Shinichi Suzuki, the father of the Talent Education Movement that has swept the music world, was drafted by the Japanese military during World War II and assigned to manage a plant that prepared cypress wood for airplane manufacture. He knew nothing about managing a manufacturing plant nor about assembling airplanes. But he understood people and decided early on to treat the workers at his plant as if they were members of his own family. He started every workday at the plant by playing the violin to the assembled workers. After playing, Suzuki would often provide some gentle advice: be kind to your spouse, teach your children, save money. He concluded early on that the employees knew far more than he ever would about cypress or airplanes and that his role was to help them "want" to do their jobs better.

Suzuki seemed genuinely interested in the needs of his employees. Most were terribly poor and many of their homes were in disrepair. He authorized the use of excess cypress from the plant's operations to keep all the workers' homes in decent condition. Full-time carpenters were sent out from the plant to work on employees' homes. Suzuki also knew that most of his employees had no financial reserves and worried greatly about their security. He promised the workers that if they devoted themselves to raising the plant's output, he would share the dividends with them. When the plant's output did go up, he gave each worker 500 yen, an amount at the time that would give them security in the event of an emergency. The plant's efficiency rose even higher. Newspapers took notice, printing articles about the air force plant managed by a musician.

Suzuki's secret was simple: he cared about his employees and built warm personal relations with them. Concerning this he said, "During our short lifetime, being devoted to the same task with everyone helping each other creates a deep refreshing feeling, and both the employee and the employer care about each other."[3] After the war, these same principles of caring and empathy became the heart of Suzuki's world-famous music education methods.

Establishing goodwill in relationships outside the company also has many tangible benefits. Goodwill facilitates sensitive negotiations and reduces the need for costly oversight. In the spring of 1997, Volkswagen relied on the goodwill of its executives at its Czech subsidiary, Skoda, to win approval to assemble cars from kits in Russia. In a similar case, managers at the Swire Group in Hong Kong used their goodwill relationships in the People's Republic of China to establish numerous joint ventures in that country. Global leaders at virtually every company use goodwill to promote their companies' self-interests. What separates effective global leaders from the rest of the pack is their creativity and strategic foresight in doing so. The manager of materials purchasing and transportation for the U.S. petroleum company we worked with in China shared some interesting insights into establishing and leveraging connections in China:

> Relationships are everything. China has laws to stop you from doing anything it wants to stop. You need the relationships to help you figure out how to get things done. Initially, we hit the shore ready to work, as opposed to ready to get the relationship going. This means that you end up first contacting the government when you have a problem. This starts things off on a bad note. . . . Another problem is that when most experts have something go wrong they send Chinese nationals to solve it. So the government people never see or interact with you. So take the time to go down there and say, "We are going to be starting an operation here and we are not anticipating any problems, but our operations are so big that I know that they are going to come; and what I am here to do is to introduce myself to you and say first of all that if anyone working for us does anything wrong, here is my card for me to help you work that out." The relationship here is always something you have to work on. The primary objective should be to meet the government agencies, the police department, the customs, the social security bureau, and so on. . . . For example, I probably go out to dinner or have drinks with the local head of Chinese customs once every two weeks. We have a relationship where we can say, "Hey, what are you doing tonight?"

Goodwill can go a long way in determining the stability of joint ventures, in promoting dialogue with customers and governments, and in facilitating strategy implementation. In the example above, goodwill came only after personal relationships were established with the appropriate local officials. It would be naive to suggest that the local Chinese initiated these relationships; it would also be naive to suggest that they came naturally and easily to the American manager. He had to work at them. But over time, friendships emerged. There was a bonding of sorts. Emotional connections were made. And these connections have served the manager and the American subsidiary well by producing goodwill.

Emotional Connections and Business:
Some Concluding Comments

Establishing emotional connections is essential for you to maximize your effectiveness as a global leader. However, developing emotional bonds with people is not the same as "going native." Leaders who are interested in people, who are excellent listeners, and who are familiar with local conditions do not have to become like the people they are with. While you need to change the parts of yourself that interfere with communication and are obstacles to empathy, you cannot lose sight of your position as a leader. Rather than passively accept local input, consider it carefully and weigh it against the greater needs of the global corporation. While you should keep an open mind, never forget who you are or what you represent.

Exemplar Global Leader:
Jon Huntsman, Jr.

Jon Huntsman, Jr., vice chairman of Huntsman Corporation, provides an excellent example of a global leader who connects emotionally with employees. A graduate of the University of Pennsylvania, Jon helps run the company his father, Jon Huntsman, Sr., started in 1970. As of 1997, Huntsman Corporation was the largest privately held chemical manufacturing company in the United States, with annual sales of $4.5 billion and 7,000 employees in 21 countries. Before assuming his responsibilities at Huntsman Corporation, the 38-year-old Jon Huntsman, Jr. had served as U.S. ambassador to Singapore. At the time of his confirmation, he was the youngest U.S. ambassador this century. He also served as U.S. Deputy Assistant Secretary of Commerce.

Jon Huntsman, Jr. became interested in international affairs while his father worked as an assistant to Richard Nixon. When 11 years old, the younger Huntsman happened to be in the White House visiting his father who worked as a special advisor to Richard Nixon. While at the White House, Jon Jr. met Henry Kissinger as he was on his way to a secret meeting in China. When he asked Kissinger where he was going, the statesman replied, "China." Before that moment, China had seemed little more than a word to the young Jon, not a real place with real people. Yet here was someone Jon knew who was actually going there. This experience had such a profound effect that the young boy began to study Asian history and Asian languages. Jon Huntsman, Jr. has spent a total of 15 years studying Mandarin and now speaks it fluently. His commitment to international study and business relations has not gone unnoticed: he was recently named by the World Economic Forum in Switzerland as a Global Leader of Tomorrow.

As vice chairman, Jon Huntsman, Jr. is responsible for much of the company's strategy. Despite his high-level responsibilities and personal financial resources that have the potential to separate him from rank-and-file employees, Jon has worked especially hard to stay connected to them. Jon is unusually humble and is always quick to point out that Huntsman Corporation was essentially built on acquisitions that resulted from the failures of such giants as Shell, Texaco, Monsanto, Eastman, and Hoechst Celanese. Jon is conscious of the most common reason for these failures of which his company has taken advantage. Most occurred because the companies involved could not get the full commitment of their people.

To get a better sense of the human side of Huntsman Corporation, consider Jon's description of how he handles the month of December. Every December, Jon and a team of senior executives visit every one of the company's facilities just to meet with employees.

> We are gone every single day in December before Christmas. We visit every Huntsman factory, every facility around the world. We shake everyone's hand. We talk to every child and spouse and learn about what they are doing in life. Where are you going to school? What do you like doing? Is your family happy? What can we do for you?

We also give them each a Christmas gift. Maybe it's a television, or a stereo, or a cruise. We want them to know how much we appreciate them. We want to make our employees feel they are the most important people in the universe. We honestly believe this.

Making these visits is never easy. We are gone the entire month. My wife always says that I am sick half the month of January just recovering from the pace. I suppose she is right. But I love the visits. We all derive incredible energy from them. We love the people. There is a burst of energy you get being in a room full of people.

We have grown so fast and have become so big I worry that if we grow any larger we simply won't be able to visit every employee. This is a real concern. The relationships with people are critical.

Jon's ability to connect emotionally with employees creates immense benefits for the company. One of the most important is that it brings senior managers face to face with the realities of their own organization and business. The visits, according to Jon, "help me immensely because when I get out there in the factories, talking to the people who make it happen, I get a much better understanding of the bigger picture, of what we are all about as a company."

Not only do senior managers get a much better sense of local conditions, but their visits engender a level of employee commitment to the company and senior management that is second-to-none in the industry. This in turn creates a much more open atmosphere where insights and ideas can percolate up from the factory floor.

Making these visits is also important because it lets us connect with our people on a personal basis. We honestly believe that the best ideas we come up with have to come from the factory floor. We tell them we want to hear from them. I give them my card and tell them they should feel free to call me. Some of them do. When they have met me, shaken my hand, and talked to me, they feel they know me. I want them to be comfortable enough to call me when they see a problem or when they have an idea that will help the business. I challenge them. I say, "Here is my number. If you have a good idea, a way to work more efficiently, call me." And they do.

Jon's commitment to his employees is a year-round endeavor, an essential part of the company culture.

And this is not just a Christmas thing. When we are in Texas, we will go out and buy everybody a big thing of gumbo and sit down and eat with the blue-collar folks. And so they know we really mean it. . . . We want our employees to feel like we're in this together, that they matter, that there is a sense of empowerment there.

At Huntsman Corporation, emotional connections extend beyond the company. Jon Huntsman, Jr. is also passionate about his relationships with his customers.

Just as we try to show our employees that we care for them, the same thing is true for our customers. No one is more important in our world than customers. For us, customers, whether large or small, are the most important people in our universe, and we make them feel that way. We want to maintain that mentality, even if we're making lots of money. It means making our customers feel that if we can't service them, if we can't give them the best price, if we falter there, then we basically failed in an area we consider to be the most important for the family. We take it very personally when we hear that a competitor is giving a better price or service. Because of our relationship with our customers, they sit down and tell us when there is a problem. . . . There has to be a personal connection. It takes time and it takes personal interaction.

Clearly, there is more to Huntsman's success than relationships. The company has a very smart management team that has made some extremely well-timed acquisitions. They have achieved substantial synergies and are known industry-wide for running tight operations. Yet in an industry known for its brutal downturns, dedicated employees and loyal customers have made an enormous difference. Without the goodwill of employees and customers, Huntsman would be far less successful than it is today.

Integrity

Integrity forms the bedrock of excellent character and is essential in establishing genuine emotional connections with people. We define integrity as having and demonstrating a strong commitment to personal and company standards. This includes ethical behavior as well as loyalty to the company's agreed-upon values and strategy.

Both personal and company standards are substantially more prone to compromise overseas. When far removed from corporate oversight, most managers face increased pressure to modify their personal ethics and alter their unit's standards to appeal to local values and demands. In many cases, such "flexibility" can bring short-term gains. Yet despite the opportunities for short-term advantage, the global leaders we studied were most effective when they consistently maintained the highest ethical standards in personal and company matters.

Ethical Personal and Company Standards

Ethics is a tricky subject for most people. Ethics involves moral decisions about right and wrong. Although some kinds of behavior are black-and-white, judged similarly in all cultures, gray areas dominate the international landscape. While all managers inevitably confront ethical issues, global leaders face them regularly. Global leaders deal with ethical questions on two broad levels. The first involves those external activities by which your company is evaluated in the outside world. In these cases, you—as a representative of your company—can contribute positively or negatively to your company's ethical image. Second, ethical behavior includes internal activities involving your company's own units and employees. In these internal activities, your appearance of ethical or unethical behavior is limited to associates within your company. Without appropriate, ethical behavior inside *and* outside the company, neither you nor your company can lead over the long run.

External Relationships. Ethical behaviors in relationships outside the firm pose particularly difficult challenges in a global context. One thing to consider is the difference between dominant behaviors within the national culture (i.e., *descriptive* ethics) and the judgments of what behaviors *should* be, irrespective of culture (i.e., *normative* ethics). Clearly, you need to understand the ethical norms in the country and markets where your company operates; not surprisingly, these norms can differ significantly. For example, in one noteworthy case in 1996, Malaysia's trade minister, Rafidah Aziz, informed a conference that bribery and other forms of corruption were normal business practices in his country. While the minister's statement shocked some conference participants, it described fairly well the business conditions of his country. As with issues of corruption, standards concerning environmental degradation, employment rights and benefits, product and service quality, and so on, can vary enormously from country to country.

Problems occur when you encounter descriptive ethics that differ significantly from you normative ethics. When your ethical standards are different from the norms of behavior in a particular country, you and your company have three basic choices: (1) you can avoid doing business in that particular country; (2) you can maintain your standards and risk being placed at a competitive disadvantage versus firms that follow the prevailing norms; or (3) you can change your standards and play the game the way the locals do. Our experience suggests that this last option, maintaining a checkerboard approach to ethical standards, is not sustainable in global companies.

One incident reported to us by an international vice president at a large U.S.-based bank underscores the importance of establishing and adhering to strict global ethical standards. The bank, although relatively inexperienced in international business, had seen huge opportunities to expand its business portfolio in Southeast Asia. Within a short time, it had negotiated a position as lead lender in a major power plant being built in the region. Over time it provided more than $800 million in financing for the project. Delay followed delay, and after some years, the power plant was still not operational.

Rather than write down the loan, the U.S.-based vice president instructed the bank's country manager—an American—to become actively involved in moving the project along. The manager pressed the lead contractor, who explained that a huge stumbling block was the refusal of the district water commissioner to finish the final water hookups to the plant. The banker decided to meet with the water commissioner himself. Feeling unsure how to proceed in the upcoming meeting, the banker asked an American friend for advice. The friend advised his banker friend that all local government officials were corrupt and that "grease" money would open the right doors.

The banker took matters into his own hands and arranged a meeting with the water commissioner at the best restaurant in the city. In preparation for the dinner meeting, the banker purchased a fancy wallet and placed in it fifty crisp $100 bills. A limousine was sent for the water commissioner to take him to the restaurant, where he was met at the front door by the banker. The water commissioner was seated first. As the banker sat down, he popped out of his back pocket the previously prepared wallet. It hit the floor with a thud, and the banker then picked it up. He looked inside, and finding no identification, turned to the water commissioner and said, "This is not my wallet. It must be yours." He then slid the wallet across the table. The water commissioner looked inside, paused, and then slid it back saying, "This must not be my wallet either. Mine had $25,000 in it." The story would be incomplete without mentioning that, unbeknownst to the banker, the water commissioner had hired a photographer to record the entire episode for future use. (As a postscript, the banker was saved by good fortune. At the time there was considerable unrest in the country in question. Within a week of the incident in the restaurant, the government fell and the water commissioner was out of a job. But the banker had learned an important lesson on crossing ethical boundaries.)

Once ethical boundaries have been crossed, others will almost certainly exploit the breach. Global leaders and large multinational companies are high-profile targets and must develop global standards of conduct. When matters of ethical misconduct come to light—even in remote locations of the world—their impact inevitably surfaces in the company's home country as well. Questionable behavior in one country can rarely be contained. Eventually the entire world finds out. Global leaders understand that global companies have global reputations.

When moving into ethical backwaters, you will find that your government provides limited guidance. The 29 countries of the OECD agreed in 1996 to make it illegal for corporations to claim bribes as tax deductions.[4] The U.S. government tends to be stricter than most in regulating conduct. U.S. corporations are bound by the provisions of the Foreign Corrupt Practices Act (FCPA), which prohibits U.S. companies from bribing foreign government officials or officers of political parties. While the FCPA does not technically affect foreign subsidiaries, in practice it applies to the degree that policies or money can be traced back to the U.S. parent company. In November 1997, the OECD extended its regulation of corporate "gifts" by agreeing to a complete ban on bribery. The rules, while in many ways similar to those covered by the FCPA, were extended to cover executives at state-owned enterprises as well as members of parliament.

Despite the direction provided by some governments, most managers know that there are abundant gray areas not formally covered by the act. For example, where does one draw the line between a gift and a bribe? In countries like China and Saudi Arabia, where does the government end and the private sector begin? Further, how should activities of joint-venture partners be interpreted?

To get around the ambiguity and to minimize corporate exposure, an increasing number of global leaders are pushing to adopt strict, company-specific codes of conduct. Because the tremors of ethical misconduct are often felt around the world, stringent global policies on gifts and gratuities have become more common. In some cases, most notably Wal-Mart and General Motors, policies forbid all gifts beyond the most nominal of trinkets. While such policies may make sense in a domestic context, they can severely restrict global competitiveness and in some cases may go too far. In fact, U.S. companies are losing the business war in many parts of the world because of unnecessarily restrictive global gifts-and-gratuities policies. In international contexts, for example, a manager's inability to pay for a customer's dinner or a round of golf is viewed with disdain.[5]

Finding a balance between what is ethically unacceptable—bribery, for example—and what should be negotiable is a critical and challenging task for global leaders. As a global leader, you must continually raise questions about what is appropriate and what is not. Tough cases must be championed and aired in the open within your company. In-house education and training programs must be promoted to inform employees of nonnegotiable policies.

Giles Branston, general counsel for General Motors' Asia Pacific Organization (APO), is an example of someone who pushes these efforts. He has organized a multipronged approach for APO employees: all employees are informed of local laws governing corruption, and all receive clear guidelines on facilitating payments. Members of the APO Strategy Board also regularly attend a workshop on ethics sponsored by the general counsel's office. In addition, a special ethics committee has been organized to review difficult cases within the region. In contrast, Motorola takes a different approach. It has created 83 different case studies that it uses to sensitize and train managers in ethical conduct. The cases are presented at Motorola University management programs along with solutions provided by professional ethicists and former Motorola CEO Bob Galvin.

Despite the best training, though, most decisions are left to the people who are closest to the issues. Because people ultimately make their own choices between right and wrong, global leaders have no choice but to epitomize high ethical standards. The importance of these standards was articulated to us by Mikell Rigg McGuire, vice president, International, for Franklin Covey. "You must have in place your own fundamental values, both the company's and your personal ones; otherwise, you are probably going to let other countries' values overtake yours."

Internal Relationships. High ethical standards are also required for behavior *within* the company. Matters such as worker safety, fairness in hiring and promotions, and freedom of expression are all part of the environment you help create for employees. Figuring out what standards to embrace in personal conduct and what standards to hold employees to is a huge challenge.

National culture has an enormous impact on how local managers interact with their employees. One study, for example, showed that men in Hong Kong and Taiwan were more likely than men in Canada and Japan to discriminate against women. The same study found that Canadians were less likely to show concern for the employment security of their employees than were managers in Hong Kong and Taiwan.[6] A different study found no cultural differences in the ethical standards of British versus Chinese managers working in Hong Kong.[7] In yet another study, older managers in the United States, Japan, Korea, India, and Australia were shown to place more value on trust than did their younger counterparts.[8] Each one of these studies shows what global leaders have long known: *ethical norms governing relationships between managers and employees differ significantly from country to country.*

To avoid conflicts and the giving of offense, as a global leader you must be committed to high personal standards in all your internal interactions in the corporation. Your standards of personal conduct cannot vary from country to country. You cannot get away with establishing more tolerant standards for sexual harassment in Thailand than in Canada. All of your employees around the world must be treated with the same degree of respect.

It is the inconsistent treatment of people across countries international boundaries that causes managers to lose respect within their organization. In many companies we work with, a significant credibility gap exists between what top management says and what employees actually believe. Sometimes the problem is the result of out-and-out unethical behavior. However, more often than not, supposed ethical failures stem from communication problems which are exacerbated by cultural differences.

As you assume leadership responsibilities in a growing number of cultures, the potential for you to misunderstand or to be misunderstood increases exponentially. Your personal conduct in matters that involve employees is particularly open to scrutiny. Just as companies develop global reputations for ethical conduct, your reputation for how you treat other employees follows you throughout the world. Other people's perceptions of you can either enhance your ability to lead or essentially shut down your leadership capability.

Champion Your Company's Core Strategies around the World

At the same time as they adhere to a high standard of personal ethics, the most effective global leaders in our study firmly and unequivocally embrace their company's core strategies around the world. They understand that strategies built on such core elements as product quality, total customer service, and leading-edge technology should not be changed from country to country. They view their role as one of articulating what the company does and does not do, and acting as both a preacher and teacher in getting the message out.

The more you push into global markets, the greater the pressure to alter your core strategies. As you enter developing countries in particular, you may be tempted to improve short-term profits by cutting features or services. In setting up KFC's first restaurant in China in the late 1980s, Tony Wang quickly realized that Chinese customers generally did not place a high value on corporate standards for quality, service, and cleanliness. Whether the washrooms were cleaned every hour or every day had little impact on sales. Whether cooked chicken sat under a heat lamp for twenty minutes or two hours did not appear to concern Chinese customers. Yet Wang also understood that KFC's ability to attract new franchisees around the world depended on its ability to ensure globally consistent standards. If Wang lowered standards, profits in China would rise, enhancing his own image. Yet Wang refused to pursue this option. He unequivocally supported corporate policies. His commitment to the company not only gave him enormous credibility at corporate headquarters but also among subordinates. Because his employees in China knew he would not compromise the company's interests, their respect for and commitment to both Wang and KFC increased.

Even if you are not in a position to dismantle your company's core strategies, you may be tempted to criticize your company's strategies and your leaders. The farther you are from home, the greater the temptation to pander to local appetites for scandal or dissention. We witnessed on numerous occasions managers who fell victim to this temptation. At one meeting we attended in Brazil, a visiting vice president of a Fortune 50 company told local managers about a litany of problems she perceived with the corporation's CEO. She went on to criticize the company's strategy and suggest several of her own alternatives. Why did she do this? She no doubt believed there was merit to her comments. But clearly she also felt a need to be accepted by an unfamiliar group of people. She wanted to be looked up to, and critiquing the CEO and the company's strategy might well have seemed a way to demonstrate superior intelligence and insight. She also believed it highly unlikely that her words would ever make their way back to headquarters. In her mind, she had a license to sound off.

After the meeting we privately asked the participants what they thought. There was universal condemnation of the visiting executive. While the visiting executive thought local managers would be impressed with her insights, they viewed her instead as disloyal and arrogant. They had expected a leader who would give them direction and fire up their commitment. Instead, the meeting had been a major disappointment for them.

In reality, with few exceptions, leaders are also followers and must support company policies and management. Robert Kelley describes the fine line between leading and following:

> Many effective followers see leaders merely as co-adventurers on a worthy crusade, and if they suspect their leader of flagging commitment or conflicting motives they may just withdraw their support, either by changing jobs or by contriving to change leaders.[9]

In a recent survey of 705 employees at 70 U.S. companies, 64 percent of respondents said that they were regularly skeptical of what management said.[10] We are convinced that this widespread problem is due largely to the fact that too many managers spend too much time attacking the organizations they work for. Global leaders know that undermining your company or colleagues brings your *own* character into question. Dennie Welsh, formerly general manager of IBM's Integrated Services Business, explained it bluntly: "If you are not committed to the strategic imperatives of IBM's vision, you will be asked to exit the company."

Integrity Engenders Trust and Is Good for Business

Integrity is clearly good for business. While high ethical standards may result in some short-term loss of business, in the long run, high standards almost always help. Dave Colton, vice president and counsel for Phelps Dodge Exploration Corporation, a wholly owned subsidiary of Phelps Dodge Corporation, is in a good position to assess the importance of high ethical standards. With annual revenues approaching $4 billion, Phoenix, Arizona–based Phelps Dodge is one of the world's largest producers of copper and copper products, such as wire and cables. In 1997, the exploration company had projects underway in 26 mostly developing countries, including Chile, Peru, Brazil, Mexico, Zambia, Madagascar, Thailand, and Indonesia. Colton, who is on the road 60 to 70 percent of the time, is familiar with all these projects.

> Some in our industry might believe there are short-term benefits working in a country with weak environmental standards.

However, in the long term, it hurts them. As a general rule, senior government employees in developing countries are smart. They do their homework when negotiating with foreign mining companies. When a company chooses not to follow standards, the world knows. In this business, reputations are global and last for decades. It is far easier to stay on the high ground than to have to climb back up.

From my experience I strongly believe that if a company is going to be global, it has no choice but to adopt consistent global standards of conduct. These standards should be equal to or greater than those set in the country that has the highest standards and not based on the lowest common denominator. By the nature of our business, we are in a given location for a long time. In this business, relationships—either with the government or a partner—are everything. Companies without high ethical standards find themselves in trouble very quickly.

A leader who lacks integrity can do serious damage to a company much faster than a leader who does not have a good strategy. Short term compromises—whether in matters of environmental degradation, bribery, shoddy product quality, or abusive labor practices—may bring temporary benefits for the misguided decision maker and his or her business unit, but invariably cost both dearly in the long run. Such compromises can undermine relationships with customers and government agencies, and tarnish the company's reputation for years to come.

Integrity is important not only for external relationships, but is critical in bringing out the best in a company's employees. Case in point: Du Pont in China. In 1997, Du Pont had extensive operations in eight different cities in China and employed, either directly or indirectly, over one thousand people. Du Pont, like other companies, has worked hard to earn the commitment of its Chinese employees. Beijing-based Sonny Matocha, managing director of operations for Du Pont Greater China has some unique insights on the role of integrity in leadership.

In China, people do not naturally differentiate between management and leadership. They have a tendency to do what they are told and it is a kind of mentality that Americans don't easily relate to. But this is part of their culture, their history. In the past, they have been told that the managers are the leaders, so management has automatically come to mean leadership. And so they don't differentiate between the two and do not fully understand the implications of true leadership. This has been compounded by the many instances where their superiors have not kept their commitments. One of the results of this is that the Chinese have come to listen to the words of superiors, but gauge their interpretation and personal behavior based on the manager's actions. While they do not challenge authority, they are very cynical about it. They tend to do their jobs, nothing more.

If you want to lead in China, your employees must believe in you. They must trust you fully. Once this happens, their productivity, commitment, and creativity go way up. But they must see you as an ethical, trustworthy person, who will not compromise no matter what.

We are vigilant in holding firm to the highest of standards, and our expectations in China are no different than any other place in the world. All employees here go through regular ethics training. And the top management here follows it up with visible behavior. We have regular audits and we never stop asking questions. We go with salespeople on calls and see how they are interacting with customers. We check on prices of locally purchased items. Are our purchasing people paying more than the prevailing rate, and if so, why? You have to be constantly vigilant. Rules need constant reinforcement. Only by doing this can you get people to move from the letter of the law to the spirit of the law. It is at that point that you can have enough trust to bring people to a higher level of performance.

Maintaining high ethical standards is clearly good for business as well as for your career. In our survey of Fortune 500 companies, the ability to consistently display high ethical standards was rated the strongest leadership determinant by high potential managers. The message is clear: the highest integrity is demanded of all global leaders. Warren Buffett echoed this sentiment in a recent speech:

> When looking for managers, I basically look for three things: integrity, intelligence, and energy. The problem is that if they don't have the first, the other two will kill you. Why? Because if someone doesn't have integrity, you really want them to be dumb and lazy. It is only if they have the first, that the second two really count.[11]

Exemplar Global Leader:
Lane Cook

Lane Cook, general manager of DSL de Mexico, has faced a series of ethical challenges throughout his career. Although a U.S. citizen, Cook has spent much of his adult life working in Latin America, first in Argentina and later in Mexico. In 1994, Cook was hired by DSL, a California-based international shipping company with $300 million in annual revenue, to work in its Mexico City office. DSL has facilities throughout the United States as well as in Hong Kong, Taiwan, Korea, China, and Singapore. The company focuses on consolidated shipments for the retail industry and counts major retailers like Wal-Mart, Hills Department Stores, Target, and JC Penney as its main customers.

In 1993, after breaking off from its local joint venture partner, DSL opened a small office in Mexico City as a first step in positioning itself for the increased trade that the North American Free Trade Agreement (NAFTA) was expected to bring. During the fall of that year, Cook was hired as operations manager at DSL de Mexico. When he arrived, DSL managers and staff were working 18-to-20-hour days. As U.S. retailers expanded successfully south of the border, the company's success boomed. Within 10 months, Cook returned to the United States and was given full responsibility for all of DSL's business in Mexico.

On the basis of growth projections, Cook won approval in December, 1994 to lease a substantially larger, modern warehouse/office complex just off the north-south highway connecting Mexico City with Laredo, Texas. Two days after the contract was signed, Mexico moved to devalue the peso.

Between December 20, 1994 and February 1, 1995, the peso's value fell almost 40 percent against the U.S. dollar. The devaluation paralyzed business.

> DSL's business was general, nonfood merchandise, and after the devaluation all people were buying was food. That's all they could afford. The devaluation cost us between 20 and 30 percent of our domestic volume, and over 50 percent of our import volume.

By late summer of 1995, the Mexican economy was beginning to show signs of stability. Many at DSL believed that the worst was over. These hopes were dashed when, in July 1995, the company's largest U.S. account began building its own Mexican distribution and warehouse facility, only one-and-a-half miles from DSL's building. Cook reflected on the loss of business:

> The account represented a huge percent of our business in Mexico, as we hadn't had much time to diversify. We put a lot of investment in our new warehouse facility for the account. . . . All of a sudden, we have a huge fixed cost that would support five times the volume and we still couldn't pay the rent. . . . With the loss of that one account, we were down from about 80 percent capacity to about 25 percent capacity in our facility.

With so much unused capacity, and costs already cut to the bone, Cook was under enormous pressure to raise revenues. Cook believed that the key to growth was in developing local business. Here, the company faced steep competition.

> We have trucking companies in Mexico that are slow, often late, and prone to lose some cargo on the way. This is actually a common occurrence here and this is what many customers are used to. If most customers can find a shipper who can move $100,000 of cargo for 300 pesos [$40] cheaper, they'll switch. . . . We are not the cheapest. We use a lot of computers and special tracking systems. We have systems that our competitors and many customers don't have. The market in Mexico is probably ten years behind the U.S. in terms of service technology, so what we offer is new to Mexico.

In May 1996, Cook made a sales visit to SuperMart,[*] a medium-sized, Mexico City–based general merchandise retailer. SuperMart had been in existence for 60 years and had revenues in excess of $150 million. After several meetings with José Hernandez, SuperMart's 58-year-old traffic manager, Cook proposed that DSL manage all of SuperMart's import shipments from Asia.

Under normal practices, SuperMart would take possession of the goods in Asia and contract with DSL for shipping to Mexico via the United States. DSL would in turn buy freight space across the Pacific to Long Beach, California and then arrange ground transportation for the shipments through its Laredo, Texas facility and on to Mexico City. Cook's office in Mexico City would select the transportation company that would bring the freight from the U.S. border to Mexico City.

Hernandez seemed convinced of DSL's capabilities, and he and Cook spent considerable time negotiating fees and other arrangements. Cook explained what happened next:

> After about three weeks of meetings and several late-night dinners, Hernandez promised us the contract at an agreed-upon price, but only on the condition that he select the trucking company in Mexico. I thought this was a little peculiar. I later heard a rumor through a mutual contact that Hernandez had a bank account here in Mexico City as well as an account in Laredo and that the trucking company he selected promised to make a kickback to his American bank account whenever a shipment was made. The Laredo bank would then wire the money to Hernandez's Mexico City account.
>
> I approached Hernandez and asked him point blank if it was true. He denied the rumor categorically. Yes, he had a bank account in Laredo, but so did many wealthier Mexicans who worried about the stability of the peso. Quite frankly, I think he was a little offended that I raised the issue.
>
> I have thought long and hard about this. On the one hand, the Mexican trucking company he suggested quoted me competi-

* A disguised name.

tive rates. I wasn't sure we could do much better. As a result, part of me said, who cares if the rumor is true? I can't impose my ethics on everyone else. It's really his problem. On the other hand, I was thinking that if what I heard was true, the trucking company he wanted to use should be able to lower its prices by that amount to make DSL that much more competitive.

If I didn't respond favorably, I was pretty sure that SuperMart would take its business elsewhere. Unfortunately, this was the type of account we needed to see DSL through the tough times in Mexico. Although there definitely are a lot worse things we could be involved with, I was troubled by it and wondered what exactly to do. It's difficult to separate rumor from fact and then separate my ethics from someone else's.

After considerable thought, Lane Cook decided to let José Hernandez determine the selection of the trucking company for SuperMart. It was one of the toughest calls he ever made.

I decided in the final analysis to let it go. I did everything I could do to verify the rumor, but hit a dead end. Then I thought, even if the rumor was true, DSL wouldn't be paying any more nor would SuperMart. If I knew it was happening in my own organization I would not allow it. But, given that it's not in my control and I am not sure it's happening, there's not much I can do.

The SuperMart saga was Cook's first but not last foray into the gray area of international ethics. Less than a month after resolving the SuperMart issue, Cook was confronted with another troubling dilemma involving a different customer.

A very large client of ours had a history of always looking for opportunities to discount our invoices. They would save huge piles of our invoices and then confront us by asking, long after the fact, whether the goods were actually delivered. We would say, "Of course." Then they would say, "Prove it." Some of the invoices might be a year old, and we'd have to go back and find proof of delivery a year later. About 90 percent of the time we could, but there would be a few times when we couldn't find the right paperwork. Still, we knew that they had received it. So when we couldn't prove it, they would try and discount our invoices. They weren't at all embarrassed, but to me it was obvious what they were up to. When we're making a 10 percent margin and then discount a couple of invoices, really quickly we're out a lot of money. So this happened on-and-off for a long time.

I started thinking that we ought to bill them service time or something if they were going to make me do all this work. Then, not long ago, I found a paid invoice from this same customer that I learned was overbilled. We were very busy and it was an honest mistake. They had already paid us and had not realized that we had charged too much. With other customers, I would have adjusted it right then and there. But this time I truly felt that they had dishonestly discounted me. It was a major dilemma for me.

After struggling with what to do, Lane Cook decided to notify the customer of the over-billing and offer a credit. He was not thanked for his honesty. Furthermore, the customer's scrutiny of DSL's invoices continued, but he never regretted taking the high road—the honest route.

In July 1996, Cook uncovered what he thought was a theft ring in his warehouse. Dealing with this was another major challenge, as Cook related:

We had an employee, I'll call him Raul, who worked in receiving. This meant that he was responsible for unloading and counting boxes coming into our warehouse off of trucks. Once the boxes were counted he would sign off on the customer's invoice so that we were all sure of the count.

There were a couple of occasions when he would be one box off. In other words, his count coming in didn't match up with the actual number going out. There weren't a lot of boxes involved, but we saw two or three incidents where the same vendor would be off a box. Every case involved electric table fans worth maybe $20 a piece.

Raul was 28 years old, married with one child. We were paying Raul the equivalent of about $100 a month. He didn't have a high school education and I know he must have been struggling financially.

My suspicion was that he probably had an agreement with the driver that was delivering the products from the manufacturer. Maybe the driver would say, "Hey, I know we're supposed to deliver 20 fans but here's 19. Mark it down as 20. I'll sign off on it and you sign off on it. When it comes back out of the warehouse the count will be off by one, but they'll blame it on the warehouse staff."

I only had a suspicion. We have six security people during the day and two at night. It's possible they were in on it, too. I don't think it's something we can ever prove the way we would want to in the U.S. before taking action. It wasn't easy to know what to do.

After careful consideration, Lane Cook decided to fire Raul. He explained his actions:

When you handle as much as a million dollars of freight in a week, and you get paid 1 percent of the volume of that, you're easily going to eat up your whole revenue with pilferage. You've got to be extremely careful.

It always starts out small. We had a ring that we caught in our facility involving the manager of our security company. We had a security company where the general manager, under the pretext of checking on his night guards, would go into our warehouse at about 3 a.m. He would pull up his car and the security guards would throw about four or five boxes in the trunk every night. Then they would sell it. It all adds up quickly. In Mexico City, the police and security guards are often the most corrupt and dangerous people.

Whenever I think in personal terms about firing someone making $100 a month, I feel really bad. But when I think in business terms, I realize that I'll pay more if I keep him. If we can't be cost-competitive we'll eventually have no business at all. At that point no one will have a job.

Lane Cook's experiences in Mexico City are not atypical for managers working overseas. International managers face a constant stream of decisions—some small, others large—involving suppliers, government agents, customers, and employees. The answers are not always easy. Knowing who to believe and what to do requires a degree of moral grounding that might not be required at home. Cook was guided in his decision making by his commitment to three principles: first, that he had a moral obligation to ensure that his customers were not being cheated; second, that he not engage in any activities that reflected negatively on his company in Mexico or elsewhere; and third, that his actions be such that they would be approved by his peers and superiors however exhaustively they were examined.

Cook's reputation as someone with rock-solid integrity has served him well both in Mexico and in his reputation at head office. While he continues to confront various ethical challenges, their frequency seems to have diminished. The locals no longer test him as they did when he was new to the job. After almost three years as general manager, he is now widely respected by his employees. Theft is down and productivity up. And business is up, too. DSL de Mexico is now the choice of knowledgeable local and international retailers who want a shipper that provides high-quality, no-strings-attached service. In January, 1998, Cook returned to the United States and another promotion. He is widely respected as someone who was able to excel in one of the world's toughest markets.

Conclusions

Character plays an important part in global leadership. The two main elements of character are emotionally connecting with people and demonstrating a high degree of integrity. Combining these two dimensions of character produces global leaders who are superbly skilled at building trust and goodwill—both inside their companies and outside, in the communities in which they live and work.

Notes

1. For more information on Nobuyuki Idei's leadership style, see "Sony's Idei Finds Winning Path: Reject Tired Thinking." *Wall Street Journal*, May 14, 1997, p. A18.

2. From the Fort Lauderdale *Sun-Sentinal* newspaper, as cited in *Parade Magazine*, January 2, 1994, p. 6.

3. S. Suzuki, *Ability Development from Age Zero* (translated by Mary Louise Nagata), 1981. Secaucus, NJ: Warner Brothers Publications, p. 69.

4. For an excellent review of the OECD's efforts, see "Who's Bribing Now?" *Christian Science Monitor*, April 16, 1996.

5. GM's policy allows for workers outside the United States to accept meals and outings to comply with local business norms. For more information on GM's "Revised Policy on Gifts, Entertainment and Other Gratuities" see "New GM Rules Curb Wining and Dining." *Wall Street Journal*, June 5, 1996.

6. Mee-Kau Nyaw and I. Ng, "A Comparative Analysis of Ethical Beliefs: A Four Country Study." *Journal of Business Ethics*, 1994, 13, pp. 543–55.

7. K. H. Lee, "Ethical Beliefs in Marketing Management: A Cross-Cultural Study." *European Journal of Marketing*, 1982, pp. 58–67.

8. G. England, "Managers and Their Value Systems: A Five Country Comparative Study." *Columbia Journal of World Business,* 1978.

9. R. Kelley, "In Praise of Followers." *Harvard Business Review*, November-December, 1988, p. 144.

10. *Business Week*, May 16, 1994.

11. As quoted from a speech given to students at the Marriott School of Management, Brigham Young University, 1996.

six

SAVVY

Savvy is an essential characteristic of global leadership. Whether Old World explorers or modern-day business executives, global leaders possess unique knowledge and skills that set them apart from the rest. They know what to do and how to get it done. Again and again, we heard about the importance of savvy in our interviews. Whether in Frankfurt or Chicago or Singapore, employees described exemplar leaders with statements like "He just seems to know what to do," or "She has a golden touch—everything she does is a success."

What exactly is savvy and how can it be articulated? We uncovered two critical dimensions of savvy through our research. First, leaders exhibit *global business savvy* when they recognize global market opportunities for their companies. Second, global leaders know how to capitalize on these market opportunities by accessing the full resources of the worldwide organization. We call this *global organizational savvy*. To be an effective global leader you must create value for your company by recognizing global market opportunities and knowing how to capitalize on them.

Our model in Figure 2.6 shows that savvy relates to both the duality and dispersion dynamics. Business savvy requires a solid knowledge of the drivers of globalization and localization; it requires the ability to assess each activity and process along the company's value chain for its optimal global or local configuration. As such, business savvy is tightly connected to the duality dynamic. In contrast, organizational savvy focuses on gathering information and influencing decisions beyond the limits of the global leader's command and control. As a result, organizational savvy is tightly linked to the dispersion dynamic. In this chapter we explore both dimensions of savvy and discuss their impact on global leadership.

Global Business Savvy

Maximizing Value

Global business savvy is essential for the simple reason that for-profit companies must make money for shareholders. Your impact as a leader rests on your ability to maximize value creation for your company, to make money on a worldwide basis—ideally, lots of it. As Homi Patel, vice president and general manager of manufacturing at General Motors Powertrain, puts it: "Globalization is ultimately about growing the business and making money. A global leader has a vision of doing business worldwide with the ultimate goal of making money." This view is common in many leading companies. "Business results are the bed rock of leadership at Motorola," says Pat Canavan, corporate vice president of global leadership and organizational development at Motorola. At IBM, Dennie Welsh, formerly general manager of the company's Integrated Services Business, counseled new executives that "to succeed at IBM, you need a successful profit-and-loss track record. Net income is a better measure than gross profit because you have to control everything." At these companies, as at many successful businesses, results are the sine qua non of leadership.

Why are business results so important to leadership? Two reasons: the first is practical; the second is psychological. From a practical perspective, managers who create the most value are generally rewarded with higher compensation and more rapid promotion to leadership positions.[1] In many companies, you simply cannot get into a global leadership position without a track record of making money. From a psychological perspective, business results generate credibility and respectability for the manager: when a division makes money, the division president gets the credit. When the company's stock is doing well, the CEO is lauded as a great leader. When the company's fortunes fall, those same individuals are viewed as failures.

The Power of Global Mindsets

Leaders with global mindsets view the world—not just the home country—as the arena for value creation. Their world is a borderless marketplace.[2] The global convergence of product preferences, increasingly intense international competition, and overall growth in international trade exert huge pressures to assess how international market opportunities benefit your corporation as a whole, rather than a particular home or host country.[3] Companies as diverse as Electrolux, Michelin, Hoechst, and ICI have led the way by becoming essentially stateless competitors; they integrate operations tightly throughout the world, and over 75 percent of their sales are generated outside the home country. For global companies like these, the sun never sets.

This relatively new vision of stateless competition forces you to rethink the role of countries as you formulate business strategy. Global leaders continually pound away at the importance of global markets when meeting with employees. In virtually every stump speech by GE's Jack Welch, Kodak's George Fisher, Sony's Nobuyuki Idei, the LG Group's Bon Moo Koo, and Nokia's Jorma Ollila, the crucial importance of global markets is emphasized. Intense competition at home and rapidly growing demand in developing countries have compelled these leaders to look beyond traditional markets. Whether companies have worldwide operations or focus on single markets, thinking globally is essential for all business leaders.

Recognizing Global Market Opportunities

To develop global business savvy you must move beyond simply *thinking* about the world to actually recognizing global market opportunities for your company. Making money is ultimately about winning in markets. Global leaders recognize three types of global market opportunities: (1) arbitrage opportunities involving cost and quality differences in production inputs; (2) new market opportunities for the company's finished goods and services; and (3) opportunities to maximize efficiencies by reducing redundancies.

Arbitrage Opportunities. Global leaders who scour the world for the cheapest and highest quality inputs of production give their companies an enormous advantage in the marketplace. Cost differentials for land, energy, labor, and raw materials differ widely from country to country. For instance, one recent study by the German Institut der deutschen Wirtschaft showed that industrial labor averaged $31.76 per hour in western Germany, $20.26 per hour in France, $17.50 per hour in the United States, and $14.63 per hour in the United Kingdom.[4] Fully loaded industrial labor costs in western Germany may be 50 times higher than comparable costs in parts of India. Although global leaders must balance labor cost differentials with labor productivity measures, real cost differences exist and can be exploited by global companies. A good example of a company that pays close attention to labor cost differentials is Singapore Airlines, which performs all software development work in Madras, India and conducts its major aircraft maintenance work in low-cost Xiamen, China. Another example is American Airlines, which processes all of its U.S. tickets in low-cost Barbados.

The same arbitrage opportunities apply for raw materials and components, which global leaders can often source from international markets at lower costs, even after factoring in quality. Global leaders recognize that by combining first-world process technologies with third-world costs, they can gain huge competitive advantages.[5] Not surprisingly, statistics suggest that trade flows of intermediate goods are enormous. Recent estimates by the World Trade Organization are that roughly one-third of world trade is intra-firm among MNCs, another one-third is trade among national (non-MNC) firms, and a final one-third is trade involving MNC exports to non-affiliates.[6]

Determining sourcing locations involves complex calculations and difficult tradeoffs. Take automobile components, for example. If you are a manager at Honda, you may be interested in either making or buying bumpers for cars manufactured and sold in the United States. To determine the make or buy decision, you must know the cost of labor, cost of steel and plastics, U.S. import duties for finished bumpers, business tax rates, shipping costs, exchange rates, currency stability, and so on for a wide range of countries. Global leaders know they need this type of data in order to weigh a range of input factors. Labor costs, for example, are far less important in the auto industry (at companies like Nissan and Toyota, labor represents less than 9 percent of total variable costs) than in the apparel industry (where labor may represent 35 percent or more of total variable costs). Global leaders proactively search for input cost and quality differences between countries to maximize arbitrage opportunities.

The ability to recognize global cost and quality differences increases when procurement activities are coordinated across geographies. You can learn a great deal about global market opportunities when your procurement people in Hong Kong regularly talk to your purchasing people in New York. For example, IBM's Willi Stark is the general manager of a joint venture personal computer company that IBM has established with Great Wall Trading Company in China. According to Stark, more than half the value of the computer is imported into China. "We can only purchase from corporate-approved, worldwide vendors," explained Stark. "This way we know we are getting the quality we depend on at prices that are the best anywhere. Not having to worry about purchasing also saves me a lot of time." IBM has the advantage of economies of scope.[7] Scope advantages enable companies to better exploit differences in international raw material and intermediate goods markets as well as in capital markets.[8] Global leaders seek out these types of global arbitrage opportunities.

When companies take advantage of arbitrage opportunities, suppliers often have no choice but to globalize their own operations. Take the airline industry as an example. Over the past ten years, the industry has moved quickly to globalize operations through the expansion of route networks and the increased use of alliances. Globalization has also allowed airlines to lower costs through global purchasing. In terms of fuel purchases, a growing number of airlines including British Airways, Lufthansa, and KLM have moved toward centralized purchasing. As a result, fuel suppliers have been forced to restructure how they service their airline customers. In the fall of 1997, Exxon Company, International announced the formation of EssoAir to manage all non-U.S. aviation fuel sales and service. Based in Leatherhead, outside of London, EssoAir has consolidated in one location the aviation fuel businesses that were traditionally based with the country affiliates. Although airlines continue to use EssoAir's country-specific phone numbers, all calls are routed to the central office in Great Britain. While client service is provided in each customer's native language, the EssoAir representative is actually located far away in Leatherhead. Centralization allows for better internal communication, more reliable service, and faster and better decision making. Using proprietary computer software and innovative telecommunications technology, EssoAir believes that not only can it reduce costs, but that it can actually provide significant improvements in customer service compared to its old, affiliate-based approach.

New Market Opportunities. Not only must you be skilled at recognizing arbitrage opportunities, but as an effective global leader you must also identify new markets for your company's goods and services. If you want your unit to continue to grow, you have little choice. The big markets are all international. By the mid-1990s, the U.S. economy accounted for just under 25 percent of the world's GNP; Japan for over 15 percent; Germany for about 8 percent; and the U.K. for just under 5 percent.[9] The message is clear: no single country represents more than 25 percent of the world economy. If you want to increase revenues, look to overseas markets.

Leaders such as David Glass at Wal-Mart, Hisashi Kaneko at NEC, John Pepper at Proctor & Gamble, and Jean Monty at Northern Telecom have relentlessly expanded their companies into new geographic markets. Beyond these high profile cases, examples of leaders who seized the initiative to globalize operations can be found throughout the world. In Australia, leaders like Tony Hancy at Andersen Consulting demonstrate an ability to recognize emerging market opportunities far away from the head office. Beginning in the late 1980s, Hancy, a managing partner and head of Andersen's Australia-based strategic services practice, began pushing the firm into the emerging markets of southeast Asia. Hancy's initiatives were very different from the norm established by competitors that had moved into Asia directly from their U.S. bases: McKinsey's drive into Asia was spearheaded by its Los Angeles office, Bain's Palo Alto office managed that company's Pacific Rim expansion, and Monitor's expansion into Asia was supervised out of Boston. Not so for Andersen, where an Australian manager with an ability to recognize market potential seized the initiative and pushed the practice where it had never been before. Partners in Melbourne now supervise virtually all of Andersen's Asia Pacific strategic services practice.

From management consulting to telecommunications equipment and consumer products, market opportunities are rapidly globalizing. Even the industries most country-focused in the past, such as airport management, are turning global as executives come to realize that global sales are the route to sustained revenue growth. NV Luchthaven Schiphol, for example, has long run Amsterdam's famed international airport. Regarded as one of the world's finest, the airport is favored for its cleanliness, efficiency, and top-of-the-line retail outlets. For years, Alexander Zeverijn, Schiphol's development director, has scoured the world for opportunities to sell his company's unique design and management skills. One big payoff came in May, 1997 when Schiphol USA signed a 30-year contract with the Port Authority of New York to run the International Arrivals Building at John F. Kennedy International Airport.[10] Assumptions that some industries are inherently country-bound are proving very shortsighted.

Global markets also provide the potential for companies to increase product features or underwrite the development of entirely new product offerings. Global leaders do this through the globalization of technology. An example of this kind of leadership was unveiled on April 14, 1998 when Gillette launched its new MACH3 razor. The company spent six years and $750 million to bring the MACH3 to market. By comparison, only nine years earlier, Gillette had spent $200 million to launch the twin-blade Sensor razor. Three hundred million dollars was budgeted to market the MACH3 during the first year after its launch alone. Of this amount, two-thirds was targeted for international markets. The company estimated that, by the end of 1999, MACH3 would be sold in one hundred countries. By comparison, it took five years for Sensor to reach this milestone. Clearly, Gillette would never have spent so much time and money on the MACH3 without the promise of strong global interest in the product.

Accessing global markets helps companies amortize costs associated with new product development. From aircraft to semiconductors, the costs associated with developing a new generation of products can be huge. In civil aircraft, Ron Woodard, president of Boeing's Commercial Airplane Group, estimated that the cost to develop an entirely new superjumbo transport ranges from $12 billion to $15 billion. Even the cost to develop a derivative superjumbo based on the 747 was estimated at being in excess of $5 billion.[11] Unfortunately, no single national market is large enough alone for Boeing to fully recoup these costs while at the same time providing competitive prices for airline customers. For companies like Boeing, global markets serve as a means of amortizing these enormous capital and technological investments.

Efficiency Opportunities. Global leaders understand that globalization provides opportunities to maximize value through increased operating efficiencies. These come through the elimination of redundancies, the use of company size as an advantage, and the capturing of economies of scale. The ability to shave off costs through cutting redundancies has been a major driving force behind Jack Smith's international expansion efforts. As General Motors' CEO, Smith has launched a $2.2 billion international expansion that includes building nearly identical auto assembly plants in Argentina, Poland, China, and Thailand.[12] In this case, process technology is being standardized so that robots, software, and computer systems are identical across all four plants. This saves money by eliminating costly duplications in system design and process engineering.

By eliminating redundancies, global leaders are also better able to exploit company size. One advantage of size comes from the ability to consolidate demand and negotiate lower prices with outside vendors. It is not simply finding the cheapest inputs around the world, but being effective at pressuring vendors to offer volume discounts. For example, ITT's *Yellow Pages* centrally manages its worldwide purchasing out of an office in Belgium. Substantial cost savings result from centralized purchasing, primarily involving paper. Paper represents a substantial variable cost, given that directories are up to 1,000 pages long and are often printed in runs of hundreds of thousands of copies. Not only can the central purchasing office take advantage of world spot markets for paper, but it can use its substantial buying power to cut special deals with paper suppliers.

Global leaders are able to maximize efficiencies by reaping the benefits of economies of scale. In disparate industries such as consumer electronics, medical diagnostic equipment, shipbuilding, commodity chemicals, and automobiles, firms reach maximum production efficiencies when volumes *exceed* the potential demand of virtually every national market. In the petroleum industry, for example, technical developments in refining shifted plant capacity from about 500 barrels per day in the early 1920s to well over 100,000 barrels per day by the mid-1950s. Since then, the optimal size of refineries has grown, albeit at a lower pace. But in refining as well as countless other industries, global markets have become essential if leaders want to maximize efficiencies.

In many cases, increasing production volumes move companies significantly down learning curves. We all learn through repetition; in some industries, learning has a direct impact on efficiency. Civil aircraft is a good example. Airbus's first A300 aircraft took an estimated 340,000 person-hours to produce; its eighty-seventh plane took only 78,000 person-hours.[13] In Airbus's case, global markets lead to lower prices for customers.

Global leaders understand the direct relationship between the benefits of exporting and the level of international market efficiency for the company's tangible assets (components, finished products, etc.) and intangible assets (services, management, etc.).[14] In a perfectly borderless world, with free trade in goods and services, and free information, exporting would be the economically preferred international strategy.[15] While the world is not perfectly borderless and while few markets are perfectly efficient, globalization is both a driver behind and a result of increasingly efficient international markets.

Managers at companies like Unilever have moved to take advantage of opportunities to maximize internal efficiencies by reducing redundancies and centralizing production. Consider the production of seed oils. Common seed oils include corn oil, sunflower oil, soybean oil, cottonseed oil, palm oil, and various blends. In Europe, the seed oil industry has traditionally been nationally oriented with lots of small-scale, inefficient plants. European integration has changed all that by allowing Unilever to shut down country-focused plants in favor of more efficient regional factories. Vassili Goudes, commercial director of Minerva (historically Greece's largest edible oil producer) explains how this gives Unilever a competitive advantage:

> The Greek consumer seed oil market is dominated by Minerva, which has an estimated 20.5 percent share of the market, and Elais (a division of Unilever), which has approximately 26.5 percent market share. The total Greek market for seed oils is approximately 110,000 tons. Of this amount, about 50 percent or 55,000 tons is devoted to consumer markets. Unilever has large seed oil plants in Northern Europe that run 150,000 tons per year. This is three times the entire consumer demand for all seed oils in Greece. How can we compete? Transportation costs helps offset some of their production efficiencies. But we all know competition is only going to increase. Greeks are now paying a premium for seed oils. Over time, prices will almost certainly fall off. Unless we do something significant we are going to lose market share to Elais.

Recognizing efficiency advantages is often difficult for managers. In many cases, managers have worked in and around the activities in question for decades. They have become *too* familiar with how things are run and find it difficult to imagine any other organizational configuration. In contrast, savvy global leaders constantly search for new and better ways of organizing activities with the objective of maximizing efficiencies.

Critical Knowledge Areas

To recognize global market opportunities, you must have a broad and deep knowledge base. This should include an understanding of external markets as well as your company's competitive positioning. Savvy global leaders master fundamental business principles in their quest to uncover global market opportunities. These include:

- *international finance*, including an understanding of foreign exchange management and global financial markets;
- *international accounting*, including an understanding of financial statement consolidation and differences in national accounting standards;
- *international marketing*, including an understanding of country differences in market size, segmentation, distribution, branding, and advertising norms;
- *international human resource management*, including an understanding of employment norms and expatriate selection and management;
- *international operations*, including an understanding of differences in production techniques and technologies;
- *international relations*, including an understanding of national and regional politics, business-government relations, and the role of nongovernmental organizations such as the World Bank and the International Monetary Fund;
- *international economics*, including an understanding of fiscal, monetary, investment, and employment policies of key countries;
- *international industry conditions*, including an understanding of the strategic capabilities and intent of key and emerging competitors,

trends in customer demands and key technologies, and the relative advantages and disadvantages for globally integrated versus locally standardized competitors;

- *international strategy*, including an understanding of competitive positioning, alliances, exporting, and FDI options.

Knowledge as a Moving Target

A vast body of knowledge and a large pool of subject matter experts support each of these activities; entire university courses and small libraries are devoted to each topic. As we discussed in Chapter 2, developing business savvy requires an enormous commitment to learning—a commitment not just to understanding compartmentalized business subjects, but also to developing a deeper understanding of subtle interrelationships between knowledge areas. Gaining a feel for how the pieces fit together is critical in identifying and weighing global market opportunities.

Beyond developing a breadth and depth of global business knowledge, you face another, more daunting challenge. The pieces of the knowledge puzzle change continually. Two types of change are noteworthy: (1) changing paradigms, and (2) changing conditions. First, changes in paradigms are uniquely unsettling and more common than ever. Whether it is total quality management, core competencies, or generic strategies, there are increasingly frequent shifts in what you are expected to *know* and *do*. Second, frequent and substantial changes in customer needs and market conditions are unavoidable. Understanding market trajectory and the speed and extent of change across multiple markets is a daunting task and yet essential for you to maintain global business savvy.

Savvy and the Global Organization

To stay on top of market opportunities, you have no choice but to get close to customers. George Fisher, chairman and CEO of Kodak stands out in this regard. In April 1997, Fisher announced that his company would open a new executive office in Hong Kong. The office, run by Assistant COO Carl Kohrt, is intended to bring Kodak closer to emerging technologies and markets. In announcing the move, Fisher said, "It is not enough to think globally, we must operate globally if we are to truly capitalize on the growth opportunities we see in markets outside the U.S."

While global leaders have a breadth of knowledge and global awareness of opportunities, they still have no choice but to rely on local people for input. Despite some successes at companies like Kodak, in most cases local employees are much better at getting close to customers and markets than are expatriates. Local employees often have an instinctive sense of the markets, and an ability to establish strong long-term relationships with decision makers and knowledge generators. Many are also very smart about business. In a business world that is changing too rapidly for any one leader to keep up with, the savvy of local employees must be tapped. The challenge for global leaders is to *focus* these localized skills and insights in ways that maximize organizational learning while at the same time they exploit the company's existing strengths. It is a delicate balancing act. Sonny Matocha, managing director, operations, for Du Pont Greater China, has some interesting insights into tapping local skills in maximizing value.

The Chinese people have a great history of savvy. They know how to make money. They have a longer history at doing it than Americans and Europeans. What I want to do is use Du Pont's global management process to help them focus their skills without changing who they are. Leadership is about getting people to focus on what they are good at, not destroying it. In China, we need to blend Chinese savvy with our processes. The challenge is to get them to go beyond repeating instructions to actually owning the value creation processes. This is the essence of global leadership.

Exemplar Global Leader:
Steven Holliday

Steve Holliday, managing director of British-Borneo Oil & Gas Ltd., provides a great example of a leader with global business savvy. Holliday, age 40, joined British-Borneo in the summer of 1997 after a 19-year stint with Exxon Company, International. British-Borneo, a British oil and gas exploration and production company with £1 billion in annual revenue, has had international operations in Southeast Asia for many years. Its recent focus has been on the North Sea and the Gulf of Mexico. Over the last two years, British-Borneo has positioned itself as one of the leading independents in deep-water areas of the Gulf, acquiring in a series of deals, the Morpeth, Allegheny, and King Kong developments in the region as part of an aggressive international push.

After graduating from Nottingham University, Holliday, a British national, joined Esso U.K. After a series of promotions, he left Great Britain for Exxon Company, International's headquarters in the United States. By 1995, he was in charge of all of Exxon Company, International's drive for new gas business in Asia Pacific and the former Soviet Union. In this capacity, Holliday oversaw strategic planning and negotiations involving a wide range of government agencies and business enterprises. Before leaving for British-Borneo, Holliday was supervising nine major joint ventures in start-up or operating stages throughout Asia Pacific and the former Soviet republics. It was a job that put him on the road constantly.

Holliday has a unique perspective on global leadership. At Exxon, he was a non-American working for one of the largest U.S. multinational companies. This presented some unique challenges in Asia where, more often than not, locals treated him as though he were American. Now at British-Borneo, he is again spending much of his time overseas, but this time the locals usually get his nationality right.

Holliday's extensive exposure to cultural differences taught him the importance of business results as a means of demonstrating leadership. According to Holliday,

> Business results are clearly tied to someone's ability to lead. But the connection is a little complicated in the gas business. Actually generating short-term revenues is not a particularly good measure of success because, as an example, in my previous job there was least a five-year gap between when we started spending money and when revenues started coming in. There were also a lot of people involved in these projects. So figuring out how I, or someone else, specifically contributed to profits five or ten years from now was really not possible. But what was and is important is being regarded as someone who makes things happen.

> If I want to be thought of as a real leader, I need to be known as someone who has made a major contribution to things that will eventually make real money for the company.

> I find it much easier to lead people when I have a track record of getting things done. When I have a good track record, people generally believe that if they have a good idea, I'll support them and open doors for them to implement what they want to do. I use my enthusiasm and energy to attract these types of people. The best leaders attract or create the best people on their team.

Holliday is convinced that there is much more about market opportunities than "playing global chess" with competitors. Business opportunities must be assessed and weighed according to straight economics before applying any other biases in favor of one market or another.

> When I think of global business, I think of a world full of markets and opportunities. British-Borneo is driven by attractive opportunities. When we see a profitable opportunity, we have the speed and flexibility to go after it. Globalization opens new opportunities to us as both a traditional exploration and production company and more particularly as a company that can help provide innovative solutions for the industry. British-Borneo has built a business based on the implementation of strategic thinking to produce a competitive advantage.

Critical to making things happen is an understanding of business fundamentals. Holliday strongly believes that the best global leaders have a deep, almost intuitive understanding of how their businesses work.

> Global leaders need a very good overall perspective of what their business has to offer. They need to know how their business is positioned, they need to understand its capabilities, and figure out what their business can and cannot do both now and in the future. The big picture issues are critically important. For me to be really effective as a leader, I need to understand how business fundamentals drive and shape the core. I cannot forget

that the objective is making money. The objective is not doing a job; rather, doing a job is a means to an ends. I need to constantly and objectively ask, "What are the economics and business fundamentals behind making money for the company?"

I have worked with many people who are uncomfortable getting into business fundamentals. They lack the confidence to explore new or different opportunities for the company. Let me illustrate with an example from Australia. A few years ago when I was working at Exxon, the Australian government decided to privatize the country's power business. Despite the fact that this could have been an excellent business opportunity, our local people in Australia assumed that we wouldn't be interested. For some reason they believed that the power business was not part of Exxon's core and that the company should pass on the opportunity. How did they get this idea? It's possible someone somewhere had said the company wasn't interested in power generation and the message was passed on until it was perceived as law in Australia. But they were just wrong. We had been extensively involved in the power business in Hong Kong for years. At a minimum, the opportunity needed evaluation.

If you have business savvy you have to recognize opportunities and not rigidly adhere to nonexistent "laws" to guide your thinking. One thing I try to do as a leader is encourage people not to put constraints on what we do. When they see an opportunity I want to hear about it. Let's look at it, even though it may not be a core business opportunity.

The challenge is not in getting people to understand the company's "core" business. Most people can explain this to you automatically. The real challenge is in getting people to understand what drives the core business and, more particularly, what might enhance it. Of course if you extrapolate too far, you can get into trouble. I am not talking about starting every day with a blank sheet of paper. But I am suggesting that we push the conventional wisdom and keep asking questions and open our minds to innovative and sometimes daring possibilities. This type of thinking, if it can be made to work, will make all the difference between British-Borneo continuing to beat the competition or drifting into becoming an "also-ran" in the industry.

Holliday provided an example of how combining an understanding of business fundamentals with some lateral thinking can enhance company profitability. His example was taken from the Black Point power plant in Hong Kong.

> Oil and gas companies have for some time been moving into power generation all over the world. In Asia, in particular, gas resources have been uneconomic to actually develop because of the absence of local markets for gas. The region has a history of dependence on coal and oil for electrical generation. But, as the economies of the region have continued to grow, the demand for power has increased substantially. A lot of oil and gas companies have waited for power companies to come along and build a power station. While they wait, the gas resources in the ground continue to lose value. As a result, backing into a power company, even a joint venture, or in some way taking a power station on your self, is one way of monetizing those gas resources earlier than would otherwise happen. Over the past five years, many of the major companies have begun to move in this direction.

> Interestingly, Exxon's major power business in Asia is a joint venture with Hong Kong–based China Power and Light Company that supplies about two-thirds of Hong Kong's electric power. The venture was actually started before this recent surge of oil companies into power generation. It required a lot of foresight and business savvy. Now, having gotten into that venture, it is possible to springboard into power projects on the mainland of China. The demand for power in China is insatiable. Discussions are currently underway with the Chinese about becoming a major supplier of gas-powered electrical generation. Because of its foresight years ago, Exxon now has a leg up on the competition in China.

Recognizing business opportunities is always a challenge. It requires the combination of an intense desire to build the business and sound business judgment. On this matter, Holliday offers some interesting insights.

> Intuition and gut feel are essential in recognizing market opportunities. It's not that the intuition of great leaders is always right but rather that it is right more often than not. Intuition is a combination of natural talent and personal confidence generated from experience.
>
> A good example of intuition and quick thinking is seen in British-Borneo's movement from the shallow water shelf into deep-water Gulf of Mexico. In 1994, the deep water Gulf was being recognized as containing some high potential fields, but was an area dominated by the majors, using proven and expensive technologies. Because of the costs, the independents were not active there. But British-Borneo recognized that there were likely to continue to be a number of smaller discoveries in the deep water that the majors would not be able to develop economically. If the company could apply a low-cost approach, there might be a niche business opportunity. Discussions were held with Atlantia Corporation, which at the time was offering simple tripod structures for use in the shallow water of the southern North Sea. During discussions, it became apparent that Atlantia had some thoughts about constructing a mini tension-leg floating platform that would be tethered to the seabed and could be used in deep water. It was an order of magnitude, lighter and cheaper than the ones previously built by the majors.
>
> British-Borneo, spotting the potential to attach smaller, sub-100-million-barrel fields, offered to sponsor further research with Atlantia. This subsequently developed into an exclusive arrangement to utilize the technology to develop prospects offshore in the deep-water Gulf. Sure enough, the initial hunch that there was an angle there through the technology opportunity paid off. It enabled British-Borneo to build a position in the deep-water Gulf by first reaching an arrangement with Shell

to take over a discovery of some 40 to 50 million barrels seen as uneconomic. British-Borneo, using this new technology, was able to turn it into an attractive commercial development called the Morpeth Field. Apparent drilling success has recently been combined with revised estimates that the field holds some 77 million barrels of reserves. This has been a stepping stone for the company which now has two further developments and has built, from a standing start, an enviable position in this high-potential area with a current share in about 100 deep water licenses.

This is an example of where there was an intuitive judgement up front followed by some good, solid technical work and then the ability to think swiftly, move quickly, and negotiate a deal. If you wait until everything is perfectly certain, it's probably too late from a competitive perspective. The correct intuition of great leaders means that they end up not wasting a lot of time on misplaced data collection.

Holliday is convinced that demonstrating business savvy requires not only business skill but also communication skills. Peoples' *perceptions* of how savvy you are really matter. In Holliday's words:

Although people respect hierarchy, you still have to prove yourself no matter what position you are in. You have got to demonstrate to people that you have an intellectual contribution to make to the debate and if you are new to your position, either coming in from outside the company or from another part of the company, people will always start off wondering how much you really have to contribute.

Let me give you an example. When I was working at Exxon, there was a guy who joined us in a senior position in the power generation business. He came from Exxon's chemical business where he was highly respected. He had a great record. When he arrived in his new job he made what was, in retrospect, a big mistake. He started off by telling people that he didn't know anything about the power business. I think he was trying to come across as a humble guy who was looking for help. But people understood his message quite differently. They interpreted what he said as, "Hey, don't take me seriously. I have nothing to add and you don't really need to listen to me." His approach was honest but ended up backfiring. He signaled the people who worked for him that he wasn't competent. And that clearly was not the case. As a result of this, it took him longer than it should have to become a major contributor to the business.

Unfortunately, you cannot separate perceptions of competency from the ability to lead. I am not suggesting that you can't pose questions to people who work for you. But I am saying that you need to communicate your competence and priorities very quickly.

In order to stay on top of business opportunities and practices, Holliday is passionate about learning. In his view, reading and studying are essential to maintaining global business savvy.

I read a lot, mostly external material. We subscribe to a considerable number of periodicals. I also rely on an excellent screening service. I do it so that I can be prepared. Being able to speak knowledgeably is so important when negotiating with companies or government officials. It's not always possible to live in every country I deal with. Sure, it would be better if I had lived in China or Turkmenistan but that is not always possible. Reading and asking lots of questions helps me fill in the blanks.

In my new role at British-Borneo, growing the global business absolutely requires knowledge and insight. We are focused on global opportunities where we are able to fully utilize the key talents we can offer in creating value through technical innovation coupled with quick decision making and action.

Global Organizational Savvy

Beyond a mastery of global business markets, you also need an intimate knowledge of your own company. Global organizational savvy is required to mobilize your company's resources to capture global markets. Understanding and working with complex global organizations requires a set of skills that many managers lack. One senior human resource manager at AT&T expressed a concern shared by many global leaders at other companies: "Here, we are heavily steeped in technological, engineering, and financial thinking. Most of our people are not so comfortable on the organizational side of the business. Yet you have to understand your organizational side as critically as your hard asset side."

Many managers we interviewed spent an inordinate amount of time familiarizing themselves with company policies and programs to the detriment of developing a sound understanding of the fundamental strengths and weaknesses of their companies' far-flung operations. They understand company rules, but not where critical knowledge and capabilities can be found within the company. A good example of this lack of familiarity with the global organization was found in our meeting with the chief financial officer of a highly successful European company with major interests in Latin America. When asked if he could identify the types of products sold by the company's large Brazilian subsidiary, the CFO could think of only four products. In fact, the subsidiary sold over 30 different products, and the four he mentioned represented less than 20 percent of sales. Many decision makers know a great deal about the global organization in an abstract sense, but often lack detailed knowledge of what is really going on in key markets.

Lack of organizational knowledge is an even bigger problem if you are posted outside the head office. In overseas divisions far from home base, employees often have only a limited sense of what the company is all about. Local managers are often not known by, nor do they know, key decision makers at head office. Not surprisingly, their effectiveness in anything but the most local tasks is severely limited.

Yet even expatriates with lots of head office experience risk getting cut out of the information loop once they take an overseas assignment. One U.S. country manager for an American automobile company in Asia complained that although he had been gone from Detroit for only two years, he felt totally lost in terms of what was going on back home. The people who sponsored his overseas assignment had either been reassigned to other jobs or had largely forgotten their promises to keep him informed. Not surprisingly, he felt isolated organizationally and uncertain when it came time to make decisions. While his subordinates turned to him for direction, he hesitated in making decisions in what for him was an organizational vacuum.

Critical Knowledge Areas

Familiarity with the global organization is critical to effective decision making. To lead effectively, you need to know such basics things as:

- the product lines offered by key subsidiaries;
- the cost structures and overall competitiveness of key subsidiaries and how they compare to the organization as a whole;
- the location and quality of technological resources (both hard assets and people) within the global organization; and
- the location of managerial and employee talent within the global organization.

Knowing these dimensions of the organization gives you a much better feel for what your organization can and cannot do.

Beyond a factual knowledge of what the organization *can do*, you also need a clear understanding of what your company *wants to do*. Figuring this out is not a simple task. First and foremost, you need a familiarity with the backgrounds, interests, and personalities of the key decision makers in your company. In most cases, company objectives and personal interests are not in perfect synch.

In one U.S.-based medical products company we worked with, head office managers spent endless hours worrying about European integration. The company had six manufacturing subsidiaries spread across Europe. Many had been in operation for over 60 years as autonomous, stand-alone subsidiaries. While each of the six subsidiaries manufactured and sold the same four product lines, significant differences existed in product specifications, pricing, and services provided. The company's U.S.-based head of international operations decided that the tradition of autonomy needed to change. With European integration putting pressure on businesses to rationalize their operations, the time had come for this company to act. A meeting with the six country managers was called, and they were charged with working out a rationalization plan within four months.

When four months passed and no action occurred, the head of international operations stepped in. Instead of manufacturing four product lines in six countries, he decided that manufacturing would be focused in four countries: France, Germany, Great Britain, and Italy. Each subsidiary in these countries was given full European responsibility for one of the four product lines. This approach created clear winners *and* losers. The two subsidiaries facing the ax, one in Spain and one in Denmark, fought hard to have the restructuring overruled. Furthermore, even the so-called winners were unhappy, because three-fourths of the divisions in the surviving subsidiaries were also dismantled. The reorganization struggled to get off the ground. Resistance to change was enormous, morale plummeted, and customers were ignored. Within a year, the head of international operations was fired.

The decision to reorganize was not itself the problem. In fact, the reorganization made perfect sense on paper. When asked why the reorganization failed, country general managers cited two reasons. First, the sweeping changes brought about by European integration had been overestimated by the head office. In the minds of the country general managers, distribution, tax, and branding differences between countries continued; as a result, the reorganization's economic rationale was weak. Second, the subsidiary managers felt that the U.S. head of international operations had picked the wrong countries for the European product mandates. France was given responsibility for product line A because it was the strongest of the six countries in making product A. However, the French general manager thought that his subsidiary was stronger in product B than in A. Furthermore, he viewed product B as more strategically important to the global aspirations of the company than product A. Germany, given responsibility for product line B, really wanted product line C, and so on. The end result? A global disaster for the company. Business savvy without a keen sense of organizational realities is the formula for failure.

An understanding of different personal interests must be weighed against each individual's power base in the organization. Determining who is gaining and who is losing power is never easy. Factors to be considered include:

- The decision maker's external constituency (relationships with shareholders, customers, bankers, etc.).

- The decision maker's internal constituency (relationships with the Board of Directors, superiors, peers, subordinates).
- The decision maker's degree of dependency on others to implement change.

Understanding the different interests and powers that permeate global organizations is time-consuming and requires substantial interaction. The majority of the most effective global leaders we met spend at least half of their time visiting the troops in the field. They want to see and be seen. Bob Galvin, chairman of the executive committee of Motorola's board of directors, is an exemplar in this area. He is known for walking around manufacturing plants and talking to employees, whether it be the plant manager or the individual who mops floors. In his words, "I believe that every Motorola site around the world has a 'character' that is unique. I have long encouraged our top managers that they need to appreciate the *flavor* of the company's different plants."

Lack of familiarity with the global organization means that while managers may have administrative titles, they may not actually lead. People in the trenches almost always know more than the manager and become resentful when their input is not valued. In extreme cases, the failure of managers to seek input generates significant employee contempt. This is a particularly acute problem overseas when headquarters managers show up once a year as part of an around-the-world junket. Ernie Gundling at Meridian Associates calls this "typhoon management." The managers sweep in like a typhoon, mess things up, go away, and then the locals have to rebuild all over again. Even expatriate country managers can face serious problems. Through little fault of their own, language differences and cultural insensitivity often prevent expatriate managers from fully understanding local conditions.

Mobilizing Resources

To mobilize a global organization's resources, you not only have to understand how and why the organization works, you must be known by the essential corporate decision makers. Getting the attention of the top decision makers in your company is a critical prerequisite for effective global leadership—

without such recognition, you will have a hard time securing control over key organizational resources.

Developing a high profile within the company necessitates that you serve on key global committees, participate in task forces, and attend critical meetings. You must become an active participant in two-way communication networks involving head-office and subsidiary decision makers. It is a mistake to assume that position alone is sufficient to automatically secure these contacts. Substantial personal effort is required on your part.

The importance of personally seizing the initiative is illustrated in the story of two senior managers we met in the course of our research. One gentleman was the European general manager of a Japanese consumer electronics giant. The manager was a British national who, by the time we first met him, had worked for the Japanese parent in Europe for eight years. He was the most senior non-Japanese manager in the company and the first non-Japanese to hold the title of regional vice president. During our meeting, we indicated that we were going to Japan the next week to meet with his boss, who was the worldwide head of consumer electronics for the company. Suddenly the man's face turned red. He seemed very worried. He then asked a favor. "When you see my boss," he said, "can you ask him how I am doing?" We were surprised that this senior manager didn't know himself how he was doing. So we decided to ask several more questions.

Q. How often do you travel to HQ in Japan?

A. Every three months.

Q. Do you speak Japanese?

A. Only enough to get by. I can maybe take a taxi and order a basic meal but that is about it.

Q. When you go to Japan, who do you meet with and what do you talk about?

A. I meet with my boss, the same man you will be visiting next week. He asks questions about our sales targets. But he already knows the numbers. I fax them to him every week. And no matter whether we are on target or not, he says the same thing: "We need to accelerate sales." He never seems impatient. In fact, he is hard to read. I honestly don't know whether he is happy with my performance or not.

Q. Do you sit on any HQ committees?

A. Of course not. All of the meetings are in Japanese.

Q. Does your boss ever ask your opinion on strategic issues?

A. Not really. Headquarters controls product design. They send us the designs just before they introduce a new product in Japan. I can drag my feet on certain products I feel wouldn't go over well in Europe. But basically, I am here to do what they tell me to do.

Q. Do you have much contact with your peers running other regions?

A. We usually have some overlap during my visits to Tokyo. But that's all.

The European general manager felt as if he were working in the dark. He felt insecure as a non-Japanese and, even after eight years with the company, did not know how to read the global organization in general, or his boss more specifically. When we visited his boss in Tokyo the next week, we were surprised by his impressions of the European general manager. "He is doing a fine job," he told us. "I just wish he would take more initiative. He seems reluctant to come forward with ideas for new products. Europe should be playing a much bigger role in our overall global strategy."

Both the British general manager and his Japanese boss seemed disconnected from the global organization. While we could fault the Japanese boss in Tokyo for not really knowing his British subordinate, perhaps more of the fault rested with the British general manager. He took no initiative to assert himself in the global organization. He did not make himself or his ideas known. He waited to be invited in, but by hesitating made himself less attractive to superiors. Unfortunately, within six months of our interview, the British manager left the Japanese company.

Managers only develop organizational credibility *after they first demonstrate* business savvy. Your employees, no matter where they are in the world, must have confidence that what you ask them to do makes good business sense. Too often this is not the case.

Many managers we interviewed in the field indicated that they thought no one at head office was thinking globally. They did not understand the local business or organization. In their minds, they were anything but credible global leaders.

Without credibility, you will never evolve into a leader who can effectively mobilize organizational resources—both within and outside your jurisdiction. A case in point is Eugene Lee, president of Siemens-Asahi of Japan. In the late 1980s, Siemens—which had been exporting medical equipment to Japan for decades—merged its medical equipment business with Asahi Medical in an effort to get into R&D and production in Japan. (Siemens owns two-thirds of Siemens-Asahi; Asahi owns the remaining third.) Mr. Lee talked about the challenges of running a subsidiary and building credibility inside and outside the subsidiary:

> If you are hired to run a subsidiary, you should not have to worry about head office. But in reality, you have to constantly fight for the subsidiary. In Japan, the staff is always watching. If you are not fighting for them and alongside them, you are out in their minds. There will always be negotiations with the parent. Headquarters will always want to get involved . . . . Headquarters wants to be the hub. I have had a lot of fights with HQ. The problem is that if we waited around for HQ to make decisions or come up with ideas, we would have been bankrupt long ago. But it takes time to effectively build a company . . . . As we have built our organization and proven that we know how to run our business, the parent's attitude has shifted from skepticism to support. I now think we can influence Siemens' world strategy, but it is still a constant series of negotiations with HQ.

Accessing Resources. Contacts and credibility are precursors to the actual mobilization of resources. Getting things done requires going out of one's way to call on people outside the normal organization chart who can make things happen. Robyn Mingle, who was director of human resources for the Eastern Hemisphere at Black & Decker in 1996, explained it best:

> Organizational savvy is more than understanding the organization chart. Some of our people are just plain uncomfortable going outside reporting relationships. We believe that sometimes, in order to get things done, you have to pick up the phone and call individuals who don't fit in the normal hierarchical organization chart. There is a hierarchy in organizations that doesn't always work and managers in Asia are just now get-

ting used to working with those unknown relationships. Global teamwork is critical and you may lose the game if you are too narrowly focused on the local organization chart. The name of the game for B&D is to use the resources that are available globally—your impact will be greater.

Exemplar Global Leader:
Tony Wang

One of the best examples of organizational savvy is Ta-Tung (Tony) Wang. Born in Sichuan province in the People's Republic of China in 1944, Wang left with his family for Taiwan when he was five years old. He completed an undergraduate degree in Taiwan and later moved to the United States for graduate work. Upon graduation, he went to work for Kentucky Fried Chicken. In 1986, he was made vice president of KFC Southeast Asia, headquartered in Singapore. From this vantage point, Tony argued to his superiors at corporate headquarters in Kentucky that KFC had a competitive edge over any other major U.S. fast-food chain in developing the Chinese market. Chicken, not beef, was preferred by the Chinese; furthermore, Tony reminded his superiors, the poultry industry was one of the top priorities in China's agriculture modernization program.

With approval from then KFC president Richard Mayer, Tony started an intensive investigation of the food service industry in China. He quickly learned that there was no fast food industry in China and that the supply of chicken was limited and likely to be expensive. He also determined that government investment regulations were "completely impossible for us to understand. In fact, trying to do so is a total waste of time." Not only was it impossible to figure out government regulations, but winning approval for operating licenses, leases, and employment contracts looked like it would be a nightmare, given the disorganized and uninterested Chinese bureaucracy. At this point, Tony could have easily stopped, or called for more research, or waited for greater clarity. Instead, he chose to move forward.

Tony wanted to find a local partner that could provide access to a secure supply of chickens that would meet KFC standards. R. J. Reynolds, which at the time was KFC's parent, had some contacts with the Ministry of Light Industry in Beijing. By tapping into the parent company's contacts,

Tony was led to the Beijing Corporation Animal Production (BCAP). Although BCAP produced breeds of chicken that were approved by KFC, the company had essentially no exposure to Western business or fast food operations; it did not itself have any money to put into the venture; and it had no close contacts with the Beijing city agencies that would be essential to set up the restaurant.

Recognizing BCAP's shortcomings, Tony began searching for another partner with ties to the Beijing bureaucracy. The Beijing Tourist Bureau seemed an ideal choice. It had helped expedite the construction of new hotels in Beijing and had participated as a joint venture partner with Western companies. Tony said of his initial contact with the Tourist Bureau:

> When we first contacted the Tourist Bureau, they were very skeptical. They had been involved in very big projects . . . and were controlling 100 hotels at the time. Many people thought that we wanted them as a partner because of their connection with tourists, but this was never the case. We wanted the Tourist Bureau because they were very well connected, they knew how to work with Western business and because Beijing has a high degree of autonomy in tourist matters.

To convince BCAP and the Tourist Bureau to become KFC's partners, Tony offered a guaranteed 5 percent return on their equity—much better than they were able to get domestically. This move was exceptional, not only for KFC but for the entire industry as well; the credibility he had established with Mayer had earned Tony the freedom to make this unprecedented gesture.

To open a restaurant, KFC needed a "License to Execute a Business Activity." This required signatures from officials of the District government, the Commerce Department, the Taxation Department, the Health Department, and the Food Supply and Logistics Department. Tony knew that these agencies were not coordinated with each other and that approval would be a sequential process. Tony also learned that the license was necessary before a lease could be signed. In 1987, there was no guarantee that a satisfactory location for a store could ever be found; virtually every appropriate building in Beijing was occupied. Furthermore, Chinese regulations stipulated that KFC would have to guarantee the income of any workers left jobless if and when KFC moved into a new facility.

After countless site visits, Wang learned that a three-story building across the street from Tienanmen Square might be available. Securing the location would require the mayor's personal approval and, given its proximity to the Great Hall of the People, quite possibly the effective approval of the Politburo. Wang was uncertain whether the move would prove brilliant or provoke a backlash that might lock KFC out of China for the foreseeable future. To make matters worse, BPAC and the Tourist Bureau were getting cold feet, sharing the fear that a high-profile location might lead to a government backlash. Despite the obstacles, Tony decided to move forward, full speed ahead.

As negotiations proceeded on the building, the city agency that controlled the lease asked Tony for 10 years' rent up front. The fee was $1 million, in cash.

> I asked the local negotiators how they came up with the $1 million number. All they would say is that $1 million was the amount of money it would take to finish the building. My Chinese partners said, "That's crazy. Don't sign." Of course I didn't have signing authority for $1 million from KFC. But I said to them on the spot, "Let's do it." And we did it.

Although Wang did not have signing authority for the amount of money demanded, his commitment of the company to the deal was never questioned. He knew who to call and what to say. The money arrived in Beijing a few days later.

To train KFC-China's new employees, Wang relied heavily on videotapes and printed material produced in Singapore for new hires. He knew exactly where to look for this material. He also had excellent contacts with regional KFC managers and knew who to tap for assignment to Beijing. Familiarity with the personalities of trainers and potential store managers enabled Wang to avoid costly conflicts with local hires and speed the training process.

And the results? According to Wang, "It was a fantastic success. KFC got all its money back in less than a year." How did KFC get its money back when almost all sales and profits were in soft currency RMB? Wang accessed the parent company's world-class counter-trade skills. By this time KFC had been sold to PepsiCo, which also owned Taco Bell and Pizza Hut. Between KFC and these other chains, there was a huge, ongoing need for employee uniforms. Most of KFC's soft currency profits in China were used to buy uniforms for export to the United States and other countries.

Without Wang's global organizational savvy, KFC would never have moved so quickly and so profitably into China. It would never have found such able partners. It would never have secured a lease for one of the most prime locations in Beijing. It would never have trained new employees so quickly. It would never have repatriated profits so effectively.

Interestingly, 18 months after opening the Tienanmen Square restaurant, Wang left KFC. He went on to work in senior executive positions for a number of Asian and American firms. In 1995, Wang left the corporate world to run FICA (Franchise Investment Corporation of Asia) in partnership with American International Group, Inc. (AIG). Among other activities, FICA won franchise rights for Beijing and Shanghai for Kenny Rogers Roasters. This time Wang moved forward without a local Chinese partner. KRR had no experience in China and could provide little support in menu design, pricing, and the supply of key food ingredients. Virtually every decision was left to Wang. In the summer of 1996, Wang opened KRR's first restaurant in Beijing. Soon a second followed, this one with country-western music and a large dance floor. No other KRR restaurant in the world had a dance floor, and Wang did not know of any other establishment in the city with country-western line dancing. When asked if headquarters approved the concept, Wang's response was typical: "I didn't ask. I thought it was a great idea and so I did it." When asked if the concept has been a success, Wang responded: "It has been successful beyond my wildest dreams."

Conclusions

Demonstrating savvy requires that you have a high level of global business and global organizational skills. Savvy involves recognizing new markets and mobilizing organizational resources in a manner that significantly increases shareholder value. Unfortunately, many managers have limited skills in the business of making money for their companies. They lack the interest or motivation. They are weak on organizational skills. They limit their interests to employees and projects close to them, expressing little or no interest in what the company is doing in distant, unfamiliar markets. Furthermore, they dislike internal politics and disdain internal networking. These managers have a place in organizations, performing useful, if narrow, duties and helping sustain their companies' ongoing viability. However, they are not—and perhaps never will be—savvy global business leaders.

Demonstrating global savvy is no easy accomplishment. At one level, it involves factual knowledge of the world of business and of people and organizations. Yet it also demands a level of understanding that is much deeper. While savvy is built on foundations of factual knowledge, it includes a broader understanding of complex relationships and judgments about what is and isn't important.

Companies around the world are struggling to find managers with global business and organizational savvy. Don Sullivan, president of General Motors' Asia Pacific Organization, estimates that he spends 70 percent of his time either hiring or mentoring managers for country and regional jobs in Asia Pacific. A problem for Sullivan is that GM is so large that most managers who are pulled into international assignments have had no profit-and-loss experience, or for that matter, exposure to geographically diverse networks of decision makers. Unless they are lucky, there are few places for them to learn global business and global organizational skills.

General Motors is not atypical of the companies we worked with. Most managers are very limited in their ability to recognize global market opportunities and get the organization to work effectively around the world. While savvy is critical in global leadership, alone it is not enough. Recognizing market opportunities and knowing how to mobilize resources is rarely sufficient to actually win people over. As we have tried to make clear, exhibiting character, embracing duality, and demonstrating savvy are all required.

Notes

1. While research has demonstrated cultural differences in the emphasis companies place on short-term versus long-term value creation, we found that, broadly
defined, value creation is a significant objective in all cultures.

2. See, for example, K. Ohmae (1985), *Triad Power: The Coming Shape of
Global Competition*. New York: The Free Press; W. Holstein (1990), "The Stateless
Corporation." *Business Week*, May 14, pp. 98–104.

3. This point is strongly argued in S. Ghoshal (1987), "Global Strategy: An Organizing Framework." *Strategic Management Journal*, 8, 425–40, and Morrison, A.
(1990), *Strategies in Global Industries: How U.S. Businesses Compete*. Westport, CT:
Quorum Books.

4. As referenced by H. Banks (1997), "Global Deregulation." *Forbes*, May 5,
p. 131.

5. See Doz, Y., Asakawa, K., Santos, J., and Williamson, P. (1996), "The Meta-
national Corporation." Paper presented at the Academy of International Business
Annual Meeting, Banff, Canada, September 26–29.

6. "Trade and Foreign Direct Investment." Report by the WTO Secretariat,
October 9, 1996.

7. For a more complete discussion of economies of scale and scope see D. Teece
(1980), "Economies of Scope and the Scope of the Enterprise." *Journal of Economic Behavior and Organization*, 1, pp. 223–47; S. Chatterjee and B. Wernerfelt
(1991), "The Link between Resources and Types of Diversification: Theory and
Evidence." *Strategic Management Journal*, 12, pp. 33–48.

8. For a discussion of scope advantages through raw material and intermediate
goods markets, see R. Caves and R. Jones (1985), *World Trade and Payments* (4th
ed.). Boston: Little, Brown & Co; M. Porter (1986), "Changing Patterns of International Competition." *California Management Review*, 28, pp. 9–40. For discussions of scope advantages in capital markets, see R. Aliber (1971), "The MNE in a
Multiple-Currency World," in *The Multinational Enterprise*, J. Dunning (ed.).
London: Allen and Unwin; G. Ragazzi (1973), "Theories of the Determinants of
Direct Foreign Investment," *IMF Staff Papers*, July, pp. 471–98; D. Lessard
(1985), "Transfer Prices, Taxes and Financial Markets: Implications of International Financial Transfers within the Multinational Corporation," in D. Lessard
(ed.), *International Financial Management: Theory and Application*, (2nd ed.). New
York: John Wiley & Sons.

9. *World Bank Atlas, 1994*. Washington, D.C.: The World Bank.

10. B. Newman, "Dutch are Invading JFK Arrivals Building and None Too
Soon." *Wall Street Journal*, May 13, 1997, pp. A1, A8.

11. R. Woodward, "The Value of a Growing Airplane Family." From a speech given at the Farnborough International Air Show, September 2, 1996.

12. For more information on GM's international expansion plans, see Blumenstein, R. (1997), "GM Is Building Plants in Developing Nations to Woo New Markets." *Wall Street Journal*, August 4, pp. A1, A5.

13. S. Vachani (1996), "The Boeing Company, 1996." Boston University.

14. For a more complete discussion of transaction cost analysis see D. Williamson (1975), *Markets and Hierarchies*. New York: The Free Press.

15. A. Rugman (1985), "Internalization Is Still a General Theory of Foreign Direct Investment." *Weltwirtschaftliches Archiv*, September, pp. 570–75; C. Galbraith and N. Kay (1986), "Towards a Theory of Multinational Enterprise." *Journal of Economic Behavior and Organization*, 7, pp. 3–19.

three

THE PATH

TO GLOBAL

LEADERSHIP

seven

BECOMING THE NEXT GENERATION OF GLOBAL LEADERS

Now that we have described the key characteristics of effective global leaders, let's examine four powerful ways you can develop them. Our recommendations are based on the research we described earlier, as well as on a recently completed survey of over 100 additional firms concerning their global leadership development activities.

As we mentioned in Chapter 1, virtually all companies need more global leaders than they have, and most need ones of even higher caliber than they have now. You may recall from Chapter 1 that 85 percent of firms feel that they do not have an adequate number of global leaders and 67 percent feel that the global leaders they do have need additional skills and knowledge before they meet company standards.

Since there aren't enough capable global leaders in most companies, the key question for you is: "Do I have to be born with global leadership capabilities or can I develop them?" The strong consensus of opinion from our interviews and surveys is that global leaders are born, *then* made.

Perhaps the easiest way to illustrate this is with an analogy given to us by one of the European managers we interviewed. This manager pointed out that even if someone was born with hands perfectly gifted for playing the violin, that gift would remain unrealized if those hands never held a violin. In addition, the individual's *full* potential might not be realized without opportunity *and* training. A great violinist is the result of superior talent, abundant opportunity, and excellent education and training. However, the best training and all the opportunity in the world can not make someone with ordinary hands into a world-class violinist.

This analogy suggests several points. First, not everyone has the ability to become a global leader, so companies are not likely to give opportunity and education to just anyone. To get the opportunities and education you need, you must demonstrate both interest in and capabilities for global leadership. Second, even with natural talent, you need to recognize opportunities and take advantage of development and training to maximize your potential. Third, even though you may rise steadily toward the top of your organization, the top may not be high enough to give you a worldwide competitive advantage unless you take an active and systematic approach to your development as a future global leader.

The basic mental process of developing into a global leader involves getting your mind around the whole world—not just one country. For most of us, it can take some pretty hard knocks before we are prepared to stretch our minds far enough to accommodate the entire world. Those hard knocks come most often—and most productively—from direct confrontations with new and different terrain. The contrast between the new terrain and the familiar landscape of the past is frequently the catalyst that forces us to redraw our mental maps.

This basic process of redrawing and stretching our mental maps was brought home to all three of us on a recent trip we took to Japan for an international management conference. Since one of our trio, Stewart Black, had lived and worked in Japan before, he decided to take the other two to a traditional Japanese restaurant for dinner. Most traditional Japanese restaurants have similar entry ways. The design consists of a thin wood-and-glass sliding door that opens onto a foyer on the other side. The runners at the bottom of the door, along which it slides, are typically not recessed; patrons must step carefully over them as they enter the restaurant.

Stewart warned both Allen Morrison and Hal Gregersen about the door runners and the need to step over them, so as not to trip. Once they found what looked like a nice, traditional restaurant, Stewart opened the sliding door and carefully stepped inside. Allen, who is about the same height as

Stewart, followed, also making sure to step over the door runner. The next thing anyone knew there was a thunderous crash in the entryway that reverberated throughout the entire restaurant. Everyone inside turned to see what had happened. Hal, who is just over 6'5", on seeing his two colleagues negotiate the entry so easily, had tried to step quickly through the door, only to smash his head on the top of the door frame. The impact had nearly knocked Hal out and caused patrons to wonder momentarily if an earthquake were starting.

The most interesting part of this story is that the next day, when we went to another traditional Japanese restaurant, the exact same thing happened. It wasn't until the third time that Hal remembered that he needed to duck as he entered. In a sense, it took getting smacked in the head hard and twice for Hal to rearrange his thinking about what he needed to do to successfully enter a traditional Japanese restaurant.

Most of us are like Hal in this instance. It takes getting smacked in the head, hard and probably more than once, before we are ready to rearrange our mental maps. Hard knocks to the head are not always pleasant, but they are necessary. They help us see the limits to our mental maps; they help us understand that to become effective global leaders, we must stretch and redraw those same maps. We need to be able to adjust our mindsets in order to embrace the constant dualities and tensions of global and local business demands. We need new maps to help us thrive in the turbulent environment of global business and take action when uncertainty reigns. We need a good shake-up in order to learn how to emotionally connect with people who are different from ourselves and engender their good will. We need broader mental maps to understand people of various ethical frameworks and demonstrate integrity in a way that inspires their trust. And finally, we need new and expanded mental maps in order to hold all the business savvy required to recognize global opportunities and to marshal the worldwide organizational resources necessary to capture those opportunities.

One of the key reasons that inquisitiveness is such a differentiator between successful global leaders and those who struggle with worldwide responsibilities is that it ignites and fuels the motivation to go through this process. Inquisitiveness actually makes head-cracking experiences that rearrange and stretch our minds *fun*.

In our research throughout Europe, North America, and Asia we found that four strategies, when properly used, can develop global leaders: *Travel,*

Teams, Training, and *Transfers.* These "Four T's" are not only development strategies, they are also opportunities to shine and have your global leadership brilliance noticed. In examining these development strategies, keep in mind that companies do *not* believe the Four T's are a means of turning anyone and everyone into effective global leaders; instead, they believe that they are the primary way to maximize the capabilities of *high-potential* individuals.

Development Strategy #1: Travel

In our interviews, many of the individuals we interviewed talked about the power of extensive foreign travel in developing various global leadership characteristics. In particular, many mentioned the power of travel in developing global business savvy and emotional connection. As one manager explained, "There's nothing like being in India to help you understand the opportunities and challenges. Nothing compares to sitting down to dinner with someone from Bombay to help you really relate to them."

Most companies use foreign travel as an important and effective developmental tool. In a study we conducted along with Mark Mendenhall and Gary Oddon, 55 percent of Japanese firms reported that they use extensive foreign travel as a key to developing global leaders, while only 40 percent of European firms and 27 percent of U.S. firms use extensive foreign travel for this purpose. We want to be clear that while Japanese, American, and European executives traveled about the same amount, development expectations of that travel differed significantly across countries.

A manager at a consumer products firm spoke to the issue of how much foreign travel many executives experience:

> Last Monday, I ran into a colleague who had been waltzing around the world for 44 days—a personal best. His dog didn't even know him when he came home. That's the tradeoff. You're on the road to learn the details of the business.

As this quote suggests, logging more miles is not the key for global leadership development. Many people log all the miles they care to, with no free time to use the frequent flier points they accumulate. The key to becoming a global leader is not the *quantity* of foreign travel, but the *quality*. To be effective, travel must put potential global leaders in the middle of the country—its culture, economy, political system, market, and so on—without the corporate cocoon of a Western-style luxury hotel, car and driver, and choreographed itinerary.

For example, an interview with an executive of a large retail store revealed that he had traveled to Japan more than 20 times in the last three years. Each trip was approximately one week long, which translates into a cumulative five months in Japan. In that amount of time, this individual could have acquired substantial insights and knowledge about a wide variety of Japanese cultural, economic, and political issues. However, as the conversation progressed, it became clear that the executive did not really understand the country at all. Further probing into his past visits revealed that the executive was always met at the airport, always stayed at the same luxury hotel, always had a car and driver to take him to appointments, always had a bilingual employee with him, and always had his entire itenerary set up by the local office prior to his arrival. In short, this executive had experienced the same week 20 times. In spite of the opportunity the frequent trips to Japan provided, this self-created cocoon guaranteed that little learning would take place.

John Pepper, CEO at Procter & Gamble, sets a completely different example for his employees. Rather than insulating himself behind the typical perks of limousines and dutiful staffers, John Pepper tries to visit five families in each country to which he travels. He wants to talk with the families and learn how they use household products. Typically, he visits these families *before* he ever goes to his hotel or office. His actions communicate the message that international travel should be used as an opportunity to learn more about the various countries, cultures, and consumers that make up P&G's global marketplace. His travels in France helped him rearrange his mental map concerning the French preference for front-load washers and their resistance to top-load washers. This in turn helped him embrace the duality of managing a new cold-water detergent brand on a global basis, while at the same time finding a way to meet the local needs of getting the detergent to distribute evenly throughout the wash when used in front-load washers. Eventually, this led to an innovative solution. The company developed a new system based on a plastic ball, designed to be filled with detergent and placed in a front-load washer along with the dirty clothes.

During the wash cycle, the detergent is distributed evenly through small holes in the ball.

International travel can be made more effective in developing global leaders in two specific ways: (1) taking detours and (2) getting wet.

Since contrasts are often the things that help us stretch and rearrange our mental maps, it is important to get off the beaten path and take detours. The following quote from a senior executive in a British oil company reflects how effective global leaders approach travel as a developmental opportunity:

> When I travel, I try to experiment as much as possible. When I am in Beijing, I like finding someone who can take me down the dirty back alley. I like going to grungy local restaurants and back alley bars. I don't want to take the tourist route. Recently, when I was in Turkmenistan, I asked our guy to take me to the local market and then to a local bar. I loved it. I ask people unconstrained questions: Why do you do that? How do you do that? Sometimes they are offended, but often they are extremely pleased that you asked.

Getting wet really amounts to diving deep into the waters of the society in terms of what shopping, education, homes, and so on, are really like for the people who live there. This is in effect what John Pepper accomplishes by visiting the homes of real people rather than having local office staffers provide reams of market research data on living styles. If you want to get wet, look for opportunities to engage all your senses—sight, hearing, smell, taste, and touch. Engaging all your senses makes the difference between merely observing and actually experiencing a new place when you travel to it.

At 3M, Margaret Alldredge described how managers are encouraged to dive deep into the society and learn as much as possible from their travels so they can share their insights with others. 3M has formalized a process for disseminating the lessons gained from international travel. After an international trip, the traveler organizes a "brown bag lunch" to present what he or she has learned about the country visited. Knowing that one must make a presentation enhances the motivation to extract lessons worthy of presenting to peers back home, and as a consequence, enhances the level of learning during international trips. In addition, the presentations facilitate vicarious learning within the firm and enable others to build from a higher base of knowledge when going abroad.

As you think over the international trips you've taken, and future trips you may anticipate, consider the following questions:

1. What "detours" have you taken or plan to take relative to
   - eating (shops, open markets, stores)?
   - lodging (hotels, inns, apartments)?
   - recreation (sports, camping, hiking)?
   - entertainment (theater, dance, music)?
   - shopping (markets, stores, centers)?

2. How deeply have you plunged into the country in terms of
   - people's homes?
   - transportation?
   - religion?
   - education?
   - cultural activities?
   - government and politics?

In summary, foreign travel must be somewhat frequent if it is to be used as a global leadership development tool; however, whether your company has a formal program such as 3M's or not, you need to take steps to enhance the *quality* of what you learn from your travels. Take detours. Be willing to venture off the beaten path. The fact that a path is beaten means it's unlikely you'll learn something on it that competitors don't already know. Remember, if you do what you've always done, you'll learn what you already know.

Development Strategy #2: Teams

Most executives we interviewed regard working in global teams as an even more powerful developmental strategy than travel. This is primarily because the intense and prolonged interaction with individuals of different backgrounds in a team context presents one with constant opportunities to face different or contrasting terrain in terms of values, business models, decision-making norms, and leadership paradigms. This mode of intense and prolonged contrast forces team members to examine their own values and business paradigms, a process that is easier to avoid on short international trips. On international trips, you can easily seek a safe harbor from the strange smells, words, traditions, and perspectives by never leaving the familiar surroundings of the local Hilton Hotel or Hard Rock Cafe. When you are part of a task force, safe harbors are harder to come by.

We found that 60 to 70 percent of European and American executives felt that global task forces or project teams composed of diverse members (e.g., functional background, nationality, culture, ethnicity) were an important developmental strategy. In contrast, only 20 percent of Japanese executives felt this way. This may reflect the history and practice of most Japanese firms, which use project teams composed almost exclusively of Japanese nationals even when the project's scope is global in nature.

Black & Decker Eastern Hemisphere illustrates the effective use of teams. Four years ago Black & Decker successfully implemented a new, 360-degree performance appraisal feedback system in the United States. Two years later the president of Black & Decker Eastern Hemisphere, Tracy Billbrough, had a team of executives examine whether the 360 system should be implemented in the region. The team represented human resources, operations, finance, marketing, and sales, as well as different nationalities in the region. Cultural issues such as Asia's stronger orientation toward hierarchy—and the associated lower level of comfort subordinates felt about giving feedback to their superiors—made the decision one that required careful consideration. In the end, the division went ahead with the 360 system and successfully implemented it by making a number of modifications for a better fit with the local environment.

Tracy felt that the team experience helped him better understand how to emotionally connect with people from different cultural backgrounds. He said it also raised his awareness of how important emotional connections were in inspiring the goodwill and effort required for successful implementation. In conclusion, he noted that the experience helped him gain a deeper understanding of how to balance the tensions of global integration (such as the corporate drive for a performance and appraisal system that would apply around the world) with local adaptation (such as the decision to ensure confidentiality by literally shredding subordinates' written feedback concerning their superiors once it had been analyzed by the human resources department).

In thinking about past or future global task force or project team opportunities, consider the following questions:

1. How much experience have you and your team members had working with people
   - of different cultural backgrounds?
   - of different functional backgrounds and training?
   - of different company backgrounds (company size, industry, life cycle)?

2. How much training and education have you and your team members had relative to
   - general team dynamics?
   - cross-cultural communication?
   - multicultural and cross-functional team effectiveness?

As these basic questions suggest, adequate experience, education, and training among the team members are critical factors in successful global teams. In our experience and travels we have seen debris from numerous global teams that crashed and burned because the members were thrown into the situation without adequate experience or training. You wouldn't send a Piper Cub pilot to fly a 747. Both are airplanes flown by pilots, but there is a qualitative difference just as there is between domestic and global task forces and teams. So always be sure you understand how large a leap is expected of you. Be certain you have adequate training for the global team challenges you do take on.

Development Strategy #3: Training

Most of the executives we interviewed indicated that formal training seminars and programs play a central role in their global leadership development. This is because good training can provide an intense experience within the context of a structured learning environment. Real experiences such as travel and teamwork are rich in lessons to be learned, but their real-time nature can frustrate all but the most determined attempts to reflect on and learn from them. By its very nature, training is based on explicit lessons, facilitating the learning process for participants.

From a company perspective, training is viewed as a powerful developmental tool for high-potential employees. A large majority of the firms in the survey plan to increase the money spent on programs designed to "globalize" their management and executive ranks. Virtually no firms planned to reduce their investment in global leadership development programs.

Recently, Sunkyong, a Korean conglomerate with $25 billion in annual revenue, launched its "Global Leader Program" as a key vehicle for training its future global leaders. The program draws participants from all of Sunkyong's worldwide business and includes both classroom and action learning experiences. In a recent global action learning project, teams of participants went to China to examine liquid natural gas opportunities and challenges. Upon their return, participants presented their findings to senior management. Among a variety of things they discovered, perhaps the most valuable was learning that the Chinese government often based its recommendations of potential business partners not on compatility or competence, but on political expediency. Having learned this, Sunkyong did some extra homework on a potential partner the Chinese government was backing for a joint venture, helping them avoid a costly mistake.

Y. S. Kim, one of the participants we spoke to, felt that exposure to various people through the company-provided training program enhanced his organizational savvy. He came to know people and their capabilities throughout the company. He expressed confidence that he could draw on this understanding and the far-flung resources in the worldwide company to tackle future complex projects that exceeded the capabilities of his immediate set of subordinates.

In looking at the programs your company offers, you should consider the following themes: (1) Participants, (2) Content, and (3) Process.

Participants

Look for programs in which participants come from outside your home country. Fortunately, companies increasingly bring managers and executives together from throughout their worldwide operations. While many firms still offer "regional programs" that draw participants primarily from within a region, the clear trend is toward offering global programs. For example, Exxon conducts its "Global Leadership Workshop" for high-potential managers twice a year and draws only half of the 30 participants in each program from the United States. The rest come from its affiliates throughout the world. In addition to drawing in participants from around the world, IBM has also conducted an eight-day program at its training sites outside the United States. A typical program involving 26 to 30 participants will have 13 to 16 different nationalities represented.

For managers at companies anywhere, the value of attending programs with international participants include the following:

- International participants have different perspectives and practices. This helps people open their minds and embrace new perspectives.
- Participants from different countries have knowledge about customers, competitors, governments, markets, and economies that can be of value to each other.
- The networking and relationship building opportunity the program provides facilitates the sharing of valuable information long after people return home. This can greatly strengthen a firm's efforts to coordinate and integrate its worldwide activities.
- Participants develop a much broader perspective on their company's global challenges and opportunities.

We did, however, find regional differences in terms of the emphasis placed on training programs. European firms place more emphasis on executive education and training than do either American or Asian firms. Interestingly, of all the major nations, Japanese firms place the least emphasis on executive training, while Korean firms spend a higher proportion of revenue on executive education and development than any other national group of companies. Korean managers spend an average of 14 days a year in education and training programs. European firms also place a much stronger emphasis on seminars and programs with in-company participants than do American or Asian firms.

Content

In terms of content, you should look for programs on the following topics:
- global vision and strategy;

- designing and structuring organizations;
- process reengineering;
- management of change; and
- global team leadership and effectiveness.

First, look for programs that address how effective *global vision and strategy* are formulated and communicated. This relates to the Global Business Savvy and Global Organizational Savvy elements of the global leadership model. As you seek out or are presented with training opportunities, you may want to pay special attention to programs designed to enhance global analytical abilities. Leaders cannot generate inspiring visions if they miss important global, competitive, economic, social, or political drivers.

Second, look for programs that examine *designing and structuring organizations* for global reach. Successfully positioning a corporation in the international marketplace calls for a deep understanding of the tensions between global integration and local responsiveness. In most companies, both approaches are necessary. Global integration capitalizes on economies of scale, scope, and opportunities for reduced costs. Local responsiveness is also required because customers in different countries and regions do not have identical preferences and tastes. In many industries, customer demand for customized features and services has, if anything, increased. This theme relates directly to the Global Organizational Savvy, Balancing Tensions, and Embracing Uncertainty dimensions of the global leadership model.

Third, look for programs that focus on *process reengineering*. Technology, especially information technology, makes it possible to totally redesign not just jobs, but entire business processes, thereby making possible quantum leaps in productivity and added value. This theme relates to the Global Organizational Savvy dimension in our global leadership model. In addition, information technology can sometimes help you balance the tensions between global integration and local responsiveness.

Fourth, look for programs that examine the effective *management of change*. In today's business environment, the only constant is change. While you can lay out new directions, visions, or strategies with relative ease, none of these make any difference unless they are well executed. Consequently, a key difference between winners and losers in the marketplace rests not so much on the content of particular strategies but on the ability to execute and implement change. This relates to the dimensions of Embracing Uncertainty and Global Organizational Savvy in the model.

Fifth, seek out programs that examine *global team leadership and effectiveness*. The increasing complexity of the business environment dictates that one person cannot know all the requirements. Cross-functional and cross-cultural teams are and will become an ever bigger part of organizational life. The ability to lead these teams effectively is becoming a critical differentiator between winners and losers in the marketplace. This theme relates most directly to your skill at Emotional Connection, which you will rely on as a global leader.

Process

Our analysis of company training programs also revealed two important process trends. The first is the increased emphasis on learning partnerships. Many firms are decreasing the use of "canned" programs, whether provided by universities or consulting firms. Increasingly, companies want customized programs and are working with proven external providers who deliver the desired content and work effectively in partnership with clients.

Consortium programs are an interesting outcome of this tendency to customize programs developed with partners. For example, we are involved with several consortia. These consortia typically have six to eight member firms. Member firms share the following characteristics:

- They currently have international operations.
- They seek to expand their global presence.
- They highly value the development of future global leaders.
- They do not compete directly with each other.

Each firm has a representative on the consortium's advisory board. We work with the advisory board to design a program that meets the general and common global leader development needs of all participating firms. Typical participants have the following in common:

- They are nominated and selected internally by each member firm.
- They have high potential for significant leadership responsibilities.
- They occupy now or will occupy in the near future positions with international responsibilities.

- They demonstrate a strong commitment to learning and further personal development.
- They come from throughout the firm's divisional, functional, and geographic units.
- They are typically 30 to 50 years old.

The typical consortium has the following structural characteristics:

- Member firms send approximately five participants to each program.
- Each program is usually two weeks long.
- Member firms make an initial two-year commitment to the consortium.
- Programs are run between two and four times each year, so a given firm sends a total of 20 to 40 participants over two years.
- Each firm selects one representative to serve on the advisory board.
- The advisory board meets two times a year to review program content and structure and provide input into upcoming programs.

Firms which do not have comprehensive systems for developing future global leaders and which do not have scores of high-potential managers find the consortium approach highly effective at meeting their needs. While as an individual you may not be in a position to decide if your firm participates in a consortium, you may be able to introduce the idea to key decision makers, and benefit by being one of the initial set of participants.

Companies in consortium programs cite several reasons for their participation in lieu of more traditional, "in-house" programs. First and foremost, companies cite cross-fertilization: the opportunity for their high-potential employees to be exposed to individuals from other industries. The fact that none of the firms involved compete with each other allows for in-depth discussion of challenges and best practices. In addition, participants are able to leverage the relationships developed during the program long after its formal conclusion. Companies also like the consortium approach because it lowers the per participant costs by leveraging the collective purchasing power of all the consortium firms.

A second process trend is the increased emphasis on "action learning"—the exact definition of which varies from firm to firm. In general, however, action learning involves some project, case, or exercise that relates to the real problems, challenges, or opportunities the firm and program participants face. For example, we worked with TRW to design its Global Leadership Program, which has three distinct segments conducted over approximately six months, including a trip to an important emerging economy and an examination of a strategically important company challenge there. The projects were defined and sponsored by TRW's president, Peter Hellman.

Summary

You should consider several points concerning training as a method of developing global leadership skills. First, training programs can be a powerful development approach. You should take advantage of and seek out the best opportunities your company has to offer. Second, look for opportunities to interact with participants from throughout your firm's worldwide operations. Seek out one to two weeks of training every year. Third, seek out programs that emphasize international strategy and vision, organizational structure and design, process reengineering, change management, and global team leadership. Fourth, pay special attention to programs developed in partnership with your firm, including consortium programs. Finally, look for programs that have action-learning components to them. Placing yourself in programs with these attributes will enhance your global leadership development through training.

Development Strategy #4: Transfers

When we talked with exemplar global leaders, we asked them a very simple question: "What has been the most powerful experience in your life for developing global leadership capabilities?" Given the diversity of the respondents in terms of nationality, functional experience, and educational background, we were amazed at the consistency of response. *Eighty percent of these individuals identified living and working in a foreign country as the single most influential developmental experience in their lives.* This is a remarkable consensus, given the respondents' diversity of nationalities, functional experiences, and educational backgrounds.

The Power of International Transfers

International assignments are the most powerful means of developing global leaders because (1) working in a foreign country provides mind-stretching experiences and (2) because those experiences are hard, if not impossible, to avoid. An international trip might be three weeks long, but many international assignments are three years long. Unlike the short-term experiences of travel, you do not have the option of waiting things out and avoiding the real fabric and texture of the country and culture. You cannot retreat into familiar territory when the workday is done, as you can in many global teams. During an international assignment, whether at home or at work, you are constantly surrounded by new, unfamiliar, and often unsettling terrain. Unlike training programs, international assignments do not provide the safety of a simulated environment. During an international assignment, you have to grapple with real people, real problems, real goals, and real consequences for success or failure.

While these sometimes bruising, head-rattling experiences are inevitable during an international assignment, individuals react in different ways and not every person gains the potential developmental benefits. There are four basic reactions to something like smacking your head against the doorways of an unfamiliar restaurant: (1) "duh," (2) "ouch," (3), "hum," and (4) "aha!" Each is quite telling in terms of an individual's global leadership potential.

Individuals with zero latent global leadership potential are easy to spot during international assignments because they don't even realize that they've run up against the new and unexpected. They smack their heads, rell around a moment ("duh") and then plow forward, oblivious to what has happened. As a consequence, they learn nothing that might help them with future global leadership responsibilities.

Those with the "ouch" response realize they've smacked their heads but end up changing their worldviews little or not at all. They have little global leadership potential because they put the pieces back together just as they were before they were shaken up. As a consequence of such thick-headed-ness, these individuals don't learn even the most basic cross-cultural or country-specific lessons, let alone any advanced global business lessons.

There is some hope for the third group. When they smack their heads, not only do they realize it but they react by saying, "Hmm. What can I learn from this?" This reaction reflects at least a moderate amount of global leadership potential because these people will at least learn to duck once they've smacked their heads a few times. That is, individuals with some global leadership potential at least learn country-specific lessons. For example, living in France for three years, they learn how to negotiate with French unions or deal with French bureaucrats. They come to understand that things get done differently in France than at home. Individuals with a moderate amount of global leadership potential recognize that the mental maps they grew up with are not always universally applicable. Learning these country-specific lessons and allowing for changes in one's mental maps make for a good country specialist, but do not guarantee that the person will develop into a great global leader.

Individuals with great global leadership potential react very differently to jarring unforeseen circumstances. They are the "aha" people. That is, when smacked in the head, individuals with global leadership talent *do not* ignore the shake-up, *do not* merely reconstruct their original mental maps, and *do not* just create unique mental maps for each new country specific situation. People with global leadership talent say, "Aha! I just smacked my head. This is good! This means there is something to learn." This reaction unfreezes their minds and disrupts their mental maps. When these individuals put things back together, they do so in a different way. Individuals with great global leadership talent create "modifiable" general maps. Instead of drawing a mental map that says, "When in Japan, duck upon entering a restaurant," they create mental maps that say, "When moving around the globe, check the height of doorframes and duck when necessary."

In other words, high potential global leaders identify variables that seem to change from country to country and that have important consequences. *They create a general map, but do not expect it to be accurate in all specific situations.* Rather, they know it is contingent and have identified those factors that are likely to change, and whose change can have a significant impact.

As a consequence, individuals with high global leadership potential not only learn country-specific lessons while on assignment, but they move beyond them to broader perspectives. They learn that *what works in one country doesn't necessarily work in another* and that *what is a mistake and doesn't work in one country is not necessarily a mistake or won't work in another.* High-potential individuals learn this not only at an intellectual level but at a behavioral level. That is, they can do more than merely spout these phrases—they actually change their behavior and worldview.

Given this mental process, it is easier to see why international transfers are such a powerful developmental experience. As a senior manager in Sunkyong emphasized, "Nothing can compare to living and working in a foreign country in terms of what has shaped my global business perspective." The daily challenge of living and working in a foreign country virtually guarantees a few hard knocks, and therefore the opportunity to exhibit and develop this adaptive mental map-making process. This is why future global leaders might be best thought of as global explorers, because they constantly forge into new frontiers and update mental maps of the territory. This is the essence of the developmental power of international transfers.

Enhancing the Effectiveness of International Transfers

Given the power of an international assignment in developing your global leadership capabilities, we should encourage you to take the next available overseas position you can, but we must also caution you. When it comes to international assignments, most U.S. firms are mediocre at best and often quite poor at selecting, training, sending, and repatriating managers. The costs that firms and individuals bear because of poor international assignment policies and practices can be quite severe. For example, each failed assignment costs an average of $250,000 in direct expenses, such as moving, transfer, and travel.[1] Furthermore, this figure does not begin to take into account the indirect costs of damaged reputations, dissatisfied customers, demoralized employees, and missed business opportunities.

For most firms, these problems are only the tip of the iceberg. From our research, we know that 20 to 30 percent of those who stay the full term of their assignments are nevertheless considered unsatisfactory performers (or "brownouts") by their companies. Given the high costs of expatriates (an average of $400,000 a year for salary, housing allowances, cost of living adjustments, and other expenses), a firm with just 300 expatriates could be wasting $30–$40 million annually on unsatisfactory performers. Bringing these people home, however, may not solve the problem. In many cases, capable local managers have not been developed. Bringing brownouts home without capable local replacements can make a bad situation worse.

But the problems don't stop with failed assignments or brownouts. On average, one in four managers returning from a successful assignment leaves the firm within a year after repatriation. Not only must the firm spend time and money to replace the individual, but it receives no long-term return on the $1 million or more it has invested during the average three-year assignment.

All these problems can combine to set off a vicious circle that can erode or even destroy a firm's global competitive advantage.

- Failed international assignments, rumors of brownouts, and repatriation turnover problems can lead the best and brightest throughout the organization's worldwide operations to view international assignments as the "kiss of death" for their careers.
- This "kiss of death" problem makes it difficult to recruit and send top-quality candidates, and this in turn increases the likelihood of more failures.
- This decreasing quality of candidates and performance can cause the firm to send fewer and fewer people outside their home countries on assignment, which in turn can lead to coordination and control problems as well as information exchange problems.
- Ultimately, this vicious circle can lead to a dearth of future global leaders with vital international understanding and experience. This in turn can in turn lead to even poorer strategic planning and implementation and to an ever-worsening global competitive position.

Many managers and executives no doubt feel that such a dire scenario is unlikely in their own firms. For those who are not vigilant, however, the price is high because this type of vicious circle can easily start and is nearly impossible to stop. All things considered, we are left with several conclusions:

- There is no substitute for the development power of an international assignment. (In fact, in some firms, such as Motorola and Samsung, an international assignment is now a requirement to get into top management positions.)
- Many companies do a poor job of setting you up for success in an international assignment.
- You can do a variety of things to manage a successful international assignment and maximize its global leadership-development potential.

Accepting

There are two keys to selecting and accepting the right international assignment. The first is to begin with the end in mind: ask yourself, "How will I use and leverage this international experience down the road?" Without a good answer to this question, you may still successfully complete a given assignment, but lose most of the assignment's developmental potential. The second key is to ensure that you and your family are in a solid position to adjust successfully to living and working in the foreign country. Figure 7.1 provides a list of questions addressing factors that research has linked to successful cross-cultural adjustment and performance. The more questions you can answer "yes" to, the greater the likelihood of your success overseas. A predominance of "yes" answers is particularly important if the answer to the last question is "no," that is, if you will be going to a country with a culture quite different from that of your home country. The greater the difference in culture, the more important are the personal family, job, and organization factors of success.

Personal Factors

- *Technical skills*—Do you have knowledge of the tasks and technical information required by the assignment?
- *Managerial skills*—Do you have the general ability to work effectively with and through others?
- *Low ethnocentricity*—Do you have a strong tendency to tolerate other beliefs and behaviors and not insist that your way is by definition superior to that of all others?
- *Flexibility*—Do you tend to try new food, activities, forms of entertainment, etc., and can you easily replace old favorites with new ones when the old ones are not available?
- *Willingness to communicate*—Do you persist in efforts to understand and be understood independent of foreign language fluency?
- *Sociability*—Do you tend to be comfortable in new social situations and seek out mentors who can provide guidance and feedback?
- *Conflict Resolution*—Do you tend to keep both your own and others' true objectives in mind and seek out solutions to conflicts which can satisfy each party's objectives?

Family Factors
- Is your spouse willing and excited to go?
- If you have any children, are they over the age of 13, and are they excited to go?

Job Factors
- Job discretion—Will you have freedom to decide what goals to pursue and how to achieve them in the overseas job?
- Job clarity—Do you know what is expected in terms of task outcomes?
- Low job conflict—Are there few conflicting or competing expectations?

Organizational Factors
- Predeparture training—Will you receive at least two days of both general cross-cultural training and country-specific training prior to leaving for the international assignment?
- Postarrival training—Will you receive at least three days of logistical, job-related, and culture training during the first six months after you arrive?

Environmental Factors
- Will you be going to a host country that has a culture quite similar to your home country culture?

Figure 7.1   Factors Influencing Successful International Assignments

Training

Many U.S. executives assume that business is business and good management is good management, so a candidate who has been successful in the United States will succeed in France, Hong Kong, Brazil, or anywhere else. As a consequence,

- Only 40 percent of American firms offer any predeparture cross-cultural training for their global managers (a figure half that of Japanese, Korean, and European firms).
- Even at those firms that do offer cross-cultural training, the training is not very rigorous in nature—averaging only a half-day in length.

- Eighty percent of U.S. firms do not provide training for spouses.
- Few U.S. firms offer any significant cross-cultural or country-specific training *after* arrival in the international post.

However, business is *not* simply business, and what made you a success in New York will *not* necessarily lead to success in Hong Kong. Furthermore, well-designed cross-cultural training programs enhance your job performance, speed your adjustment to the new culture, and improve the development of cross-cultural managerial skills.

In general, training effectiveness requires matching the training approach to your specific situation. Three factors can call for more extensive predeparture and postarrival training. First, examine the difference in the underlying values and ways of doing business between your "home country" and "destination country" (often called *cultural toughness*). Second, examine the degree to which you will be called upon to internet personally with members of the local populace such as employees, government officials, customers, and suppliers (often called *communication toughness*). Third, analyze the extent to which the new job is different from what you have done in the past (often called *job toughness*).

In considering your training needs, however, do not limit yourself to just predeparture training. While important, it has its limitations. Predeparture training should focus mostly on basic, day-to-day, survival-level concerns, because you and your family will encounter these issues as soon as you step off the plane. As time passes in the new country, you and your family will need less training on day-to-day survival issues and will, instead, need an understanding of the deeper cultural aspects of the country. While you should get some cultural training prior to an international assignment, in-depth cross-cultural training is most effectively delivered *after* you are "in-country." Mastery of "culturally tough" concepts does not automatically come with time. Thus, postarrival training is needed to help you master these elements. Postarrival training is particularly effective because:

- You will be more motivated to learn because you will have since bumped into the more subtle and important aspects of the culture.
- You will have direct experience with the local culture, which will provide you with a foundation for learning deeper cultural values, norms, and ideas.

- You will be in an environment where you can immediately apply in the workplace what you learn in the training seminar.
- You will be in an environment that itself lends a "reality" factor to the training content that does not exist when training is undertaken in the home country prior to the assignment.

In terms of timing, most predeparture training should be completed a month before departure, and in-country training should not begin in earnest until you have spent two to four weeks in the country. This is because just before and immediately after arriving overseas, you and your family will be overwhelmed by all the logistics of the move and have little energy or attention to focus on retaining knowledge from the training programs.

Adjusting

Support and contact with the home office during the international assignment is critical. Too many expatriates feel "out-of-sight and out-of-mind," and this usually results in repatriation turnover problems. We have several recommendations to help you adjust, gain support during the assignment, and ensure that you can leverage it into greater global leadership opportunities:

- **Stay connected**. Even though you may be tempted to take "home leave" and go off with your family to new and exciting countries for vacation, make sure that all of you have time periodically to remain connected to people back home. Repatriation adjustment at work and home will be difficult anyway, so take the time to reduce the "out-of-sight and out-of-mind" phenomenon.
- **Find some anchors**. Throughout the assignment, it is important to maintain some anchors, such as writing in a journal, exercise, religious worship, or other familiar pursuit, to keep things on a somewhat even keel.
- **Get a cultural mentor**. You need someone—preferably a host country national—who knows all the cultural road signs and traffic rules, and can both guide you and give you feedback as you form new mental maps and behavior patterns.

Repatriating

Repatriation may be the least talked about and most difficult aspect of international transfers. Without effective repatriation, you will have difficulty taking full advantage of your overseas experience as a global leader. As noted before, approximately 25 percent of managers completing successful international assignments leave their firm within a year after coming home. The following quotes reflect why the repatriation problems are so severe:

> Coming back home was more difficult than going abroad because you expect changes when going overseas. It was real culture shock during repatriation. I was an alien in my home country. My own attitudes had changed, so that it was difficult to understand my own old customs. Old friends had moved, had had children, or had just vanished. Others were interested in our experiences, but only sort of. They couldn't understand our experiences overseas or they just envied our way of life.
>
> —*Expatriate spouse returning from three-year assignment in Vietnam*

> If you look at repatriation as a "homecoming," you're setting yourself up for failure. My company left me dangling in the wind, so to speak. I think that is wrong. I took a real demotion when we came home. No one in the company volunteered anything. I had to initiate everything. I fell through the cracks in the system—if indeed there was a repatriation system in this company. Why can't companies deal more efficiently and compassionately with employees returning from overseas assignments?
>
> —*American expatriate returning from a four-year assignment*

To some top executives and line managers (especially those without international experience), these comments may seem a bit overstated; however, 60 percent of American expatriates experience "reverse culture shock" during repatriation more severe than the original culture shock they experienced when they went overseas.

Many expatriates and their families expect a "hero's welcome" after returning home from a successful international assignment. However, most are lucky to receive *any* welcome at all. In fact, one American expatriate told us that he actually lost his "identity" during repatriation. Apparently he did not exist on his own company's records for three months after his return. He found out about the problem from a credit firm when he was denied two critical loans (house and car) because he was unemployed! While this might seem like an atypical case, it is not. In fact, if you are like most expatriates returning home to America, you will be functionally unemployed when your airplane lands. You might be on the company's records, but you may no longer have a real position in the firm.

Monsanto has been often cited for the attention it pays to repatriation issues, and the company now has a one-day repatriation program that all employees must attend. Samsung, though it has not received the same kind of recognition, places an even greater emphasis on repatriation issues. All returning Samsung managers spend one *month* in a repatriation program designed to help them understand the dynamics of "reverse culture shock," and to capture the lessons learned while overseas. Samsung has created a giant database in which information about various countries, cultures, governments, competitors, and markets is extracted from each and every returning manager during the one-month repatriation program.

Returning expatriates at most U.S. firms are not lucky enough to have such programs available and so must rely more on their own resources. Individuals who succeed at repatriation and use international assignments to develop their global leaderships capabilities do several things right that most do wrong. Figure 7.2 is a list of what you should do; the manager quotes reflect how things usually go for most people.

Keys to Repatriation Success

- **Look for a sponsor to help with placement and reentry into the firm.**

  No one accepted responsibility for placing me back in the organization. I ended up without a job when I was expecting a promotion! My wife also gave up her job with the same company to go overseas (she had 12 years of experience). We were promised a job for her upon our return. Again, no one has helped us find one.

  —*Expatriate with 15 years of experience in the parent company*

- **Plan your repatriation three to six months ahead.**

  After being home three months I am still waiting for a permanent office. All this after 30 years of experience in the company and three international assignments!

  —European expatriate

- **Locate a suitable position.**

  When I was overseas, I felt I had an impact on the business. In the U.S., I feel as though the impact—if any—is minimal. When I came home, I was assigned to a newly created, undefined staff job where I had no friends, no contacts, and no access to management. Firms need to realize that expatriates have developed independent decision-making skills, become accustomed to having final authority, and conditioned to having their business judgment given a lot of credibility by top management. In my new job, my business judgment is much less valued than when I was overseas. Until firms change, expatriates should expect the worst when coming home to avoid disappointment.

  —American expatriate with a large commercial bank

- **Allow yourself some "downtime" upon repatriation.**

  I arrived home on Tuesday and started work on Wednesday. I haven't adjusted yet to much of anything and really feel depressed. I worked fourteen-hour days, six days a week. There was little time to look for housing, yet the company still pressured me to move out of a hotel in order to get me off the "expense" status.

  —Japanese expatriate

- **Request repatriation training.**

  We received absolutely no training or orientation concerning common repatriation adjustment problems. Just knowing about them and having a few ideas of how to effectively cope would have been of great value to us and to the company in terms of my performance.

  —Expatriate returning from Japan

- **Set realistic return expectations.**

  I went on my foreign assignment to the U.K. as a favor for the department. In return I received nothing special for the 10 months I spent away from my family and the hardship I put them through. I really expected a promotion after coming back home and did not receive it.

  —European expatriate

- **Consider family adjustment issues and the spillover effect on work.**

  My spouse has had a very difficult time coming home from Europe and living in the suburbs of America. She hates it. Her adjustment difficulty has made my life less than wonderful and my work performance less than excellent.

  —American expatriate

- **Search out opportunities to utilize your international experience.**

  Firms must value international expertise—not only appreciate it but actually put it to good use. Don't let a corporate headquarters' environment destroy the lessons, "business savvy," negotiation skills, and foreign language proficiencies which expatriates learned from the real world—a global marketplace.

  —Japanese expatriate

- **Seek out a return job with reasonable autonomy.**

  If you have been the orchestra conductor overseas, it is very difficult to accept a position as second fiddle when coming home.

  —American expatriate recently returned from the United Kingdom

Figure 7.2 Keys to Repatriation Success

Recommendations

So how can the Four T's make an impact on your development as a global leader throughout your career? We examine this question in more detail in the next chapter. Still, we should emphasize several points here.

First, even though we place the burden of responsibility for development on the individual's shoulders, we believe that senior executives have a responsibility to make sure that the company has both the quantity and quality of leaders it needs in order to ensure prosperity for years to come. Recently, Jack Welch of GE expressed this same sentiment this way, "Headquarters at GE doesn't run companies. It runs a school that teaches how to run companies, and does it so well that GE maintains a huge trade surplus in talent. That's my job. We spend all our time on people. The day we screw up the people thing, this company is over."[2]

Second, there seems to be little substitute for an international assignment in terms of developing the mindset needed for global leadership responsibilities. Because many organizations do not think about international assignments from a systematic or strategic development perspective, you must make sure that you do. Two excellent books covering these issues in detail are *So You're Going Overseas: A Handbook for Personal and Professional Success* and *So You're Coming Home* from Global Business Publishers (www.contact CGA.com, 1-888-446-4685). Not all international assignments are of equal strategic value for the organization or your personal development. In general, look for assignments that will give you the opportunity to link the local operation to regional and corporate headquarters. Technology transfers are especially likely to provide opportunities to integrate and coordinate activities between the local unit and regional or worldwide units. Think carefully about accepting an assignment that will put you out in the "wilderness" with little reason to coordinate with others. While this type of assignment and autonomy can be very enjoyable and personally rewarding, it is a better route for someone who wants to become a country specialist than for those who want to develop broader, global perspectives.

Third, take advantage of formal training and education opportunities that focus on international aspects of business. Especially seek out programs that draw participants from a variety of functional and geographic backgrounds. To the extent possible, also seek out programs that give you an opportunity to interact with individuals from other companies and industries.

Don't just wait for someone to nominate you for a program. Use your knowledge of your organization to suggest, appropriately and proactively, educational programs that can help you increase your global leadership capabilities.

Fourth, although it may not always be possible, seek cross-cultural and cross-functional team membership experiences before you seek out or accept cross-cultural and cross-functional leadership opportunities. If you do have the opportunity to lead a cross-cultural and cross-functional team, be sure to assess members' knowledge and skills relative to global team dynamics. Do not assume that all the members are equipped to deal effectively with diverse team dynamics. To the extent that skills are lacking and the team's task is important and visible, you would do well to try to get some training for the team before it becomes fully involved in the project.

Finally, make sure that you seek out detours and learning opportunities during international travels. In one sense, none of us have the time for these detours; however, from another perspective, you cannot afford not to take them. If you want a competitive advantage over others, you need to see and experience things they don't. You've got to get off the beaten path.

With these recommendations in mind, let us now examine in more detail how these strategies for developing global leadership capabilities change over the course of your career and how you can continue to pursue them.

Notes

1. S. Black, H. Gregersen, M. Mendenhall, and L. Stroh (1999), *Globalizing People through International Assignments*. Reading, Mass: Addison-Wesley.

2. T. Stewart (1999), "The Contest for Welch's Throne Begins: Who Will Run GE?" *Fortune*, January 11, p. 27.

INTERSECTING YOUR CAREER STAGE AND LEADERSHIP DEVELOPMENT

Your development as a global leader should be placed in the most capable and interested hands—your own. While companies want and need more global leaders, in a recent survey we conducted, only 7.6 percent of the firms indicated that they had a comprehensive global leader development system. Consequently, while you should take advantage of every reasonable development opportunity your company offers, you should also have your own development plan.

Your personal plan should rely heavily on the Four T's (Travel, Teams, Training, and Transfers). However, you should look at the Four T's in the context of your particular career stage. Interviews with executives pointed out some important differences by career stage in the use of each development strategy (see Figure 8.1).

Early Career Development

Individuals do not become global leaders instantly or easily, so you need to start your developmental journey as early as possible. Unfortunately, few

Developmental Activity	Early Career Stage	Midcareer Stage	Late Career Stage
Global Travel	• Awareness • Testing	• Learn • Share	• Connections & relationships • Building others
Global Teams	• Team Member • Single function/ cross-cultural • Cross-functional	• Team Leader • Single function/ global • Cross-functional	• Global team leader
Global Training	• Perspective • Awareness • Functional skills	• Perspective • General mgr. skills • Action learning • Networking	• Senior executive skills • Networking • Action learning
Global Transfers	• No P&L • Awareness • Shorter term • Testing	• P&L responsible • Cross-functional • Long-term • Testing	• P&L responsible • Global or regional • Long-term • Final polishing

Figure 8.1 Development Objective and Career Stage

companies pay much attention to the early career stage in terms of identifying and developing global leaders. If you are in the early stages of your career, look at this lack of attention as both a challenge and an opportunity. It is a challenge primarily because few systematic development strategies may exist. You may find it difficult to "sell" your development needs to individuals who have the authority to give you the development opportunities you need. However, the lack of established development programs is also a great opportunity. For example, we know of one young manager who raised the need for cross-cultural training for young managers with several executives. This young woman had a double challenge because she was in a fairly invisible job and department, and the company had done virtually nothing in the way of formal cross-cultural or international training for young managers. Not all the executives who heard this young women's arguments were persuaded, but two key executives were. As a consequence, the executives authorized the young woman to organize a seminar for younger managers. Not only was she one of the first participants in the program, but she became much more visible to other executives who in the end had to sign off on their subordinates who attended the seminar.

Travel

You may be one of the fortunate ones who even early in your career has the opportunity to travel to various countries. If you are, count yourself lucky. In our research and consulting experience, young managers' most frequent complaints concerned inadequate international travel opportunity. You should know that you will likely have to have to push hard for these opportunities. An effective backdoor method is to become involved in situations, such as negotiations, in which foreigners visit your location. These types of situations often involve reciprocal visits to their homeland and office. If you are a valuable member of the team, you may get yourself invited along on the next trip.

Keep in mind that travel early in your career is a great way to increase your overall awareness—awareness of different markets, governments, consumers, competitors, business customs and practices, etc. Published country briefings, such as those offered by firms like Craighead International (www.craighead.com, 1-203-655-1007), can be a valuable way to get up to speed before you travel to the country. This way you can ask better questions and gain sharper insights about the country.

Early in your career be careful about taking "detours." As a young manager, you do not have the same credibility as a more senior manager. Therefore, you are not as likely to be given the benefit of a doubt when someone is trying to decide if your half-day tour of the *Tsukiji* fish market in Tokyo was a great learning experience about the country's distribution system or not. This is not to say you should not take detours off the beaten business path, just take them wisely.

Keep in mind that those traveling with you are watching. Sometimes they are even deliberately testing you. For example, John Huntsman, Jr., vice chairman of Huntsman Corporation, travels with young managers to see specifically how they respond to being "out of their element."

> I'll take people on negotiating sessions overseas for technology transfer or in dealing with foreign groups who come here. You can pretty much separate out those people who can mix well with foreign groups, as against those who just clash. The personalities that seem to flourish . . . are those that are open. I mean, they're typically open-minded. They sit back before they speak, and they think about the implications a little bit more than the typical American knee-jerk reaction. And I think you see that through experience, by basically sharing the negotiating table with them, or seeing them in action with foreign delegations.

In short, traveling can be an excellent way early in your career to enhance your level of awareness and gain some visibility with senior managers. Or if you are a more senior manager, like John Huntsman, you can use travel as a way to get an early read on young managers. In either case, it's important not to read too much into the results of early travel experiences. Making a mistake or experiencing a bit of culture shock at age 23 is not foolproof evidence that you do not have what it takes to be a great global leader.

Teams

While global task forces and teams may be all the rage, they can be difficult animals to ride. As one executive from Texas observed, "It's plain dumb to try and ride big, Brahma bulls right out of the chute. You need to break in riding bucking calves first." Early in your career, it is wise to seek team membership on a single functional team that has members from various countries throughout a given region. Keeping the functional discipline constant—as with a marketing task force, for instance—will give you more time and mental energy to focus on the cultural issues that the diverse members of the team bring.

One executive recalled her early experience on a global advertising team. The team, charged with developing a global advertising strategy for a new product, was composed of members from all major regions in the world. Even though the team members shared similar technical and functional knowledge, the differences in advertising strategy in the various countries led initially to near chaos. Although everyone spoke English, it soon became clear that each member was speaking a different language. That is, the underlying assumptions about advertising effectiveness, media plans, etc., were significantly different. It wasn't until group members learned how to communicate their underlying assumptions and draw out those of others that members could finally see and understand each other.

Once you've experienced membership on a single function but multicultural team within a region, the next logical step would be membership on a cross-functional team within the same region. At that point you can leverage your understanding about the various countries and cultures of team members and begin the process of understanding how different functional perspectives can filter and affect how people see and approach various problems. You can also examine the nuances that different cultural backgrounds can have on these functional perspectives.

Later, you should look for opportunities to be a member of a multicultural and cross-functional team. In this type of team, not only do members learn how to bridge national or regional culture gaps, they learn how to bridge functional culture gaps as well. As one manager reported, "Sometimes the gap in perspective and values between finance and marketing can be as great as that between Taiwan and England."

Training

Unfortunately, few of the companies we surveyed or interviewed provide formal global leadership training for young managers. Many, however, do provide training in functional skills. Early in your career, you should take advantage of every reasonable opportunity to attend these programs. You should make an extra effort to attend, or get yourself nominated for, functional programs that have international dimensions.

If you are fortunate enough to attend a program with a global leadership or business theme, keep in mind that your main objective early in your career is to heighten your awareness and broaden your perspective on global business and leadership issues. Early in your career, you may not be in a position to immediately apply all the great content from the program. Keep in mind that senior managers will likely evaluate your ability to determine appropriately what you can apply *now* and what may be more relevant *later*. Exercising good judgment about what to do—or not do—with what you learn can be just as important as retaining the program content. In training programs we have been involved with, we have seen cases in which young managers were so excited by the content in one of our programs that they lost sight of their position in the company and exercised poor judgment in determining the line between effectively pushing the organization and stepping too far outside acceptable limits.

Transfers

The expense of international transfers causes most firms to restrict them to more senior managers. There are, however, some exceptions to this rule. For example, American Express has a program in which it selects five young, high-potential U.S. managers and five non-U.S. managers and sends them on 18-month international assignments, half the usual length. Colgate-Palmolive has a similar program.

Even if your firm does not have this type of program, you might consider what Kelly Barton did as a young manager in a software company. Kelly graduated with an undergraduate degree in Japanese Studies. She had lived in Japan for a semester as an undergraduate and was reasonably fluent in the language. Although Japan was a strategically important country and the base of her firm's Asia operations, it was so expensive to send people there that the firm had basically stopped sending expatriate managers. Kelly recognized that Japan represented an important consumer and competitor base in the video and computer game software industry. She also knew that if she could get even a short assignment there (6 to 18 months), she could gain exposure to other important Asian countries. Given the potential growth of the overall Asian market in video games, Kelly was convinced that exposure to the region would be of lasting value.

Leveraging her knowledge of how to live cheaply in Tokyo, Kelly proposed to go to Japan on a short assignment without a full expatriate package.

If the company would pay the large deposits usually required when renting an apartment in Japan, Kelly offered to go there without any extraordinary allowances, like housing or general cost-of-living increases. Through internal networking, she had already discovered two projects in the company's Japan office that were a perfect fit with Kelly's capabilities. Both projects were expected to take less than 18 months to complete.

Kelly's request was reviewed and in the end granted. Interestingly, despite her background in Japan, Kelly found that working there provided a whole new set of insights about the country. Her exposure to other Asian countries, especially China, also turned out to be a bit different from her expectations. The differences, however, helped broaden her perspective in a way that never could have happened without living and working overseas.

Kelly's experience helps illustrate the key elements of an international assignment early in your career. First, the assignment needs to focus on a single country. Unless your personal and family background is such that you have lived your life in a variety of countries, you will do well if you can effectively adjust to and perform in a single foreign setting at a time. Although the term of the assignment does not necessarily need to be short, given that the main purpose is to broaden awareness, especially of one's self, longer-term assignments may not be necessary or advisable. Early career international assignments provide unique development opportunities to create a heightened self-awareness about your specific strengths and weaknesses relative to global leadership, and they can enhance your inquisitiveness about the international business domain in general. With this development purpose in mind, it makes little sense to attach profit-and-loss or other significant responsibilities to early-career international assignments. Still, even without intense job responsibilities, these assignments are a great way for the company to get an early idea about your long-term global leadership potential.

Cautions

Regardless of what specific development opportunities you find, two cautions are in order concerning early career development. First, both you and the company should take care not to overinterpret the results of these opportunities. People change and weaknesses are overcome. Second, having raised awareness of your weaknesses, seek out guidance about how to turn them into strengths. Without this guidance, you may set off in unproductive corrective directions.

Midcareer Development

Midcareer is the most challenging stage in terms of global leadership development. This time period mixes rigorous development and serious testing. Unlike early career opportunities that are primarily developmental in nature, midcareer opportunities are quite often intended to provide significant development and a test to determine if you have the potential to become a senior officer in the global corporation.

Travel

Unlike young managers early in their careers, most midcareer managers whom we interviewed or surveyed are on the road plenty. As a consequence, if you are at the midcareer stage, you probably don't have to push for travel opportunities, but rather travel destinations. But just as the number of international trips changes between early and midcareer, so too do the purposes. International travel at the midcareer stage has two main global leadership development objectives.

The first purpose of travel is to learn. This is not to say that you can or should ignore the business purpose of the trip. There is always a business purpose to the trip—someone to see, documents to review, negotiations to conduct, etc. The business purpose of an international trip is a given. Our experience is that if you weren't capable of accomplishing whatever the business purpose is, you wouldn't be getting on the airplane. But if that's all you accomplish, then you will have missed out on the full global leadership development potential of international travel. As we have said, the best way to learn new things is to take "detours," to get off the beaten business path. The advantage of being mid-way through your career is that you are likely to have some latitude in taking these detours because of the credibility you've built up over the years.

You can enhance this credibility relative to the detours by sharing what you learn, which is the second basic developmental purpose of travel during midcareer. As mentioned earlier, 3M has formalized a series of brown bag lunches in which learnings from various international travels are shared and discussed. Even in the absence of a formal program like the one at 3M, nothing is likely to prevent you from organizing such a lunch and sharing your insights with subordinates or peers.

Consider, for example, Dale Smith. During every trip he takes to Latin America, about once a quarter, Dale makes sure to take some sort of detour. Often he'll ask a local national what cultural value is core in the country and what place, event, or activity best captures that value. To the extent possible, he will then try to visit the historical site, watch the event, or participate in the activity. Upon he return to his base in Florida, Dale always makes it a point to invite one of more of his staff out to lunch. In addition to reviewing the business results, Dale describes the detour he took and what he learned from it. In talking with one of Dale's subordinates, it's clear that not only does he convey the business results and the cultural knowledge he picked up, but he also sets an example for his staff as a leader who tries constantly to learn from new experiences. In the long run, this may have a bigger impact than any of the specific lessons Dale learns or shares.

Teams

If you are like many managers we've spoken with, by midcareer, leading "global teams" no longer has the glamour and allure it did when you were in your early twenties. Experience has taught you that global teams are indeed difficult animals to ride. Ideally, you have already had the opportunity to be a member of at least a couple of multicultural and cross-functional teams. If so, midcareer is your time to seek out team leadership opportunities.

As with team membership, it is wise to seek team leadership first of a single functional team with members from various countries throughout a given region. Keeping the functional discipline constant can be very valuable in your early global team leadership experiences. Unlike when you were younger, you no longer have the luxury of sitting back and simply observing how differently Germans and Chinese view challenges, such as establishing a global brand identity. As the team leader, you have to get people with these very different views to work effectively together. Complicating this with different functional background too early in the learning curve can be a recipe for midcareer disaster.

Executives also pointed out important risks and pitfalls that need to be managed for global teams to function as an effective developmental strategy. The first caution was the risk of asking someone to lead a cross-functional, multicultural team too early in their career or without enough experience in these types of team settings. One executive related the following:

> I knew one young woman who had lots of potential, but she got put in charge of a task force with people from four different countries and three different functional backgrounds. The team had a total meltdown, and she had no chance. She was inadvertently set up for failure and didn't even know it until it was too late.

In addition, executives pointed out the pitfall of placing individuals on global teams without adequate training in the dynamics and effective process skills relative to diverse teams. Several executives indicated that the pressure of having to deliver something without adequate "diverse team process" training led to less than optimal results. A common problem was the domination of the group by one individual or a coalition. The takeover and the associated suppression of diverse ideas and perspectives was typically justified by the offenders by the "need to get something done." However, this approach rarely resulted in superior deliverables. Therefore, be sure that team members, including yourself, have the requisite knowledge of and skills for diverse team dynamics. If you or the team members don't, do all that you can to get some training before the team gets too far into the process. It's trite but true: "An ounce of prevention is better than a pound of cure."

Effective teams figured out what was going wrong with their group dynamics and subsequently created norms for the team concerning issues such as conflict resolution or decision making. While this usually resulted in a reasonable deliverable from the team, valuable time was lost while the group dynamics were being fixed. Furthermore, the deliverable was often less than it could have been if team members had been adequately trained in the first place.

Training

We've learned from our experience and research that midcareer managers are the primary beneficiaries of formal global leadership training. Most companies we interviewed and surveyed don't currently have programs for high potential midcareer managers, but they plan to add such programs in the near future. Excellent programs can enhance your awareness and perspective concerning global business and leadership issues. If you are fortunate enough to choose the programs you attend, you should seek out those with the following three characteristics.

First, look for programs that focus on general management skills. Although in-depth functional programs with international dimensions can be of some value, programs that integrate various disciplines (e.g., finance, marketing, human resources, strategy) will provide the greatest value in preparing you for global leader responsibilities.

Second, look for programs that have action learning components. Unlike early career managers, at midcareer you want and need opportunities to apply program content. One of the best ways is to have some business challenge built right into the program. As mentioned earlier, TRW's Global Leadership Program has a significant project built into the program design. Participants actually spend over a third of the total program working in foreign countries on real company issues assigned by the president. A professional facilitator is assigned to each team to help with nightly debriefings, team dynamics, and project content in order to avoid disasters and raise the probability of the team's success. Sunkyong, Samsung, 3M, and GE all have executive development programs with substantial global action learning components.

Third, take advantage of programs that provide within- and across-company networking opportunities. One of the great benefits of Exxon's Workshop on Global Leadership is that it brings high potential midcareer managers from throughout Exxon's worldwide operations. The two-week program allows individuals to get to know each other personally and to leverage those relationships in facilitating the company's increasing efforts to coordinate activities on a global basis long after the program is over. The participation of Solar Turbine (a division of Caterpillar) in a consortium program has allowed its high-potential managers to leverage relationships with individuals outside their industry as well as benchmark itself against non-competitors.

Transfers

Despite the expense of international transfers, in our recent survey of over 100 medium and large firms, 73.8 percent of the firms plan to increase the number of managers sent on international assignments over the next five years, while 21.5 percent plan to keep the number the same, and only 4.7 percent expect to reduce the total number. Consequently, if you prepare yourself well and appropriately signal your willingness to go, you will likely be given the opportunity to take an international assignment.

So what should you look for in an international assignment to maximize its unsurpassed global leader developmental potential? First and foremost, if you get the chance to have profit-and-loss responsibility, go for it. In our interviews with individuals identified by their companies as future global leader role models, these people indicated that P&L responsibility made them wrap their minds around the overall business and how their business fits in with others across the corporation's worldwide network. These individuals explained that it was the breadth of the responsibility that helped them gain "a truly global perspective." One manager at American Express indicated that while he was running marketing in Japan, he did not completely appreciate the global aspects of the business. It wasn't until he became president of the Japan operation that his perspective became truly global.

If P&L responsibility is not possible, seek an assignment with cross-functional dimensions. Keep in mind that most senior positions in a global company require a comprehensive perspective. That is, you will need to see not just across the borders of countries, but across the borders of divisions, products, and functions within the company. An international assignment that provides opportunities in this way has the greatest developmental potential. This, however, does not mean that you should turn down an international assignment if it doesn't measure up to these ideals. Our research shows that any international assignment has the potential to help you develop and prepare for global leadership positions in ways that staying at home just can't. Many of the executives we interviewed had never experienced an ideal assignment, yet they benefited significantly from the international assignment in their global leadership development. In fact, they would always take the assignment again if given the choice between a less than ideal international assignment and no overseas experience at all.

Finally, make sure that your personal and family situation allows you to seek assignments at least three years long. Assuming you haven't lived in the foreign country before, it will take you eight to twelve months to adequately adjust to living and working there. It will also require six to nine months to prepare adequately for your return home. This leaves only a little over a year in a typical three year assignment to focus fully on the job at hand, let alone use it to develop your global leadership capabilities and create value for your firm.

While we stress the development potential of international assignments, the reality is that during the assignment you will be tested and evaluated, both in terms of your current abilities as well as your long-term potential. Thus you should do all you can to ensure that your international assignment succeeds. In addition to picking up a copy of *So You're Going Overseas*, which we recommended in the previous chapter, you may want to take a look at another book that offers a comprehensive discussion of foreign assignments—*Globalizing People through International Assignments* (www.contactCGA.com).

Cautions

The fact that midcareer global leadership development opportunities have both development and testing purposes creates one key caution. If you overemphasize the "testing" aspects of these experiences, you will likely to hyperfocus on delivering "results." This is not bad per se, and you certainly cannot ignore delivering results. However, an overemphasis on results can lead to risk-averse behavior. This is unfortunate, because in most cases the "ability to take risks and act outside the box" is a key global leader skill. Thus, becoming obsessed with "hitting the numbers" may well cause you to miss out on the development opportunities you need to reach greater leadership responsibilities. True, missing the numbers will probably lower your chances of advancing to the next level as well. However, one executive we interviewed put it this way: "Too many managers think that doing well where they are now is sufficient to move them along in their careers. I want to see them do well now and *also* demonstrate that they can learn and grow enough to be ready for the next level."

Late Career Development

Late career development is the weakest link in most companies' global leadership development efforts. Many companies falsely assume that either you have it or you don't by this point in your career. The issue is not whether you have it or not; the key issue is, how refined is what you have? Given the broader scope of senior management positions and the more strategic impact decisions at that level exert, small refinements in global leadership capabilities can produce significant payoffs to both you and your company. As a consequence, you should view global leadership development at this stage as a period of specific refinement and polishing. It will also likely be a time of final testing.

Travel

Most executives in the later stage of their careers pointed out that they had more travel demands, let alone opportunities, than they could possibly meet. As one executive at Kimberly-Clark lamented, "If I took every trip for which there was a business reason or justification, I would never be home." As a senior manager, you travel when business reasons make it compelling to do so. However, in addition to the normal business reasons for the trip, in the later stage of your career, you should focus on choosing international travel opportunities that provide the chance to do two things.

First, take advantages of trips that help form and solidify relationships. Jon Huntsman, Jr. stressed the need to travel in order to connect with business partners on a personal basis.

> We won't do business with people who we don't enjoy being with. You become friends first. Then you begin talking about business. But, we're not just going to do business blindly. We like to pick and choose. We go into a country, like in Australia, and there's the Packer family, Cary Packer. And our families are very close, and Cary's a great guy, and his son James, who's now running the business, is one of my very good friends, and that comes first. It's the relationship before the business. The business will go up and down, but we try to keep the personal relationship always intact and unharmed.

Second, take advantage trips that help you build others. There exists no way yet to "digitize" relationships and the nuances that go along with them. If you are trying to develop and build one of your managers in a foreign locale, it's hard to do that simply through e-mail, fax, or even the phone. You often have to be face-to-face for the richness of the exchange and communication to take place. Or you might be taking someone along on the trip who could benefit from the mentoring you could provide. As was true of yourself early in your career, simply listening to the descriptions of distant negotiations, governmental protocol, market situation, or competitors just doesn't have the same impact as being there in person. Take individuals with you and use travel to help build them.

Teams

Senior executives in a variety of companies said they felt a keen responsibility to select and develop future top executives. However, several expressed frustration at the difficulty of "picking stars that will really shine." Part of this frustration grew out of not having had the opportunity to personally lead a global team. Often this was because their companies had moved so quickly into global arenas that they were responsible for several global teams without having been the leader of a single global team themselves. This lack of experience caused some executives to make mistakes in choosing other executives to lead global teams. As one senior executive said to us, "I never had the opportunity to lead a truly global team. I didn't fully understand what it took. It took a couple of mistakes in selecting [global team leaders] before I really understood what it was all about."

Leading a global team can easily represent a microcosm of the dynamics of running a global organization. As a consequence, you can gain insights into your strengths and weaknesses, while you still have a chance to take care of any necessary refinements. While leading a global team before guiding a global division seems to be the ideal, at least one European executive managed to do both at the same time. He leveraged lessons learned while leading a global team to help better structure and run a global product division. If you are in charge of a global unit and have not had the opportunity to lead a truly global team, you should identify a salient business issue and put together and lead a global team. You can then leverage the lessons learned from leading the global team and apply them in your overall unit.

Finally, as mentioned before (and it's worth repeating), be sure that team members, including yourself, have the requisite knowledge and skills for diverse team dynamics. If you or the team members don't, do all that you can to get some training. And yes, once again: "An ounce of prevention is better than a pound of cure."

Training

From our experience and research, late career executives receive very few opportunities for formal global leadership training. However, a number of the companies we interviewed and surveyed believe this is a shortcoming and plan to add programs in the near future. Programs that add value for executives are not easy to design or execute. If you are in a position to choose to attend a global leadership program designed for senior executives, seek out programs with three characteristics.

First, find programs that focus on senior executive capabilities. For example, programs with a heavy dose of content that examine global strategy and structure, competitive intelligence, strategic alliances and joint ventures are beneficial. These programs should include case studies and discussions that focus on the dynamics of integrating business activities across divisions, products, functions, and geographies and on determining which business activities are best localized.

Second, look for programs with an action learning component. In order to be of value, however, these projects need to have the potential to push you, to help you identify areas in yourself in need of polish and refinement. Suppose you just returned from a two-week action learning project in Vietnam. The objective of your team project was to assess the political risk and market potential of the country. The deliverable was to be a report and presentation to the executive committee of the company about whether or not to enter Vietnam, and if so, how best to proceed. As you step off the plane, weary from a 20-hour flight, you are confronted by a reporter and TV crew. They hound you with questions about your trip:

> "Is it true that you have been investigating the potential of opening operations in Vietnam?"

"Can you confirm the rumors that you signed a memorandum of understanding while you were there?"

"Is it true that you will be closing your factory in Kentucky and moving it to Vietnam?"

"Has the U.S. government put any pressure on you one way or the other concerning your firm's activities in the country?"

How would you react to the situation? As a senior executive, you will quite likely confront such a scene. How good are your public relations skills? What if this mock confrontation took place when you landed in Vietnam? How well would you do? The point is, you want to look for programs to stretch you and give you insights about those skill areas that could still stand a little improvement. This last bit of polish is likely all you need to be a truly effective global leader. Keep in mind, however, that having come this far, and having received lots of positive reinforcement about your capabilities over the years, you will probably need a program that shocks your system, a program that stretches you, to make visible your areas of needed refinement.

Third, take advantage of programs that provide within- and across-company networking opportunities. One of the great benefits of GE's Global Leadership Program is that it brings senior managers together from throughout GE's worldwide operations. The four-week program allows individuals to get to know each other at a level that can truly facilitate a company's efforts to coordinate activities globally.

Transfers

Most companies plan to increase the number of managers sent on international assignments. They also plan to broaden the "traffic patterns" of these transfers. Instead of most expatriates coming from the home country and being sent out to various foreign units, in a hub and spoke pattern, firms are beginning simply to transfer the best person (regardless of nationality) to the position. The resulting pattern looks much more chaotic, but it better utilizes the firm's global human resources.

An international assignment in your later career stage represents an opportunity to polish specific capabilities and become personally familiar with strategic geographies. For example, all managers headed for senior positions within Komatsu serve at least one assignment in the United States. This is because U.S.-based Caterpillar is Komatsu's toughest competitor the world over. Don Sullivan, president of General Motor's Asia Pacific Organization (APO), confided that GM expects most of its growth over the next 10 years to come in Asia. As a consequence, an assignment in APO represents a strategic opportunity to learn first hand about what may well be the most important consumer region in the world for GM long into the next century.

In addition to the strategic importance of the locale, we mentioned before that our interviews with exemplar global leaders found that P&L responsibility was an important dimension in maximizing the developmental potential of an international assignment. This was especially true for individuals in the later career stage.

Cautions

Our work also uncovered an important weakness relative to late-career global leadership development: firms constantly underutilize their global talent base. This observation applies to most multinational companies regardless of country of origin: Japan-based firms underutilize their non-Japanese talent; U.S.-based firms underutilize their non-US. talent; Germany-based firms underutilize their non-German talent; and so on. Global firms cannot afford to continue to believe that the best global leaders are primarily those of the parent company's nationality. Top management at LG Group of Korea have embraced this vision. They estimate that they will need 1,400 global leaders by 2005, and they plan for an even split between the number of Korean and non-Korean global leaders. As we mentioned, traffic patterns are changing, but changing slowly. True globalization requires that firms give up the old hub-and-spoke mentality, with headquarters as the source of all global leadership talent.

Our work also uncovered a surprising lack of linkage among global leader development, turnover, and overall succession planning. Specifically, the "bench strength" in most firms is quite weak, and the development plan is either not in place or is inadequate, given the turnover levels among upper-mid- and senior-level executives. While only 7.6 percent of the firms have a comprehensive global leader development system, those that did had better financial performance than those that did not.

Conclusion

Our study of companies as they move forward into the uncharted territories of the global frontier produced several conclusions. Clearly, effective global strategies and structures cannot be formulated without capable global leaders. Even with good global strategies and structures, effective execution is what ultimately separates the winners from the losers. Successful execution of global strategies and structures is impossible without adequate numbers of high-quality global leaders. Executives in the companies we interviewed consistently complained that they have neither sufficient numbers nor the desired level of global leadership talent.

Global leaders, like athletes or musicians, need some natural talent. However, this talent must also be developed. Because you cannot become a global leader overnight, you and your company must take a systematic and multifaceted approach to the process. For the best results, your development approach should vary depending on your career stage. Despite the need for companies to take a more proactive and systematic approach to the development of global leaders, *none of the outstanding global leaders we interviewed simply waited for their companies to map out the territory and trade routes to global leadership development.* Without exception, these individuals ultimately shoulder development responsibility themselves. They not only push the global business frontiers, but the frontiers of their own careers and development as well. They use any development opportunities the company offers, request ones not offered, and create something out of nothing to ensure that they, like you, become the next generation of global leaders.

nine

MAPPING YOUR FUTURE AS A GLOBAL LEADER

Our immediate neighborhood we know rather intimately. But with increasing distance our knowledge fades . . . until at the last dim horizon we search among ghostly errors of observations for landmarks that are scarcely more substantial. The search will continue. The urge is older than history. It is not satisfied and it will not be suppressed.

—*Edwin Hubble, reflections in his last scientific paper*

We live in an age of constant discovery. Explorers in a variety of fields continue to expand the scope of human knowledge: With the Hubble telescope, we can peer deeper into space, seeing stars and galaxies that we have never before beheld. On earth, we now travel deep into the oceans, discovering sea life that was until now unknown. Yet with all this exploration, we are reminded that in spite of all that we can now see and understand, there is still so much more to learn.

Similarly, in the constantly changing global marketplace, personal and organizational frontiers stretch beyond the horizon as the vast oceans did for the explorers of old and as endless space does for astronomers today. Firms pushing into this new frontier are in desperate need of global leaders to help them forge ahead. They need global leaders who can help make sense of the changing psychology of the employment contract, shift through the opportunities and pitfalls in developing markets, and bring together cohesive and effective teams of individuals from different countries, cultures, and functional disciplines. While the challenge of global leadership is significant, the good news for you is that they are in short supply. There is a large global leadership gap waiting for you to fill it.

Mapping Your Personal Career Frontier

Filling this leadership gap is easier said than done. The turbulence of the global market not only creates competitive challenges for companies but career challenges for individuals. For example, the globalization tsunami has already smashed the employment contract of the past into a thousand splinters. No longer do organizations promise secure and predictable careers in return for loyalty and solid performance. The turbulence of today's global environment shred the reliable career maps upon which you once could chart your course. Career ambiguity has replaced the predictability of the past. The notion of long term loyalty to a single company has been washed away and replaced with relatively uncharted career frontiers.

In the predictable business world of the past, the image of captain and ship was often used to describe the corporation and its leader. The image was not complete without the brave captain sailing the company out to sea. In this scenario, the thought of jumping ship was not an inviting one. Sharks lurked below, waiting to devour anyone foolish enough to leave the safety of the vessel.

Times have changed. The symbolism of this old image has shifted. Today, the ship does not represent the company; it is your own career, and you have to be the captain. The winds of opportunity blow from many directions and the waves constantly change. In conquering these challenges, your career path will not follow a nice straight line. Instead you will have to tack right and left; you will have to keep moving, growing, and developing. These tacking maneuvers may be within the same company or they may be across different companies. Unlike what was true in the past, there is no way to reliably predict whether your career path should be navigated within one firm or across many.

By evoking this transformed image of ship and captain, we do not want to create the impression that firms do not care about retaining high potential individuals, or that they are doing nothing to generate global leader development systems. In fact, our experience with senior executives in most firms suggests just the opposite. At companies like 3M, Colgate-Palmolive, and GE, executives spend considerable time, energy, and money on developing cadres of future global leaders. As we pointed out earlier, though, our surveys of the terrain found that most firms have, at best, stitched together some ad hoc programs. Fewer than 10 percent have comprehensive global leader development plans.

This fact leads to two key insights. First, while the vast majority of companies are without comprehensive development systems, they still face a rapidly expanding need for global leaders. As a result, you may not have the luxury of waiting for your firm to develop a comprehensive plan before moving full speed ahead with your own global leadership development. Second, if most firms today do not have comprehensive development systems, then they surely didn't have them in the past. Yet, as we have tried to demonstrate, there are effective global leaders *today*. If their companies did not have comprehensive development plans, how did they become the capable leaders they are today? When we put this question to these exemplar leaders, to a person, the answer was the same: They did not wait for their companies to lay out a global leader career map. While they took advantage of every opportunity the company offered, they assumed full responsibility for charting their own career course. The path they charted anticipated the need for global leadership capabilities by several years and at time, decades. For example, Michael C. Hawley, likely the next CEO of Gillette, began his international career in 1966 by running Gillette's import-export operation in Hong Kong. Over the next 20 years, he lived and worked on five different continents. Long before most executives understood the need for a global outlook, he was already in China back in 1979 helping Gillette begin operations in that country. With executives like Michael Hawley, companies like Gillette will catch and ride the gigantic wave of globalization rather than get wiped out by it.

Today's effective global leaders have all come to the same basic conclusion: to be successful you must become your own career cartographer, your own ship's captain. If you wait for your company to figure out and implement a comprehensive global leader development plan, it just might be too late. It may be too late because many of the global leadership opportunities will have passed you by and been taken by others who were more prepared. It may be too late because if you wait, you will still be standing at the starting line as hundreds and perhaps thousands of other high-potential managers join the race.

To become your own career cartographer, keep in mind that becoming a global leader is not an overnight process. As a consequence, good first moves today produce competitive advantages tomorrow. In the tournament for global leadership, those who move first have a clear advantage. The responsibility for these early (as well as for mid- and late) career moves resides with you. One exemplar manager put it this way:

> If the global future for companies is uncharted, why should a person's global career be any different? And if winning companies cannot afford to simply wait and copy their competitors' moves, why should individuals be any different? I didn't know exactly where I needed to head in order to enhance my value the most, but I knew I couldn't wait for someone to map it out for me. I knew I had to take that responsibility myself.

While Chapters 7 and 8 described in general terms the ways in which successful global leaders develop themselves, the precise sequencing and content of travel, teams, training, and transfers is in your hands. Accurate personal assessment is the key to being able to create an effective career map.

For example, if an internal assignment is the single most powerful means of developing global leader characteristics and you haven't had one yet, are you prepared to take one on? Not every international assignment is right for you (nor are you necessarily right for every assignment) and now may not be the right time, but have you done a careful assessment of yourself and your family situation to know what assignments and timing would be appropriate? While books such as *So You're Going Overseas* are important to read once you've been presented with an opportunity, they are probably of most value long before the opportunity appears. Only through advance assessment of yourself, your industry, firm, and family can you have enough time to make the necessary preparations and changes. And only in making them early will you be in a position to both maximize the business results and the development potential of an international assignment.

Without exception, every exemplar global leader we interviewed was a self-employed cartographer, busily mapping out his or her career. Consider the path that Steve Burke charted. As mentioned in Chapter 5, Steve embarked early on a self-designed path that ultimately led to a senior executive position. He initially worked at General Mills, learning the ropes of marketing by pushing Yoplait yogurt. This experience gave Steve valuable lessons in marketing that prepared him for a career move to Disney—heading up part of its consumer products division. From the beginning, Steve tapped into employee creativity and went on to build the Disney retail store concept from the ground up. Starting with zero revenues, Steve built the Disney stores into a $500 million-a-year operation in five short years. Not willing to rest on success or familiar territory, Steve actively sought out his next position in an entirely different part of the company: theme parks.

Steve made this significant tack in his career course and ended up in France helping turn around the EuroDisney theme park in the 1990s. During this experience, he had to acquire a whole range of new skills related to park operations and European business that he had never needed when running Disney's retail stores. Working with the Paris-based EuroDisney team as well as with executives at Burbank headquarters, Steve helped put the theme park back in the black.

Steve then took his time and searched for a return assignment that would leverage his growing skill base and still provide development opportunities. He found just such an assignment back in America. Steve's first job back was identifying and building strategic synergies between Disney and Cap Cities/ABC after their recent merger. Not having worked in the television and film business before, Steve was again faced with a challenge from which he acquired new capabilities. Before long he made another move and took a senior executive position in charge of ABC's television and radio stations, requiring that he master the tricky world of programming.

Most recently, Steve has taken another significant career tack, leaving Disney for an entirely different learning opportunity. He became Comcast Cable's president. Now instead of being part of a large, established organization, Steve leads a young, upstart company in the increasingly global entertainment and communication industry.

Steve—just like Tony Wang or Gary Griffiths—never waited for someone else to take control of his career. He put himself at the helm. Of course he sought advice from colleagues and bosses to guide his choices, but he never left his ultimate career fate in someone else's hands. Further, Steve, recognizing—like all exemplar global leaders—the necessity of tacking left and right, has followed a fairly convoluted path that has crisscrossed countries, industries, companies, and functions. This kind of self-planning prepared Steve, and will prepare you, for all the unforeseen frontiers encountered in today's global business world.

Global Leadership: A Personal Journey of Discovery

While some companies do more than others to develop global leaders, in the final analysis the road to global success is a personal journey of discovery. As you sail off into the waters of the new global marketplace, you will learn volumes about markets, technology, competitors, customers, suppliers, and the like. As we have described, such learning and the inquisitiveness that produces it are at the core of effective global leadership. However, more important even than learning about markets, technology, competitors, customers, or suppliers, you must prepare for and look forward to learning about yourself.

As you sail forward, will you be like the drill rig operator in Asia who maintained his ethical standards by refusing to pay bribes of a few thousand dollars to a corrupt government official even though the opportunity costs of an idle rig are tens of thousands per day? Will you be like Jon Huntsman, Jr., and look beyond the nationality and language of people and emotionally connect with them as individuals? Will you be like Tony Wang and relish the opportunity to bring together diverse organizational resources outside your line of authority to pull off a critical global deal? In essence, are you excited about this personal journey of discovery to know where you stand as a global leader?

As you embark on your leadership journey, keep in mind Henry David Thoreau's advice to become "the Lewis and Clark . . . of your own streams and oceans; explore your own higher latitudes . . . be a Columbus to whole new continents and worlds within you, opening new channels, not of trade, but of thought . . . it is easier to sail many thousand miles through cold and storm and cannibals . . . than it is to explore the private sea, the

Atlantic and Pacific Ocean of one's being." This journey may well prove the most important one to take as we move into the twenty-first century. It will also prove the most difficult since the real journey is one of personal discovery—discovery not so much of distant markets but of yourself.

Remember Gary Griffiths' experience at the Warsaw Marriott. Gary took that international assignment with limited overseas business experience. He worked for years as an accountant in a public accounting firm before taking an accountant's job at a smoothly running western U.S. Marriott hotel property. When Gary left that world of stability and flew to Poland, he had no idea what kinds of surprises he would face. At first, he clung to the certainty of his past—when he came across familiar Mars candy bars for the first time in Poland, he grabbed five. Not because he was starving, but because he wanted to hold on to what was soothing and familiar. Yet the sweet taste of the candy bars wore off fast as Gary faced a mountain of uncertainty in Warsaw. Nearly every day, Gary faced challenges for which he had no ready answer. What do you do when:

- over 100 phones are stolen from the hotel during its first week of operations?
- a guest commits suicide in the hotel lobby by jumping from the second-floor balcony?
- you need cash to start up the hotel, but can't get a business bank account?
- one night's lodging costs a customer four million zlotys (the local currency)?
- someone attempts to pay for a night's stay and there are more digits in the price than the computer can calculate?
- you have to get truckloads of cash to the bank in a cash-starved economy?
- you have to account for purchasing $4,000 worth of food for the restaurant each day that must be picked up by a truck driver in an open market and paid for in cash?
- you can't get a phone line or refrigerator in your home for months?

For Gary, questions like these went on and on. Faced with constant uncertainty, Gary confronted more than one defining moment that forced him completely out of his comfort zone. These were the times when he was ready to give up and go home because he just wasn't sure he could rise to the challenge. But he stuck it out. He came to realize through these tough experiences that "the reality of the situation is just that, the reality." What he had been comfortable with in the past just wouldn't work in the present. As a result, he looked deep into the mirror and discovered a flicker of flexibility that he fanned into a flame—a flame that any global leader must have in order to succeed. Over time, Gary discovered that he thrived on the uncertainty and challenges of the environment he faced. He confronted the new reality of doing business in Poland by first confronting himself. If he had known in advance the exact level of craziness he was to face, and if you had asked him if he was up to it, he honestly might have said, "NO." In retrospect, he knows the experience was invaluable: "In the most important ways, I improved myself."

Experience is the forge through which ordinary people become extraordinary global leaders. It is said that the swords of the Japanese samurai are among the best in the world. Each blade is shaped in the hottest fires. The metal is folded over and over a thousand times. It is pounded repeatedly into itself until it fuses at the molecular level. Finally, it is sharpened with the greatest precision. In much the same way, we discover the real nature of our personal leadership "metal" by seeking out and confronting the greatest international challenges that lie before us. Just like a samurai sword, we become the very best when our character is forged in the hottest fires, pounded on by the most difficult experiences, and sharpened with continuous learning. There are few paths in life that offer greater opportunity and challenge than the one to global leadership. For that reason, there are few paths in life more rewarding. And for now, it is still the road less traveled. In this very personal journey of discovery, we wish you all the best.

GLOBAL EXPLORER™

Global Explorer™ is a proprietary assessment instrument of an individual's global leadership potential that we developed based on our extensive study and research. It is designed to give feedback to the individual about his or her strengths and weaknesses. It also outlines specific actions that can be taken to improve one's overall global leadership profile. The questions below are a sample of those in the official instrument. They are designed to give you a rough idea of your strengths and weaknesses. The official version of the instrument is available only through the Global Leadership Institute. You can contact Hal B. Gregersen for more information.

Assessing Your Competencies as a Global Leader

To assess your current global leadership competencies, please answer the following questions:

1. I have a good understanding of my company's business model (how it makes money).

	Strongly Disagree					Strongly Agree
1	2	3	4	5	6	7

2. I have a clear sense of other companies'
strategies in our industry.

*Strongly
Disagree*   *Strongly
Agree*

1 2 3 4 5 6 7

3. I personally know the key decision makers in my business unit/division.

*Strongly
Disagree*   *Strongly
Agree*

1 2 3 4 5 6 7

4. I generally know who to contact to get
things done in my business unit/divi-
sion.

*Strongly
Disagree*   *Strongly
Agree*

1 2 3 4 5 6 7

5. I genuinely care about and understand
people whose cultural backgrounds are
different from mine.

*Strongly
Disagree*   *Strongly
Agree*

1 2 3 4 5 6 7

6. I like to spend as much time as possible
with my employees.

*Strongly
Disagree*   *Strongly
Agree*

1 2 3 4 5 6 7

7. I consistently display high ethical standards when I represent my company to
outsiders.

*Strongly
Disagree*   *Strongly
Agree*

1 2 3 4 5 6 7

8. In conversations with other employees,
I support my company's strategy and its
leadership.

*Strongly
Disagree*   *Strongly
Agree*

1 2 3 4 5 6 7

9. I thrive in an uncertain environment.

Strongly Disagree   *Strongly Agree*

1 2 3 4 5 6 7

10. I don't like my job to have too much structure.

Strongly Disagree   *Strongly Agree*

1 2 3 4 5 6 7

11. I am very good at differentiating between those of my company's products and services that should be globally standardized and those that should be locally tailored.

Strongly Disagree   *Strongly Agree*

1 2 3 4 5 6 7

12. I recognize that a lot of what my company does needs to be modified as it enters new international markets.

Strongly Disagree   *Strongly Agree*

1 2 3 4 5 6 7

13. People say that I am constantly examining experiences and extracting the lessons that can be learned.

Strongly Disagree   *Strongly Agree*

1 2 3 4 5 6 7

14. Whenever I need energizing, I pursue new experience learning.

Strongly Disagree   *Strongly Agree*

1 2 3 4 5 6 7

15. I actively seek out unfamiliar territory and opportunities for learning.

Strongly Disagree   *Strongly Agree*

1 2 3 4 5 6 7

Scoring:

Scoring this sample instrument is relatively easy. Simply add your circled numbers together for each of the following clusters of questions.

Total score for questions 1–4:

25–28	You have excellent organizational and business savvy.
21–24	You have good organizational and business savvy.
17–20	You have average organizational and business savvy.
16 and below	You have a major deficiency in organizational and business savvy.

Total score for questions 5–8:

25–28	You have unbending integrity and an excellent ability to connect emotionally with others.
21–24	You have strong integrity and a good ability to connect emotionally with others.
17–20	You have average integrity and a fair ability to connect emotionally with others.
16 and below	You have a major deficiency in integrity and a poor ability to connect emotionally with others.

Total score for questions 9–12:

25–28	You have excellent ability to embrace uncertainty and balance tensions.
21–24	You have good ability to embrace uncertainty and balance tensions.
17–20	You have average ability to embrace uncertainty and balance tensions.
16 and below	You have a major deficiency in your ability to embrace uncertainty and balance tensions.

Total score for questions 12–15:

25–28	You have excellent inquisitiveness.
21–24	You have good inquisitiveness.
17–20	You have average inquisitiveness.
16 and below	You have a major deficiency in inquisitiveness.

GLOBAL ASSIGNMENT PREPAREDNESS SURVEY (G-A-P-S™)

G–A–P–S™ (Global Assignment Preparedness Survey) is an assessment tool designed to give individuals feedback on their strengths and weaknesses relative to characteristics that influence success or failure when living and working abroad. G–A–P–S™ feedback helps to:

1. Increase awareness of cross-cultural issues for successful international assignments.
2. Increase understanding of personal cross-cultural strengths and weaknesses.
3. Facilitate individual efforts to strengthen cross-cultural capabilities and enhance overseas success.

G–A–P–S™ feedback can help the firm to:

1. Facilitate training and education effectiveness by better matching training and education to the needs of the individual.

2. Help avoid costly mismatches of individual candidates and overseas assignments.
3. Better determine the size of the pool of candidates within the company that have high, medium, and low cross-cultural aptitudes.

G–A–P–S™ measures six key cross-cultural skills that are related to global assignment success: cultural flexibility, cosmopolitan perspective, sociability, willingness to communicate, conflict-resolution style, and leadership approach. These dimensions have been empirically shown to be related to aspects of success in international assignments such as cross-cultural adjustment, job satisfaction, organizational commitment, and job performance. The official version of the instrument is available through Center for Global Assignments (1-888-I-Go-INTL or 1-888-446-4685 or www. contactCGA.com).

Index